SPAIN
A Literary Companion

Jimmy Burns

JOHN MURRAY

First published in 1994
by John Murray (Publishers) Ltd.,
50 Albemarle Street, London W1X 4BD

The moral right of the author has been asserted

A catalogue record for this book is available from the British Library

ISBN 0–7195–5098–X

Typeset in 12½/12½ pt Bembo
by Colset (Private) Limited, Singapore
Printed in Great Britain by Biddles Limited, Guildford and King's Lynn

CONTENTS

ILLUSTRATIONS
(between pages 112 and 113)

AUTHOR'S NOTE

I owe a special debt in the preparation of this book to the late Nissa Torrents, dear friend and senior lecturer in the Department of Spanish and Latin American Studies at University College, London, who was a source of constant encouragement and help prior to her death. Generosity and kindness are rare gifts indeed, but Nissa, right up to the last moment, showed them in abundance.

Many other relatives, friends, and acquaintances were in one way or another instrumental in making this book possible. They include: Tom G. Burns, David Burns, Sir Jonathan and Lady Parker, Gregorio Marañón y Bertran de Lis, Carmen Araoz, Belen Marañón, Gregorio Marañón Moya, Professor Angel Garcia, Professor Jim Cummings, Lord Thomas, Bella Thomas, Sir Brinsley Ford, Margaret and Peter Hebblethwaite, Fr. Michael Campbell-Johnston, Professor Paul Preston, Antonio Masoliver, Agustin Gervas, Jaime de Salas, Carmen Salas, Robert Graham, Touna Graham, Farid Kiumgi, Andrew Haynes, Jorge de Persia, Antonio Muñoz Molina, Juan de Loxa, Rafael Nadal, Ian Gibson, Sol Perez de Guzman, Anna Campbell, Frances Cavero, Gillian Walton, Alma Starkie, Professor L.J. Woodward, Peter Nicholson, David Gardner, Peter Bruce, Michael Thompson-Noel.

As part of my researches I made one long journey and several additional trips to Spain in 1991–3 for which I owe thanks to officials at the Spanish Embassy, especially Miguel de Santiago and Xavier Zarzalejos, the Spanish Tourist Office, the Junta de Andalucia, and Iberia Airlines. I was given valuable time thanks to a sabbatical from the *Financial Times*, to which I am grateful to Richard Lambert, Alain Cass, and David Walker. Thanks too to the staff of the Alhambra, St Alban's College in Valladolid, the London Library, the Spanish Institute (Cervantes Institute), the *Financial Times* library, and Senate House; Karen Harker for help in typing; my agent Caroline Dawnay who as always cast an incisive eye on a first draft; and to my editors at John Murray, Caroline Knox, Gail Pirkis, and especially Kate Chenevix Trench, whose patience mixed with practical advice survived many months. To Kidge, and our daughters, Julia and Miriam, yet again, the biggest thanks of all.

INTRODUCTION

This book has its roots in an Anglo-Spanish upbringing. Much of my childhood in Spain was spent under the awesome shadow of books which were, in the main, inaccessible. My grandfather's flat, off the Avenue Castellana in Madrid, housed one of the largest private collections of books on Spain, a dimly lit library that had survived imprisonment, civil war, and exile. Ford, Dumas, Gautier, Borrow, Swinburne, Washington Irving, Unamuno, Ortega, all were to be found there in their first editions. From my playroom I could only imagine the huge, colourful and adventurous world that lay within those shelves. The library was strictly out of bounds.

I have other childhood memories of long happy holidays at a variety of family residences where Spain revealed itself at first hand in all its cultural diversity: winter and spring in Castile, summer in the Basque country and Catalonia. In the back of an old chauffer-driven Rover we motored across this wide and generous land, crossing mountains and valleys, to look at Roman ruins and Moorish palaces, to sit in on the occasional bullfight and flamenco evening, to sample food and wine in forgotten villages. We discovered the only remaining strip of empty coastline left in Spain and built a house there, near Palos in Andalusia, from where Columbus sailed to the Americas.

My Spanish mother married a Chilean-born Scot with Basque blood in him. I was brought up straddling cultures, sensitive to the different perspectives from which foreigner and native observed Spain and its people. My own views on

Spain have always been coloured by an underlying duality: I love the energy of Spain and yet despair at times at the selfish individualism of its inhabitants. I have never shared in the view that Spaniards are cruel or hot-blooded by nature, although I do feel they have a healthier way of expressing their emotions than Anglo-Saxons. I think Spaniards lack manners, but perhaps thanks to their Catholicism, they have a mystical sense of life.

Spain itself is many different countries. What I like about the Basque country, Galicia, and Catalonia are those very characteristics which set them apart from the rest of the country: the fertility of the landscape, the industry of the people, their good sense and reliability. I feel equally charmed by the Andalusians, but for quite different reasons: their exuberance, their extreme reactions to matters of love and death, all remind me of how far away I am from puritan England.

Spain – the land and its people – has perhaps been subjected to more scrutiny from within and from without than any other country in Europe. To the compiler of a book of this kind that is not without its problems. Inevitably I have been forced into being highly selective, and on the whole have let my choice of writing correspond to my own experiences and prejudices. The difficulty I have faced is deciding what to leave out rather than what to include. I hope the source list will prove a helpful guide to further reading. Generally the book is weighted in favour of foreign (mainly English and French), as opposed to native, writers in order to make it as accessible as possible to the non-Spanish, non-specialist reader. This book is neither an anthology nor a history of Spanish literature. So I have picked those Spanish writers who in my view convey a sense of their country with immediacy and clarity. The Basque country and Galicia do not feature prominently because they have inspired the least literary output of all Spain's regions.

Spain was never part of the Grand European Tour. Travel and accommodation were too uncomfortable, the food too unpalatable, the threat of bandits too real to attract the kind of visitor who from the seventeenth century onwards, elsewhere in Europe, went in search of nothing more than his own peers in a novel, mildly exotic setting. Spain attracted a different kind of traveller – mad knights, Protestant spies, pilgrims, Bible pedlars, eccentric aristocrats, philosophers, poets, soldiers. To all of them Spain proved a discovery, a strange, idiosyncratic land, not easily understood. The towns and cities did not seem to belong in Europe, nor did the landscape. The country was a mass of different regional and communal identities – and then there was Andalusia, different again from the rest of Spain, so much part of Africa, the land of Don Juan and of Carmen and of the Moorish Caliphs, where frocked travellers from colder climates found themselves transformed into men of passion.

'The history of travel writing,' Colin Thubron has written, 'is not simply an account of objective voyage and description. It is the history of an endless tension between the temperament and character of generations of writers and that of the worlds they travel through.' Much of what has been written by foreigners about Spain is heavily weighted with the prejudice which Protestants bring with them to a Catholic country. This prejudice distorts reality at times, but also sheds a new light, a necessary flicker of scepticism in a country of such intensity and excruciating self-analysis. To be fair, Spain's own writers and intellectuals have also frequently challenged the traditions passed down to them by history.

A Literary Companion to a country as culturally varied as Spain inevitably invites criticism. Why, for example, are there individual chapters on Madrid, Barcelona, and Seville and not on other cities? Why are the only wars treated at any length the Peninsular and Civil Wars? Is flamenco the only dance to be practised in Spain, and do not Spaniards play football as well as go to the bullfight? Again I must make a plea for personal choice. The three cities with chapters of their own have always struck me as presenting in microcosm the cultural variety which makes up Spain as a whole. On the subject of wars, there can be no doubt that the Peninsular and the Civil War have produced the most literature of all conflicts to have taken place in Spain, and have had perhaps the most considerable political and social impact. And as for flamenco, while it is of course Andalusian – no Castilian, Basque, Catalan, or Gallegan would claim it as part of his or her culture – it symbolises for me once again the ethnic diversity of Spanish culture.

One of the reasons that I have greatly enjoyed compiling this book is the discovery along the way of so much writing that has outlived its time and survives as relevant contemporary comment. I make no excuses for quoting in abundance Richard Ford, the most entertaining and incisive of commentators on Spain. Ford remains little known beyond a relatively close-knit circle of Hispanists; I hope this companion will help bring him to the attention of a wider audience. On subjects as diverse as Spanish cooking and Moorish culture, he remains an indispensable guide. The romantic prose of Gautier is wonderfully inventive, and though subjective, provides more amusing insights into aspects of Spain than the often over-sentimental prose of Spaniards writing at the time. Among modern foreign writers, Laurie Lee and Jan Morris's poetic images have an accuracy, as well as a beauty, that has stood the test of time. Kate O'Brien, Honor Tracy, Rose Macaulay, and Virginia Woolf bring a particular feminine touch to their perceptions, often sensitive to the inner soul that lies beneath the tough Spanish skin.

There is no shortage of fine writing on matters Spanish, far more than can be contained in a book of this size. Even writers like V.S. Pritchett, Ernest Hemingway, and George Orwell, who have more than proved their colours in other countries, seem to be charged with a special vigour by the Spanish scene. I hope I have done them justice, as well as lesser known writers like Walter Starkie and Gerald Brenan who in my view remain among the most underrated commentators on Spain. Among the Spaniards I have tended to focus on authors like Cervantes, Galdós, Lorca and Cela who happily are now available to a much wider audience thanks to translation. I have also drawn in, where space permits, those Spanish writers, who although well known in Spain, remain largely overlooked internationally, such as Azorín and Baroja.

In the latter stages of the twentieth century, Spain has undergone a radical transformation as a result of tourism and general economic development. But while on the surface there has been change, much has not really changed at all. Spain is still quite unique, a part of Europe, yet separate from it in many respects. Spaniards are still old-fashioned in spirit and in some pastimes; anarchists and little dictators still abound, as do beautiful women and their dashing suitors; food and wine have a centuries-old tradition; a good flamenco and a good bullfight remain enormously popular, as do the Catholic festivals and fairs. I hope this is the Spain reflected in these pages.

Finally, I would also like the reader to look upon this book much as Cervantes looked upon Don Quixote and Sancho Panza: a meeting of the grave and the humorous, illusion and reality. For the most part I have concentrated on those writers whose perceptions have proved and will prove to be of lasting value. I have for large sections of this book ignored politics because they do not not belong in a book of this kind which aims to identify more lasting values. The clearest exception to this is the Spanish Civil War, without question, a literary as well as a political event. On the whole, my prime purpose, in the spirit of all good companions, has been to entertain and, as often as possible, to move.

BAY OF BISCAY

ATLANTIC OCEAN

Santander

Corunna
Oviedo
ASTURIAS
Bilbao

Cap Finisterre
Santiago de Compostela
GALICIA
León
Burgos

Vigo

Valladolid
OLD CASTILE

Zamora

R. Douro
Salamanca
Segovia
Sierra Guadarrama

Avila

MADRID

Almorox
Toledo
NEW CASTILE

R. Tagus
Talavera de la Reina
Consuegra

EXTREMADURA
R. Tagus

R. Guadiana
Manzanares

Lisbon
PORTUGAL
Badajoz
Merida

Valdepeñas

Sierra Morena
Ubeda

Guadalquivir
Cordoba

Huelva
Italica
Moguer
Palos
ANDALUSIA

Seville
Granada

Sierra Nevada
Yegen

Jerez
Ronda
Malaga

Cadiz
Torremolinos

Costa del Sol

N

Gulf of Gibraltar

MEDI

A F

*To my parents, Mabel and Tom, and
to the memory of my grandfather,
Gregorio Marañón.*

1

ACROSS THE PYRENEES

First Impressions

To get to the heart of Spain, V.S. Pritchett suggested in *The Spanish Temper*, one ought to go there by aeroplane and fly to its centre.

> Spain is reddish brown, yellow, and black, like some dusty bull restive in the rock and the sand and (we would guess) uninhibited. The river-beds are wide and bleached and dry. After Switzerland this is the highest country in Europe. The centre is a tableland torn open by gorges, and on the table the mountain ranges are spaciously disposed. There is little green, except on the seaboard; or rather the green is the dark gloss of ilex, olive, and pine, which from the height at which we are flying appear in lake-like and purple blobs. For the most part we are looking down at steppe which is iced in the long winter and cindery like a furnace floor in the short summer. Fortified desert – and yet the animal image returns again and again in this metalled and rocky scene, for occasionally some peak will give a sudden upward thrust, like the twist of a bull's horns, at the wings of the plane. Flying over Spain, we wonder at the torture that time had put upon the earth's crust and how human beings can live there.

The sheer variety of landscape makes much of the rest of Europe look tame and dull by comparison. Spain's sense of identity stems from its apparent geographical inaccessibility. 'Spain is a castle', wrote the essayist Salvador de Madariaga. But it is an enchanted castle, labyrinthine and majestic. In the time it may take us to drive across an English county, Spain unfolds in what the poet Laurie Lee has described as its 'geographical convulsions.'

From the first quarter of the eleventh century onwards, one of the most popular routes into Spain was by way of the Pyrenean pass of Roncesvalles. On the Spanish side this begins in the village of Valcarlos, the valley of Charles, named after the Emperor Charlemagne. Jan Morris, who travelled to Spain in the 1960s, described the pass as the most heroic of the ten defiles that pierce the Pyrenees, 'a high demanding route, resonant with romance . . . one of the classic passes of Europe and a properly sombre gateway into Spain.' It was used by Crusaders and pilgrims after Santiago de Compostela became one of the principal places of pilgrimage in Europe. Today it is still scenic, the border a dark forest of oak and chestnut falling away to a fertile green valley, made all the more evocative by the most moving and dramatic legend of pilgrimage to Santiago, that of the knights-errant Roland and Oliver.

Historically, Roland and Oliver were killed in AD 778, crushed by rocks thrown down on them by the wild people of Navarre. But the story of their exploits was transformed four centuries after the event in the *Chanson de Roland* written by the Norman cleric Turold. In this version of the story the knights are killed by Saracens. The natural landscape evoked by the poem's soft lyricism belies the brutality of the eighth century.

> High are the hills, dark and huge.
> The valleys are deep and the waters flow swiftly.
> They sound their bugles front and rear
> And all echo to the oliphant.
> The emperor rides with great wrath
> And so do all the Franks, distressed and sorrowful.
> No one fails to weep and show his grief;
> They pray for God that he protect Roland,
> Until they all arrive upon the battlefield.

Together with him they will strike mighty blows.
What matters? It is to no avail;
They delay too long; they cannot get there in time.

Roncesvalles and the *Chanson* have become so bound up
with each other that travellers through the centuries have
been content to accept legend as part of history. In 1907,
the poet Hilaire Belloc crossed the Pyrenees on foot, noting
as he did so that any man who yet believed the *Chanson* to
have been a Northern legend 'had better come to this place
and drink the mountains in'. Belloc writes in *Many Cities*:

> I have entered Spain by many entries in the last twenty
> years: by Barcelona, coming from Africa and the
> Balearics; by Cadiz, coming in a little coastwise boat
> from Laraiche, in Morocco; by the Bay of Santander;
> by Coruna and by Vigo. More often by the mountain
> roads . . . Whenever I so enter, whether by sea or by
> land, I find rising in me the same emotions as were
> provoked by my first glimpse of a new habit in houses
> and in men and of a new culture, unique in Europe,
> which came to me in that first voyage from Africa
> when I was young. But most strongly does one feel the
> contrast and change – the interest of exploration, the
> appetite for the discovery of new things, and the weight
> of the past – most strongly does one feel all these things
> when one passes into that proud, separate, and reserved
> world, not even by a path, nor by any entry commonly
> used, but alone, through some chance high notch of the
> ridge, where, not without difficulty but without peril,
> the mountains may be crossed and an approach made to
> Aragon through one of her innumerable parched valleys.

Alexandre Dumas in 1846 chose the less dramatic border
crossing at Irun for his entry into Spain. Dumas had three
trunks laden with new clothes and white linen, and six
cases of rifles and small arms to protect him on his travels.
Honoured to encounter such a distinguished literary tourist,
the Spanish customs officers left Dumas' luggage untouched.
They did not show the same generosity towards his less
famous companions – his son, an Arab valet, and three French

artists. 'My friends spent two hours arguing with the customs officials while I smoked a cigarette with their chief,' Dumas later recalled in *From Paris to Cadiz*.

Apart from overcoming border controls, the French party's first hours in Spain were spent consuming a cooked chicken, a loaf of bread, and a bottle of Bordeaux – a gift from their Spanish guide. Not until the last crumb had vanished did Dumas turn his eyes to the Basque countryside.

> If the heights that surrounded us were mere foothills compared to the Pyrenees, they were nevertheless quite considerable mountains compared with Montmartre, their rusty-brown slopes brightened here and there with patches of yellow, red, or green, wherever the owners of this rocky land found a plot of earth large enough to cultivate laboriously, by hand, a little crop of corn, *pimento* or clover. The road itself was delightful, with sparkling brooks and pretty villages, red and white, basking in the sunshine; crowds of children laughing, shouting, swarming everywhere, while now and then · as we flashed past the open doors of cottages we caught a glimpse of a dusky interior and the serene, clear-cut profile of a woman spinning.

Once on the highroad to Madrid, Dumas was equally impressed by the cultural diversity he encountered among the people.

> In France all the wayfarers one meets in any particular district are dressed very much alike. In Spain, what a contrast! Quite apart from the priests with their fantastically enormous hats, there is the copper-skinned Valencian with his voluminous white breeches, his feet shod with *alpargatas*; a man from the plains of La Mancha, with his brown jerkin, red belt, short trousers and brightly coloured stockings, his scarf knotted crosswise over his chest and his blunderbuss at his saddle-bow; an Andalusian, whose hat, with its two silk pompoms, has a widely curving, turned-up brim, and whose customary dress is a vividly chequered coat, brilliant waistcoat, crimson tie, trousers cut off at mid-

thigh, and high, embroidered top-boots, slashed at the side; the Catalonian, the length and thickness of his staff regulated by order of the police, a silk square knotted round his head with the ends hanging down his back; all these one can recognise at sight, as well as others from the dozen or so different regions of Spain which have grudgingly consented to form one kingdom but will never bind themselves into a united people.

The endless plain of Castile, through which Dumas journeyed, provided the Spanish essayist and journalist José Ortega y Gasset with much philosophical fodder as he journeyed south from the green hills of Asturias and the Basque country by train in 1921.

Beyond, a land begins which is not land; the land without green vegetation, without botanical adornment; the yellow land, the red land, the land of silver, pure clod, naked soil marked out now and again by the high lines of poplars. The plain undulates as if in torment, and sometimes it turns in on itself forming ravines and gullies, small hills and unsuspected, but always strategically placed, the villages and towns: one overlooking two valleys, another in the bevel of a hill. Always inhospitable, always in ruins, always the church in the centre, with its fine alert tower, which looks tired, but which rests like a good warrior, on its feet, saddle sunk into the earth, elbow resting on the cross . . . The atmosphere is completely transparent, and into it, as if into an emptiness without obstacles, light pours in torrents. Thanks to this, each colour reaches its ultimate potential. There is an unacceptable prejudice which considers beautiful only those landscapes where green triumphs. I think a certain element of utilitarianism influences this perspective which is alien to aesthetic contemplation. A green landscape promises a comfortable and abundant life . . . This landscape is not green, certainly: but it is instead a panorama of coral and gold, of violet and crystalline silver. Physiologists know well enough that the colours yellow and red automatically increase our pulsations, and their numbers increase the

wider the scope of hot tones which opens up before us.
. . . Well here in Castille, they will find an inflamed
scenery which does not exist in Europe; here the red and
golden fields set pulses galloping. Moreover: the whole-
ness which each colour achieves transforms all objects –
land, buildings, figures – in pure vibrating spectres . . .
It's a world to be contained in the pupil of an eye, an
ethereal and unreal world which, like the cities created
by the shape of moonlit clouds, seems at every instant
ready to disappear, eradicate itself, be reabsorbed in
nothingness. Castille, felt as a visual unreality, is one of
the most beautiful things in the Universe.

Castile as 'visual unreality' is felt with particular intensity
in Cervantes' masterpiece *Don Quixote*. The hero of the title
is the impoverished country squire with a consuming passion
for reading books of chivalry. He is also a mad knight deluded
into believing that the world he reads about is real and not
imaginary. Such delusion prompts him into action and elevates
this very prosaic character to a level of heightened perception.
Castile is transformed in Quixote's eyes; windmills become
giants:

At that moment they caught sight of some thirty or forty
windmills, which stand on that plain, and as soon as
Don Quixote saw them he said to his squire: 'Fortune is
guiding our affairs better than we could have wished.
Look over there, friend Sancho Panza, where more than
thirty monstrous giants appear. I intend to do battle with
them and take all their lives. With their spoils we will
begin to get rich, for this is a fair war, and it is a great
service to God to wipe such a wicked brood from the
face of the earth.'
'What giants?' asked Sancho Panza.
'Those you see there,' replied his master, 'with their
long arms. Some giants have them about six miles long.'
'Take care, your worship,' replied Sancho, 'that you
are not experienced in this matter of adventures. They
are giants, and if you are afraid, go away and say your
prayers, whilst I advance and engage them in fierce and
unequal battle.'

Don Quixote is a work of fiction, but the adventures of its two main protagonists are so closely linked to the real-life wanderings of Cervantes that they have become part of history. Castile itself has always exercised literary imagination to an extent that belies its apparent barrenness. In the 1980s, the writer Nicholas Wollaston journeyed through La Mancha in the steps of Don Quixote, and found fact and fantasy easily confused.

La Mancha imparts an indefinable anxiety, a sense of travelling without firm contact with the earth. I feel a vague longing to be elsewhere. Sometimes mountains appear on the horizon like distant islands, solid land at the edge of this unwaving sea. They make me restless. If they aren't imaginary, or put there like brush-strokes to define the plain, they must be a reminder of real country somewhere.

There was nothing imaginary about the Spain William Jacob, Member of Parliament for Rye, encountered for the first time on sailing into Cadiz in 1809. Andalusia was then, as now, as different from the rest of Spain as Spain is from the rest of Europe.

After I had entered the gates, and become a little reconciled to the nauseous effluvia of oil and garlick, I was greatly struck by the extraordinary scene around me; and could have imagined almost that I had suddenly been dropped from the clouds into the midst of a huge masquerade: the variety of dresses and characters, the swarms of people, the height and externally clean appearances of the houses, with the curtains drawn across from one side to the other and the extreme narrowness of the streets, rendered still more so by the projecting balconies of painted or gilt iron grating, all produced feelings I never before experienced and which no language can describe.

Few travellers have gone to Spain with a greater sense of mission than George Borrow, a member of the British and Foreign Bible Society. Borrow sailed to Iberia (the first port of call was Lisbon) with the intention of propagating the

Protestant Bible among a nation of Catholics. His crossing in early November 1835 was not an easy one. Scarcely had Borrow found the time to muse on the magnificent appearance of the coast of Galicia – 'lofty mountains, gilded by the rising sun' – than his ship was caught in one of those treacherous strong winds that plague Cape Finisterre. During one particularly fierce squall, one of the ship's crew was knocked into the sea while attempting to haul down the yard. Borrow watched helplessly from the deck, as a bungled attempt was made to rescue the stricken sailor. The young seaman sank beneath the waves never to be seen again.

He was to sail these same seas within the year, after a brief return to England to get formal acceptance for a 'Biblical campaign'. The passage proved no less dangerous as Borrow once again found himself approaching Cape Finisterre, 'a bluff, brown, granite mountain, whose frowning head may he seen far away by those who traverse the ocean.' In *The Bible in Spain*, Borrow recorded the drama that ensued after the ship's engine broke in the midst of a hurricane.

About this time I was standing near the helm, and I asked the steersman if there was any hope of saving the vessel, or our lives. He replied, 'Sir, it is a bad affair, no boat could live for a minute in this sea, and in less than an hour the ship will have her broadside on Finisterre, where the strongest man-of-war ever built must go to shivers instantly – none of us will see the morning.' The captain, likewise, informed the other passengers in the cabin to the same effect, telling them to prepare themselves; and having done so, he ordered the door to be fastened, and none to be permitted to come on deck. I, however, kept my station, though almost drowned with water, immense waves continually breaking over our windward side and flooding the ship. The water casks broke from their lashings, and one of them struck me down, and crushed the foot of the unfortunate man at the helm, whose place was instantly taken by the captain. We were now close to the rocks, when a horrid convulsion of the elements took place. The lightning enveloped us as with a mantle, the thunders were louder than the roar of a million cannon, the dregs of the ocean seemed to be cast up, and in the midst of all this turmoil, the wind, without the slightest intimation, veered right about, and pushed us from the horrible coast faster than it had previously driven us towards it.

The oldest sailors on board acknowledged that they had never witnessed so providential an escape. I said, from the bottom of my heart, 'Our Father – hallowed be Thy name.'

Almost exactly a hundred years later, a sea crossing to Spain by Laurie Lee proved less tempestuous and more suited to contemplation. Escaping from the security of his Cotswold family home, and spurred on by the memory of twelve months labouring on a London building site and a brief but intense love affair, the young Lee had bought a one-way ticket to Vigo at a cost of four pounds. It left him with a handful of shillings to see the rest of Spain.

Lee enjoyed the two slow days' sail from the English Channel and across the Bay of Biscay, 'smelling the soft Gulf winds blowing in from the Atlantic and feeling the deep easy roll of the ship'. The crossing was spent in a romantic half-sleep, broken by the sound of the anchor rattling over the side on their arrival in Vigo. Lee lay in his bunk a little longer listening to the first faint sounds of Spain, 'a howling dog, the grasping spasms of a donkey, the thin sharp cry of a cockerel'. Then he walked up on deck and for the first time in his life saw a foreign city. This first glimpse of Spain was like an apparition.

It seemed to rise from the sea like some rust-corroded wreck, as old and bleached as the rocks around it. There was no smoke or movement among the houses. Everything looked barnacled, rotting, and deathly quiet, as though awaiting the return of the Flood. I landed in a town submerged by wet green sunlight and smelling of the waste of the sea. People lay sleeping in doorways, or sprawled on the ground, like bodies washed up by the tide.

Among the earlier visitors to Spain was a friend of Dr Johnson and a distinguished man of letters in his own right, Joseph Baretti, who kept a daily travel journal. In 1760,

Baretti survived a tedious sea-crossing to Lisbon thanks to the bagpipe playing of a fellow passenger, a Scots surgeon. Approaching the Spanish border he was further entertained by a group of flamenco dancers.

It was nine o'clock this morning when I had not yet closed my eyes. The sight of dancing and the hurry of writing had inflamed my mind too much. I got up and went into the shaking gallery, where several of the men were eating salt meat and pickled olives with the four Spanish women. An odd breakfast, I thought. The women bowed and smiled as I entered, and the men invited me to do as they did, which I declined. People say that the Spaniards constantly breakfast on chocolate. Perhaps they do when they are at home; but here the general report was effectively contradicted.

After breakfast they had another touch of the *Fandango* in compliment to me, having seen how much I had been pleased with it: a piece of Spanish civility that should not pass unnoticed. But while some were thus dancing, others were shaving in the same room. This in other countries would be deemed an intolerable want of manners; but here it is nothing. These people live truly *sans façon*, or to say better, *à la Tartare*.

It was incidents such as the these that inclined Baretti to judge Spaniards generously. It was not his intention to follow 'those peevish and insolent travelmongers, who in the countries they describe look only for such objects of blame and disapprobation.' He found Spaniards no more corrupt than the English, and included their alleged idleness in his list of 'prejudices, calumnies, and falsehoods' propagated by careless and superficial observers.

A very different view was taken seven years later by fellow Italian Giacomo Casanova, although by then the Venetian adventurer's financial and sexual decline was such as to distort any view of the country and its people. In *Spanish Passions*, the sixth volume of his memoirs, Casanova's cynicism regarding all things Spanish (with the exception of women) dominates this record of his first glimpse of Valencia:

Though Valencia is blessed with an excellent climate, though it is well watered, situated in the midst of a beautiful country, fertile in all the choicest products of nature, though it is the residence of many of the most distinguished of the Spanish nobility, though its women are the most handsome in Spain, though it has the advantage of being the seat of an archbishop; in spite of all these commodities, it is a most disagreeable town to live in. One is ill lodged and ill fed, there is no good wine and no good company, there is not even any intellectual provision, for though there is a university, lettered men are absolutely unknown. As for the bridges, churches, the arsenal, the exchange, the town hall, the twelve town gates, and the rest, I could not take pleasure in a town where the streets are not paved, and where a public promenade is conspicuous by its absence. Outside the town the country is delightful, especially on the side towards the sea; but the outside is not the inside . . .

Poor Spaniards! This beauty and fertility of your land are the cause of your ignorance, as the mines of Peru and Potosi have brought about that foolish pride and all the prejudices which degrade you.

Spaniards, when will the impulse come? When will you shake off that fatal lethargy? Now you are truly useless to yourselves, and the rest of the world: what is it you need?

A furious revolution, a terrible shock, a conquest of regeneration; your case is past gentle methods, it needs the cautery and the fire.

Anti-Catholic prejudice guided the views of William Lithgow, a combative Scot who travelled to Spain in 1620 on a voyage he hoped would eventually take him to Ethiopia, the legendary land of Prester John. His 'discourse on the rare adventures and painful peregrinations' that befell him, include a far from favourable first impression of Spain. The countryside was 'generally a masse of mountains, a barren ill-manured soyle'. Travelling was 'miserable', with poor accommodation and – in a sentiment shared not just by Sancho Panza but by every other *picaro* that has graced the pages of

Spanish literature – a lack of good food. There was, Lithgow moaned,

> No ready drest diet, unless you buy it raw. You must buy first in one place your fire, your meate from the butcher, your wine from the taverne, your fruits, oyle and herbes from the botega, carrying all to the last place your bed-lodging: thus must the weary stranger toile or else fast. And in infinite places for Gold nor money can have no victuals.

Lithgow was accused of being a spy after strolling with a group of British seamen along the shore in Malaga and was subsequently tortured by the Inquisition. Released the following year, Lithgow recovered from the rack and the water torture by taking a cure in Bath. He never returned to Spain.

A more sympathetic view of Catholic Spain was taken by another Protestant, Richard Ford, although when he travelled there for the first time with his young family it was not without some misgivings. He told the minister plenipotentiary in Madrid, Henry Addington, in a letter dated 15 September 1830, 'It is a serious undertaking to travel in Spain with three children and four women, and a great bore to break up my establishment here, but it must be done.'

Between 1830 and 1833 Ford was to travel far and wide across Spain, covering more than 2000 miles. While he never grew to like garlic, he acquired a deep sympathy for and understanding of Spain as a whole. He probably appreciated aspects of the country rather more acutely than the Spaniards themselves, even if his perspective seems both patronizing and romantic at times. In *A Handbook for Travellers in Spain* he writes:

> Spain is Spain, a truism which cannot be too often repeated; and in its being Spain consists its originality, its raciness, its novelty, its idiosyncrasy, its best charm and interest, although the natives do not know it, and are every day, by a foolish aping of European civilisation, paring away attraction, and getting commonplace, unlike themselves, and still more unlike their Gotho-Moro and most picturesque fathers and mothers.

A strong sense of realism, and of the wild, brutal nature of Spain, has never lagged far behind more sentimental accounts of the country. An anonymous young American citizen who visited Spain at about the same time as Ford, recorded a fellow traveller's account of someone who travelled forth from the city of Zaragoza and had been twice 'plundered' along the way. This was a country in which no one could be trusted and one was likely to be robbed and murdered at any hour of the day. The American listened attentively, but was unperturbed. These tales of horror, he concluded, were but a 'trifling impediment to men already resolved'. However, on the road between Tarragona and Valencia he was attacked by a group of brutal robbers. His coachman, having been struck by one of them with a stone, invoked in his agony Jesus Christ, the apostle Santiago, and the Virgin of Pilar.

All in vain: the murderer redoubled his blows, until growing furious in the task, he laid his musket beside him, and worked with both hands upon his victim.

Pepé, the lad, fared even worse. Caught by the bandits while trying to escape, he was hacked to pieces with a bread knife.

It was not a blunt sound as of a weapon that meets with positive resistance; but a hissing sound, as if the household implement, made to part the bread of peace, performed unwillingly its task of treachery.

Miraculously, the American himself escaped untouched.

In spite of stories like this, travellers were to follow the American to Spain in their thousands, testing every kind of transport available in order to discover the country and its people. For Ford, easily the most preferred form of transport was the horse.

A man in a public carriage ceases to be a private individual: he is merged into the fare, and becomes a number according to his place; he is booked like a parcel, and is delivered by the guard. How free, lord and master of himself, does the same dependant gentleman mount his eager barb, who by his neighing and pawing exhibits his joyful impatience to be off too! How fresh and sweet the free breath of heaven, after the frosty atmosphere of a full inside of foreigners, who, from the narcotic effects of tobacco, forget the existence of soap, water, and clean linen!

On one occasion Ford made a pilgrimage from Seville to Santiago and back again, accompanied only by an Andalusian servant. Another extended tour of many months took him on horseback through Granada, Murcia, Valencia, Catalonia, and Aragon, to say nothing of repeated excursions 'through every nook and corner' of Andalusia. As a result, Ford had no hesitation in recommending to the 'young, healthy, and adventurous' a lengthy horse-ride around Spain – preferably as far off the beaten track as possible – as 'by far the most agreeable plan of proceeding.'

Even with the onset of modern travel, visitors to Spain have reserved a special interest in the horse as a form of transport. It was the horse that brought to Spain Penelope Chetwode, the wife of the poet laureate John Betjeman, in 1961. To friends who urged her to visit the country, Penelope responded that her experiences of two other countries, Italy and India, were 'enough for ten lifetimes.' Her mind was changed when she read about conducted tours in Andalusia in an English Sunday newspaper. They were run by a Sevillano near the emerging tourist resort of Torremolinos. The preliminary tour was in the Serrania de Ronda. Penelope's gypsy groom, Pitirri,

> taught me to sing the Hail Mary and also a lot of words pertaining to the feeding and shoeing of horses. Every morning before starting I would write out a vocabulary to be learnt while riding along. By the time I set off on my own tour, therefore, I was equipped with a good string of nouns such as barley, straw, girth, crupper, saddle, horse-shoe, blacksmith, but not more than six past principles: I have come, I have been, I have suckled, I have eaten.

For her main tour, a six-week trek through the *pueblos* (villages) of the Sierra de Cazorla, north of Granada, Penelope

borrowed a mare from the Duke of Wellington's *finca* in
Molino del Rey. The horse was called La Marquesa, the
Marchioness. She was twelve years old, 'more or less equiva-
lent in horse age to my fifty-one years . . . so we were going
exploring together – two middle-aged ladies in Andalusia.'

Penelope Chetwode described her adventures on horseback
'like riding through the Garden of Eden before the Fall.'
Yet by the time of writing, primitive Spain – breakfasts of
pig brains grilled in pine embers, dusty tracks, and oil lamps –
was barely resisting the advent of the modern era.

Modern times were ushered in with the coming of the
railways. The first line linking Barcelona to nearby Mataro
was put into service in 1848, two years after Dumas had made
his way across Spain by horse-drawn diligence. By the early
1860s it was possible to travel by train from Calais to Alicante.

The building of the railways proved wrong one of Ford's
predictions, that Spain's 'national indolence and dislike to
change' would defeat any attempt at industrialization. And
yet the railway network did not immediately make travel
easier or faster. In his *Wanderings in Spain* (1873), Augustus
Hare noted that while Spaniards used the railways, they hated
and abused them, making them 'go as slow as possible.'
Certainly his own passage from France proved less than
triumphant. The train was derailed just as it was about to
cross the Bidassoa river, 'knocking everybody back into their
seats, and swamping sentiment in fright.' The train was
back on its tracks within an hour thanks to the efforts of
a 'multitude of peasants', and as it finally steamed across the
narrow channel, Hare found the time to meditate with more
leisure on the peculiarities of Spanish train travel.

> However crowded it may be already, however filled up
> with hand-bags and other impedimenta of its occupants,
> the new-comers, who would be scowled upon in
> England, are welcomed with smiles and willing help;
> places are at once made for them, their bags and baskets
> are confortably stowed away, and everything that can be
> supplied is offered for their convenience; every Spanish
> gentleman is willing to assist, translate, or advise; and
> if you travel in the second-class carriages, which, as in

many parts of Germany, are, in the north of Spain, often much more roomy and confortable, and generally far less crowded than the first, not even the humblest peasant leaves it without lifting his hat and wishing you a hearty 'A Dios Señores.'

The train crawls along in the most provoking way, stopping at all the small stations for two, four, ten, twenty minutes, and giving you ample time to survey the scenery. You feel impatient, but your Spanish companions are perfectly satisfied, 'it is so much safer, so satisfactory never to have any accidents.' Time is of no importance to them whatever.

In 1916, Leon Trotsky travelled by train from the Pyrenean border to Madrid after being expelled from France as a German sympathiser. His diaries provide snapshots of Spaniards at their most relaxed.

We advanced towards the interior of the Iberian Peninsula. This is not France, but something which is more primitive, more provincial, more crude. It is altogether more sociable. They drink wine from earthenware jugs. They talk loudly. The women laugh a great deal. Three friars read their breviary, and, afterwards fix their gazes on the polished roof of the train and babble. There is much here which is picturesque. The Spaniards are wrapped up in capes with scarlet linings or in gaudy chequered blankets and scarfs which cover them up to their noses. They sit there like turkeys or parrots. They seem unapproachable. In reality, they are incorrigible talkers.

The English poet and travel writer Ted Walker arrived on one of his first trips to Spain at the port of Santander. There he experienced a variety of scents, 'fresh bread and over-ripe melons, shellfish, chopped onion, red meats being cooked in sauces containing bitter dark chocolate . . . the beginnings of slow-to-simmer soups and stews, newly-crushed garlic heads releasing juice into hot olive oil; and the fragrances of late breakfasts: pungent coffee, newly-fried churros, the smoke of black tobacco'. And yet for him no entrance to Spain was made with 'anything like the same sense of excitement and incredulous wonder' as when he transferred his luggage to the Spanish train on the French border. It was in the mid-1950s, well before the advent of the high-speed train and when the joy of travelling still lay in what one encountered on the way.

> What a train! Nothing to do with Europe, clearly: rather, a century-old Mexican monster, complete with cow-catcher, brass belly-bands and a tall chimney belching smoke not of coal but of wood; a train straight out of a cowboy film, a Wells Fargo Special with bygone carriages of nice, varnished oak – one that Hopalong Cassidy might have ridden alongside to foil a robbery while Lulabelle, simpering beneath a white parasol, waved from the window. The vast engine quietly hissed and occasionally sneezed a mild, hay-fever sneeze. The driver and his fireman sat nearby on the platform, their backs to the wall in the shade, eating a leisurely snack. I watched them as I might have observed rare animals in the wild. Real Spaniards! They tore hunks of yellow-crust bread, sliced rounds of *chorizo* sausage, with wonderfully, long, flick-bladed knives, and drank wine from squeezed leather *botas* at arm's length – the glittering parabola of liquid bridging lips and fingertips exactly as described in an ancient picaresque novel I'd been reading.

Kate O'Brien first arrived in Spain in 1922, at the age of twenty-four, to take up a post as a governess. Her employers were a rich Spanish family who lived in Bilbao. The job in the 'queer melancholy' Basque town allowed her to take in a foreign country gradually. Her impressions were first recorded in *Mary Lavelle*, one of her early novels. In it, there is a description of a journey the heroine takes by train through Castile.

> Men in suits of black cotton straightened themselves to see the train go by, and sometimes a boy waved his wide straw hat. The land was blond unbrokenly; its fairness stretched without pause or hurry to meet a sky so far away and luminous as to be only in the most aerial

meaning blue. There were undulations, there were valleys; but within this spaciousness the breaks they made were like sighs which alleviate meditation; hamlets were so buff of roof and wall as almost to be imperceptible in the great wash of gold; roads made lonely curves across the quiet and bridges of pale stone spanned shallow rivers. Here a shepherd called his goats for evening milking; there a bell rang for a village funeral.

Like transport, Spanish accommodation for travellers and newcomers may not have been physically pleasing, but at least provided some entertainment. Don Quixote took a Spanish inn for a castle, and a cook for a princess. But there were other romantics who found in a *venta* or a *posada* an oriental primitiveness and excitement that helped them forget the hardships encountered on the road. Kate O'Brien had this to say about Spanish hotels in *Farewell to Spain:*

I love Spanish hotels. I speak, I repeat, only for the cheap ones, of which I know a great many now. They have their defects, Heaven knows – occasionally quite unpleasant defects of a kind which we need not discuss in this polite book. Defects of plumbing. But these are infrequent, and their like has come my way in the hotels of other countries where I have been charged more than I have ever paid in Spain and where compensatory efforts of hospitality were neither as marked nor as much to my taste as the Spaniards'. Good manners, for instance. Spanish good manners are unbeatably good, and most of the Spanish possess them. They are so especial because of the steady balance in the average Spanish character of good-will and reserve. These two things are ideal in a hotel-keeper – as in anyone. And good taste. The good taste of Spain when she isn't trying is only equalled, in my experience, by her bad taste when she is. And the latter can certainly be frightening . . . There'll be statuary that you'll never forget as long as you live, and a radio as big as a bathing-hut; there'll be oil-paintings of Sevillan ladies, and flashier strip-lighting than you've ever seen . . .

Another visitor to Spain, the Marquess of Londonderry, may have had time for similar contemplation had his travels not been so cluttered. In 1839 he set off from Malaga for a journey through the Alpujarra mountain range with a baggage wagon, two coaches, 'one for the ladies, and the other of an inferior description for the servants', a group of gentlemen on horseback, and an escort consisting of a non-commissioned officer and six lancers. The British consul to Malaga joined the party at the last minute, dressed '*a l'Espagnole*' and armed with arquebus and dagger. It poured with rain so that the party was forced to seek shelter.

The inn they found consisted of two small rooms and a kitchen entirely filled with Spanish travellers. The party by now was drenched and tired and in no mood for Spanish obstinacy or machismo.

We experienced at first the greatest brutality; no entreaties would drive the cigar squadron from its position round the fire; no money would bribe them; they were travellers, and paid as well as we, and they would give way to no one. The situation of our ladies had no affect on these ruffians.

The party was spared further humiliation by the intervention of the local mayor. He ordered the premises to be cleared of his fellow Spaniards so as to make room for the tourists. The English were given full possession of the inn. They drank bottles of claret and champagne and slept on their portable beds. The Marquess nonetheless was never reconciled to the 'wretched encampment'. Only his cook 'saved the whole party from perishing.'

In 1818, the young Bostonian George Ticknor noted: 'I have not been in a single inn where the lower storey was not a stable and the upper one so full of fleas as if it were an Egyptian course.' But he was up against the Spanish paradox and loved it. For all the torture along the way, the Spanish people amused Ticknor 'more than anything I have met in Europe', thanks to the originality of their manners and feelings. He concluded romantically: 'When you have crossed the Pyrenees you have not only passed from one country and climate to another, you have gone back a couple of centuries in your chronology.'

In 1829, the American writer and honorary consul Washington Irving embarked on a journey from Seville to Granada with his friend Prince Dimitri Dolgorouki, the Secretary of the Russian Legation. They stopped at a mountain inn and quickly struck up a dialogue with the local Spaniards. Cigars were handed out by Irving and food was served by the innkeeper's wife. The evening was spent in a warm glow of cordiality with entertainment being provided in the form of an impromptu flamenco by 'rustic belles and amateur singers': a buxom local girl, the innkeeper's pretty daughter Pepita, and a shoemaker.

Washington Irving would in time take up more luxurious quarters in the Alhambra. But the American was equally taken by these rustic scenes, even if now and again he may have embroidered them a little.

> What a country is Spain for a traveller, where the most miserable inn is as full of adventure as an enchanted castle and every meal is itself an achievement. Let others repine at the lack of turnpike roads and sumptuous hotels, and all the elaborate comforts of a country cultivated into tameness and the commonplace, but give me the rude mountain scramble, the roving haphazard manners that give such a true game flavour to romantic Spain.

In the summer of 1946 Camilo José Cela set off on foot in the steps of Cervantes in search of the heart of Spain. The region he chose was the Alcarria, in the north-east corner of Castile, a place remarkable for its Spanishness. At the time Spain was still suffering the aftermath of Civil War, and her ensuing international isolationism. Far from giving the country a sense of its own identity, literature and history had combined to obscure it. In an open letter to his friend Gregorio Marañón which he published as an introduction to *Journey to the Alcarria*, Cela explained that travel writing should be like a lesson in geography, concerned only with the truth.

> The Alcarria is a beautiful region which people apparently have no desire to visit. I walked through it for a number of days, and I liked it. It is a region of

great variety, and except for honey (the dealers buy up all that), it has everything: wheat, potatoes, goats, olives, tomatoes, and game. The people seemed like honest folk; they speak magnificent Spanish with a fine pure accent, and though they didn't know much about what I was doing there, they treated me well and fed me, sometimes scantily, but always with kindness.

While Spaniards in the twentieth century have concerned themselves with the Spanish 'soul', it is the foreign visitor who can convey a sense of the excitement of discovery. As he cleared the pass of the Pyrenees and gazed down at the landscape stretching infinitely away, Hilaire Belloc wrote movingly of geography and history in a way that conveys both the immensity of the past and the profound appeal of the present.

How often had I known that call! And yet, as I say, in that night and morning passage of the hills, I felt it more strongly than ever before. I was to see those villages which seemed part of the brown earth, and each of which had been called impertinently a museum, but should be called, reverently, a shrine. I was once more to stand astonished at the amazing pillars of sandstone as high as mountains which take the traveller aback as he turns the corner of the valley at Riglos. I was to come upon the first of the great churches which continue and grow to this day, and are the centres of this people, having in their plan, in the details of their ornament, in the uncompromising national seclusion of the Coro – like an inner mystery everywhere – the impress of something which is still of Europe and yet more individually itself than anything else of the West. For though it is a jest only that Africa begins at the Pyrenees, it is true that there begins with the Pyrenees a place sharply different from ours, in some things older, in others younger, having suffered crucifixion, having re-arisen, subjected to every vicissitude of fortune and misfortune, of glory and of humiliation, of satisfaction and regret; but, above all, enduring and fed with an inward fire. Spain.

2

THE BUMPKIN CAPITAL

Madrid

As every guide book will inform you, in Spain all roads lead to Madrid. Kilometre zero can be found in the Puerta del Sol, the gateway to the sun – a square in fact not a gate. It is a city that has never been loved much by those who seek shape and direction or even those whose romantic sense of travel has focused their attention too strictly on the unusual and the exotic. It has been admired most by those who have been prepared to take Madrid on its own terms, judging it from within rather than from without. It has appealed to liberal minds, capable of tolerating a city that is both shabby and vain, traditional and innovative, insular and yet vulnerable to the impact of foreign forces, in peacetime as in war.

If Madrid deserves the title of capital it is because it has grown to represent the many faces of Spain. Archibald Lyall remarked after a visit to the capital in the late 1950s:

> Of all great European capitals, Madrid is the one which most bristles with paradoxes and offers the most contrasts and inconsistencies. It is at once the least Spanish and the most Spanish town in the Peninsula – the least Spanish because it is the most modernised and international, and the most Spanish because, perhaps because of its four centuries as a sort of 'Washington D.C.' and of the mixed population which has flowed into it from various regions of Spain, it is a synthesis of them all. In

Barcelona one is all the time aware of being in Catalonia, and in Seville one could be nowhere except in Andalusia, but Madrid is not particularly Castilian in the sense that the smaller cities of Castile are Castilian. It is Spanish, and that is all.

When Philip II moved his court to Madrid in 1561, it was a small hill-town, with a quarter of the population of Toledo. The decision to establish the capital there was, in the words of historian Hugh Thomas, 'a fateful choice, which has for ever after affected, and severely weakened, Spain and perhaps, through example, the entire Spanish world.' Among the early visitors to the new imperial capital was Sir Richard Wyn, a Welsh baronet, who in 1623 accompanied Charles Prince of Wales on his journey to court the Infanta Maria. Wyn left this account of the town the King of Spain liked to describe as 'noble and very loyal':

The place resembles Newmarket, both for the country and for the sharpness of the air. It is but a village, and lately grown to this greatness by this King and his father's residing there. It stands very round, thick with buildings, having neither back-premises nor gardens in all the town. We were brought in at the far end of the town, which lay near the place we were to alight at. Coming through the streets, I observed most of the buildings to be of brick, and some few of stone, all set forth with balconies of iron, a number whereof were gilt. I found likewise that some of their buildings were but of one storey, and the rest five and six stories high. Enquiring the reason, I was told those low buildings were called in Spanish, Casa de Malicia – in English, House of Malice. For there the King has the privilege, that no man can build above one storey, the King is to receive half the rent, to save which charge, there be infinite numbers of houses but one storey high.

By the following century Madrid had grown in size and some of its buildings had achieved a certain imperial grandeur. In other aspects, however, it had begun to demonstrate its backwardness. Approaching the capital from the south in

October 1760, Joseph Baretti was much impressed by the Royal Palace and gardens of Aranjuez. 'I have seen a great many delightful places in many parts,' he noted, 'but none more so than the royal palace and garden of Aranjuez. A poet would say that Venus and love consulted here with Catullus and Petrarch about building a rural mansion for Psyche, Lesbia, Laura, or some Spanish Infanta.'

Later, when he crossed the Manzanares river, Baretti's generosity still pervaded his impressions. The river has been subject to criticism from Spaniards and foreigners alike: the seventeenth-century Spanish novelist Francisco Quevedo called it an 'apprentice stream'; and Dumas was to relate how he had bought a glass of water, drunk half of it, and thrown the rest of it into the Manzanares, after concluding that the virtually dry stream needed it more. Baretti was kinder: 'the fact is that the Manzanares becomes sometimes a considerable river by the sudden melting of the snow on the neighbouring hills, and is often half a mile broad in winter. Philip therefore did a very proper thing, when he built a large bridge over it, and ridiculous are those who pretend to ridicule him on this account.'

Only when he found himself closer to Madrid's centre, did Baretti adopt a more critical tone.

From the bridge to the gate of the town there is a straight and wide avenue of fine trees, which renders the entrance on that side very noble. But it is impossible to tell how I was shocked at the horrible stink that seized me the instant I trusted myself within that gate! So offensive a sensation is not to be described. I felt a heat all about me, which was caused by the fetid vapours exhaling from numberless heaps of filth lying all about it. My head was presently disordered by it, and the head-ake continued very painful from that moment. I came to alight at an inn called La Locanda del Principe, which is kept by one Zilo, a merry Venetian, and have taken possession of the highest apartment in it, that I may be as distant as possible from the polluted ground. But the whole of the atmosphere is so impregnated with those vapours, that I think them unavoidable, was I to mount to the third region of the air.

Baretti vowed never to return to Madrid until the King had succeeded in meeting his pledge to clean the town. Sewers were installed within five years. In spite of the improved hygiene, however, Madrid continued to provoke divided opinions. In 1774, Major William Dalrymple, who was garrisoned in Gibraltar, visited the capital during a five-month horse ride through Spain. His subsequent intelligence report included the following observation:

> Some of the streets, such as the Calle Atocha, Carrera de San Geronimo, Calle de Alcala etc. are spacious and handsome; particularly the latter, the entrance of which is near two hundred feet broad; they are kept perfectly clean, and well paved and lighted, lamps being placed at every fifteen or sixteen yards. The police, upon the plan of that of Paris, is well regulated . . .

Visiting Spain just over a hundred years later, Eugene Poitou showed himself unimpressed by Madrid.

> Madrid is a gloomy enough city and a paltry enough capital. It is deficient both in charm and grandeur. It has neither beauty of site – for its environs are a desert; nor the advantage and agreeableness of a river – for the Manzanares is dry during three-quarters of the year; nor memories of a storied past – for as a city it dates only from yesterday; nor monuments of art – for you would seek in vain a church or public building worthy of any interest . . .

> To Madrid has happened what happens to all cities which the caprice of a sovereign endeavours to found, without reference to the accidents of nature or the necessities of commerce; like Berlin and Washington, it is an artificial creation, living with a factitious life. Madrid – without commerce, without industries, without intellectual or political movement of its own – is but a nominal capital, which receives from without its life or impulse, instead of communicating it. It is 'la corte' as the Spanish say – that is the royal residence; it is neither the head nor the heart of the country . . .

> Its general appearance is mean and vulgar. The streets are ill-paved, the pavements few and narrow. Its shops

shine with a borrowed luxury, which comes from Paris. Brussels is more alive, and Bordeaux has more the air of a great town. The Puerta del Sol, which the Spaniards so admire, is an irregular and somewhat ugly square, of smaller area than the Place de la Bourse in Paris.

Terence Mason Hughes, an English resident of Spain in the year 1845, noted the extent to which Madrid had grown to encapsulate the country's turbulent politics. The nineteenth century alone saw international and civil wars and countless *coup d'états*. Madrid had had 'her bosom torn by domestic strife and been a seething cauldron of political turmoil', although the 'face of the city had been yearly improving, and the solution to the great problem of life has been hourly progressing, slowly, yet with visible advancement.'

Such advancement as there was however was not sufficient, in Mason Hughes' eyes, to put Madrid on the same level as the rest of European civilisation. The capital had yet to overcome its backwardness.

Confort as yet is not understood except in the higher circles, and in a portion of middle life; the numerous forced emigrations to France and England have been of essential benefit as eye-instructors; while the habits of foreign residents in the Spanish metropolis, and especially the manners and influence of diplomatic circles, have beaten down a portion of that stubborn pride in which the Spaniard wraps himself as in a cape, impervious to the slighten civilisation of the 'outer barbarians'. But it is above all the travelled Spaniard who is a powerful agent in convincing his countrymen that, so far from monopolizing the world's wisdom, they are far outstripped by societies of exterior men, and that foreign inventions have their usefulness as well as ingenuity.

The ambivalent attitude of the Madrileño to foreign influences is portrayed in Galdós' novel *Fortunata y Jacinta*, published in 1876. By then most of the buildings which today survive as old Madrid were in place. The strength of the novel lies not so much in its architectural descriptions as the way in which it captures the prejudices and preferences of the capital's inhabitants. The shawl shop run by Gumersindo and Isabel Arnaiz becomes Madrid in microcosm, both open to change and resistant to it. Their daughter grows up in 'an atmosphere redolent of sandalwood and Oriental fragrances and saturated with the vivid colours of Chinese shawls.' But by 1840, the shops that received Cantonese materials direct from China could no longer compete with the 'ones that ordered through Liverpool.' Gumersindo, brought to the edge of bankruptcy, curses the foreigner who has made hell of his life and changed irrevocably the Madrid he once knew. His wife however adopts a more pragmatic position towards Europe.

'Well, we might as well face up to the novelties,' Isabel said to her husband, observing the obsession with fashion that this society was beginning to display together with the instant desire of the Madrileños to be 'seriously' elegant. And on top of that, it was the era when the middle class was beginning to come into its own, taking up the jobs created by the new political and administrative system, buying up all the properties (of which the Church had held the title) with installment plans, thus making itself the chief landowner and beneficiary of the budget; in a word gathering the spoils of absolutism and clericalism to found the empire of the frock coat. The frock coat is of course the symbol, but the most interesting thing about this empire is the dress of its ladies, the powerful energies that flow from private into public life and decide the course of great events. Clothes, ah! Is there anyone who doesn't see in them one of the main sources of the energy of our times, perhaps even a generative cause of movement and life? Think a bit about what they represent, what they're worth, the wealth and ingenuity that the most industrious city of the world spends on producing them, and your mind is bound to catch, between the pleats of fashionable materials, a glimpse of our whole mesocratic system, the huge pyramid at whose peak sits the top hat; the entire politico-administrative machine, the public debt and the railroads, the budget and the national income, the paternalistic State and socialist trends in Parliament.

But Gumersindo and Isabel had arrived a bit too late. The novelties were in the hands of clever merchants who already knew the road to Paris. Arnaiz went to Paris too, but having no taste, he brought back horrible stuff that nobody wanted. Isabel, however, didn't let her spirits flag. While her husband began to lose his good judgement, she began 'to see a few things'. She saw that customs were rapidly changing in Madrid; that this proud court city, this indecent country town, would soon become a civilized capital. For all its ridiculous vanity, Madrid was a metropolis in name only. It was a bumpkin in a gentleman's coat buttoned over a torn, dirty shirt. But the bumpkin was about to become a real gentleman . . .

Sir Arthur de Capell Brooke gleaned some valuable information on Madrid society in the nineteenth century whilst travelling to the capital in a crowded diligence. It was the apparent weakness of its politicians for the female sex.

Our buxom companions, who were in excellent spirits, had been, it appeared, to Madrid on business which induces numbers to repair to the capital, to do what their husbands could not do, namely, to obtain certain favours from the minister, which are granted with greater facility to the female than to the male sex. This is the general system in Spain, and petticoat influence had in consequence by far the most preponderating weight in affairs. Does a person wish to obtain any situation, post, or office, to be appointed to a certain command, or to effect, in short, any object essential to his interest, and of which the government has the disposal, his rib, as a far abler negotiator than himself, is despatched to Madrid, and, repairing every day to the minister's levees, brings into play her different points of character, and the numberless little tricks which her sex in general, and the Spanish ladies in particular, know so well how to exhibit to the best advantage.

Madrid has tended to be loved rather more for its people than for its buildings. The Prado museum, however, has

always attracted praise. One of the earliest commentaries
on the building was that of Don Nicolas de la Cruz de
Bahamonde, Count of Maule, a cultured gentleman from
Cadiz who collected works of art. Don Nicolas lived much
of his adult life in the Spanish colonies of South America,
but in 1806 he was in Madrid, observing the construction,
in the Prado Avenue, of what was originally intended as the
Museum of Natural History.

> Of all the public edifices the magnificent Museum is
> the most worthy of our concentrated attention . . . the
> main frontage comprises a peristyle of six massive Doric
> columns below and a gallery above composed of twenty-
> eight Ionic columns, fourteen on each side, combined
> with twenty-eight pilasters. The jutting angles are quite
> pleasing. On the side facing the Botanical Gardens a fine
> porch is to be seen, adorned with four fluted Corinthian
> columns, unfinished . . . It would be advantageous if the
> architect, Don Juan Villanueva, in charge of the works,
> were to publish his plans as soon as the building is
> completed and compose a detailed account of a structure
> of such great merit. The frontage at present lacks light,
> but will not do so after the site has been cleared and
> the adjacent walls on the Prado Avenue demolished. The
> edifice will then make a very fine impression . . .

The building survived the vicissitudes of the subsequent
French occupation of Madrid, although the damage it suffered
meant that the Museum of Natural History never came into
being. Instead this fine example of Spanish neo-classical
architecture was restored and turned into one of Europe's
major national art galleries under the auspices of King
Ferdinand VII. On 19 November 1818 the Prado museum
was thrown open to the public for the first time.

William Clark, a fellow of Trinity College, Cambridge,
visited the Prado in 1849 during a long summer of travel
through Spain.

> The first impulse of every stranger on waking, the first
> morning after his arrival at Madrid is, or ought to be,
> to visit the Gallery. Indeed, but for that magnet, few

would encounter the slow torture of diligence-travelling through the interior, when they might go by steam from port to port all round the coast (cholera-time excepted). Let the stranger, then, having duly fortified himself with chocolate, sally forth, pass intrepidly through the midst of the soldiers who are lounging about the post-office door (fierce as they look, they won't harm you), and then take the Carrera San Geronimo, carefully hugging the shady side till you come to the Prado. The scene you left so full of life, and fans, and flirtation, last night, is now abandoned to sunshine and solitude – two synonymes at this time of year. You must, however, endure the glare for a minute or two, cross right over 'the dust that once was love', and before you stands a large, massive, but not inelegant building of red stone, with white facings and pillars, in the British infantry style. That is the Gallery. Unless your first object be the sculptures – which is scarcely conceivable – go to the door at the north end; enter, present your passport to the old doorkeeper, who returns it to your worship with a grave bow; write your name and occupation – 'proprietor' of course, even if you are conscious that the only thing you hold is the fee – simple is your portmanteau – buy a catalogue, and then go in, and walk straight forward, glancing to right and left, but pausing nowhere, till you have found the Pearl – that famous jewel of art.

The painting Clark refers to is *The Holy Family* by Raphael. He recorded his impressions too of Velazquez, whom he considered a 'genius, which can be estimated at Madrid, and at Madrid only.' Similar adulation for Velazquez was demonstrated by Edouard Manet, when he visited the Prado in 1865. He noted:

The painters of every school who surround him in the Madrid Museum, and who are very well represented, all seem second-rate in comparison with him. He is the painter to beat all painters. He didn't astonish me, he enchanted me . . .

The Prado museum was not yet in existence when William Beckford came to Madrid in December 1787. The capital, shrouded in fog, revealed itself only gradually.

About one o'clock, the vapours beginning to dissipate, a huge mass of building, and a confused jumble of steeples, domes, and towers, started on a sudden from the mist. The large building I soon recognised to be the new palace. It is a good deal in the style of Caserta, but being raised on a considerable eminence, produces a most striking effect. At its base flows the pitiful Manzanares, whose banks were all of a flutter with linen hanging out to dry.

We passed through this rag-fair, between crowds of mahogany-coloured hags, who left off thumping their linen to stare at us, and, crossing a broad bridge over a narrow streamlet, entered Madrid by a gateway of very indifferent architecture. The neat pavement of the streets, the loftiness of the houses, and the cheerful showy appearance of many of the shops, far surpassed my expectation.

Upon entering the Calle de Alcala, a noble street, much wider than any in London, I was still more surprised. Several magnificent palaces and convents adorn it on both sides. At one extremity, you perceive the trees and fountains of the Prado (avenue), and, at the other, the lofty domes of a series of churches. We have got apartments at the Cruz de Malta, which, though very indifferently furnished, have at least the advantage of commanding this prospect. I passed half-an-hour after dinner in one of the balconies, gazing upon the variety of equipages which were rattling along. The street sloping gradually down, and being paved with remarkable smoothness, they drove at a furious rate, the high fashion at Madrid; where to hurry along at the risk of laming your mules, and cracking their skulls, is to follow the example of his Majesty, than whom no monarch drives with greater vehemence . . .

If subsequent travellers found themselves drawn to the Puerta del Sol it was less to admire the surrounding architecture than to feel the pulse of the city's population gathered there. In 1837, George Borrow entered the capital on horseback, having left behind him the reserved Portuguese and the stark landscape of Extremadura. He approached it as a man journeying half lost across a desert, relying on the instinct of the animal that carries him. He found the roads leading to the capital across the Castilian plain poorly marked, especially at crossroads. He invariably allowed his horse to decide which way to go. Once inside the capital, disorientation gave way to enthusiasm for the city's astonishing vitality. Paris and Edinburgh might have more stately edifices and London nobler squares, but the population, drawn from all areas of Spain, made Madrid unique.

> Within a mud wall scarcely one league and a half in circuit are contained two hundred thousand human beings, certainly forming the most extraordinary vital mass to be found in the entire world; and be it remembered that this mass is strictly Spanish . . . with the exception of a sprinkling of foreigners . . . a population, which however strange and wild, and composed of various elements, is Spanish, and will remain so as long as the city exists.

Borrow described the Puerta del Sol as the 'great place of assemblage for the idlers of the capital, poor or rich.' Edmondo de Amicis, an Italian who wrote numerous travel books and novels, in 1870 was similarly enraptured by the human atmosphere he experienced in the crowded central streets and squares of the capital.

> Upon the sidewalks, which are wide enough to allow four carriages to pass in a row, one has to force one's way with one's elbows. On a single paving stone you see a civil guard, a match vendor, a broker, a beggar, and a soldier, all in one group. Crowds of students, servants, generals, officials, peasants, toreros, and ladies pass; importunate beggars ask for alms in your ear so as not to be discovered; cocottes question you with their eyes; courtesans hit your elbow; on every side you see hats lifted, handshakings, smiles, pleasant greetings, cries of '*Largo*' from lane porters and merchants with their

wares hung from the neck; you hear shouts of newspaper
sellers, shrieks of water vendors, blasts of the diligence
horns, cracking of whips, clanking of sabres, strumming
of guitars, and songs of the blind. The regiments with
their bands of music pass; the King goes by; the square
is sprinkled with immense jets of water which cross in
the air; the bearers of advertisements announcing the
spectacles, troops of ragamuffins with armfuls of supple-
ments, and a body of employees of the ministries, appear;
the bands of music repass, the shops begin to be lighted,
the crowd grows denser, the blows on the elbow become
more frequent, the hum of voices, racket, and commo-
tion increase. It is not the bustle of a busy people; it is
the vivacity of gay persons, a carnival-like gaiety, a
restless idleness, a feverish overflow of pleasure . . .

Martin, one of the central characters in Cela's post-war
novel *The Hive*, hears the stir of the waking city, its 'rioting
heart beat', as he emerges from a night in a brothel.

The carts of the garbage men coming down from
Fuencarral and Chamartin, coming up from Las Ventas
and Las Injurias, emerging from the sad, desolate, landscape of the cemetery and passing – after hours on the
road, in the cold – at the slow, dejected trot of a gaunt
horse or a grey, worried-looking donkey. And the voices
of women hawkers who got up early and are on their
way to set up little fruit-stalls in the Calle del General
Poulier. And the first, distant, indistinct motor-horns.
And the shouts of children going to school, satchels on
their backs and morning snacks, fresh and sweet-
smelling, in their pockets.

Madrid has always been the centre of the Spanish literary
world. The sixteenth-century writers Calderón, Tirso de
Molina, Quevedo, and Lope de Vega were all born here.
Spanish writers who have lived and worked in Madrid include
Ramón Gomez de la Serna who remarked once that 'if a
wedding or a baptism did not pass through the Puerta del Sol,
it was neither the wedding nor the baptism which God had
ordered.'
The Café Pombo was one of the most popular of the cafés

chosen by intellectuals and writers for their *tertulias*, or informal gatherings. In his memoirs, the Chilean poet Pablo Neruda recalled de la Serna's 'booming voice guiding, from his spot in the café, the conversation and the laughter, the trends of thought and the smoke.' Neruda also glimpsed the dramatist Ramón de Valle Inclán – 'an endless white beard and a complexion like a yellowing page, he seemed to have walked out of one of his own books, which have pressed him flat' – and the poet Antonio Machado, 'sitting in his favourite café [the Café Gijón] dressed in his black notary's suit, silent and withdrawn, as sweet and austere as an old Spanish tree.'

The *tertulias* had their heyday in the 1920s when literary, political, and philosophical discussions took place over endless rounds of coffee and '*copas*'. Of the best known of these cafés which survived into the second half of the twentieth century, the Gijón remained a pole of attraction for aspiring literati. Café life in Madrid by this time was no longer the preserve of the intellectual class. It had been claimed by people with less time and more money. In her book *Spanish Leaves*, published in 1964, the novelist Honor Tracy related the 'melancholy story' of the Gijón.

> Only a few years ago it was full of shaggy men and dishevelled women in various forms of fancy dress, poring over manuscripts or displaying canvasses or wrangling about life as they waved their cigarettes. I used to eye them respectfully but with suspicion, for any Spanish writer or artist I ever knew was fully occupied twenty hours out of the twenty-four in keeping body and soul together. The fame of the Gijón spread, and soon half the clientele were bourgeois, eyeing each other in the disrespectful certainty that this is not at all what they came to see . . .

No such sense of disappointment is felt by Mary Lavelle, the heroine of Kate O'Brien's eponymous novel, when she visits Madrid for the first time in 1922. The romantic young Irish nanny from Mellick falls in love with the place, its bustle, its energy, and above all its light.

> It was architecturally common; it was noisy and hot; it had a smug, prosperous glitter over it which she

suspected a more experienced traveller would call
provincial – but it sparkled with sunshine and fountains
and the most natural good manners under Heaven; the
streets were wide, the acacias green and sibilant; the
shoeblacks all told her gently that she was *guapa*, and
the sky – ah, useless ever to try to wreathe Madrid's
sky in words! Looking up at it once during the
morning – she was sitting on the stone parapet in the
King's courtyard, and had been considering his western
view with envy, the foreground of dark, descending
woods, the little dried-up Manzanares, the blond and
leafless undulations of Castile and far away, in diamond
clarity, the white peaks of the Gredos – looking up from
this out of the hot September morning, considering the
temperate transparence of its blue, its inexplicable fairy
sparkle, the sweet vague movement of its gauze of cloud,
it had struck her that here was the ideal roof for an
ideal world, here was Heaven's formula.

During the Spanish Civil War, Laurie Lee found Madrid
silent and empty, 'smothered in a pall of greyness'. With a
great sense of loss, he recalled an earlier visit in peacetime,
the 'one-time buzz of the cafés, the tram bells, the cries of
the lottery-ticket sellers, the high-stepping servant girls with
their baskets of fresh-scrubbed vegetables, the parading young
men and paunchy police at street corners.'
Visiting the city in the early 1960s, Jan Morris noted the
change that had fallen on Madrid 'like a pile of concrete':

The last of the slums have almost vanished, and Madrid
feels rich. Here are the headquarters of the powerful
Spanish banks, whose huge central offices have almost
banished from the pavements of the Calle de Alcala the
café life that once distinguished it . . . Here are the
diplomatic offices of the Americans, whose vast pay-
ments in return for strategic favours have helped to
revise the fortunes of Spain, and here too are the headquarters of the Director-General of Tourism, whose
staggeringly successful efforts to bring foreign visitors
to Spain have acted as a yeast, to ferment the outlooks
of the Spaniards. From Madrid, herself a babel of

ill-digested modernism, all rushing traffic and gaudy
cinemas, you may see how the influences of material
advance, channelled through the offices of Philip's
capital, are whittling away at the insularity of the State.

Yet Madrid's atmosphere has in other respects survived the
test of modernization remarkably well. No one who spends
more than a night in Madrid can argue with Hemingway's
outlandish boast about the capital, even if in other matters the
American author has shown a tendency to exaggerate.

Nobody goes to bed in Madrid until they have killed the
night. Appointments with a friend are habitually made
for after midnight at the café. In no other town I have
lived in except Constantinople during the period of
allied occupation, is there less going to bed for sleeping
purposes.

Madrid's centre has moved from the Puerta del Sol to the
long acacia-lined avenue of the Castellana which cuts the city
from north to south. Come June, the Madrileños will respond
to the growing heat of summer, by putting out their tables
and chairs, and taking their *paseos*. In his novel, *La de Bringas*
(1884), Galdós described the stifling atmosphere.

The month of August slowly unrolled its tedious length.
This is the month in which Madrid is not Madrid, but
an empty frying pan. In those days the only theatre
open in summer was Price's Circus, with its insufferable
ponies and its clowns who played the same tricks every
night. The Prado was the only pleasant place to be;
and in the shadow of its trees the amorous couples and
the tertulias passed the time in more than or less boring
conversations, trying meanwhile to defend themselves
against the heat with waving fans and sips of fresh water.
For the Madrileños who are obliged to pass the summer
in the city are the true exiles, and their only consolation
is to declare that at least they are drinking the best water
in the world . . .

Théophile Gautier described the area surrounding the
Prado, at the southern end of the Castellana, as 'one of the
most beautiful promenades in the world.' Again not because

of the site or the architecture, 'but because of the astonishing assembly which gathers there every morning.' Other streets of Madrid proved a source of equal fascination.

> You will be surprised, also, at the quantity of fire insurances that bedeck the façades of the houses, especially in a place where there are no chimneys and where no one ever lights a fire. Everything is insured, even the public monuments, even the churches: the civil war, it is said, is the reason for this great eagerness to be insured: nobody being certain of not being more or less roasted by some Balmaseda or other, everybody seeks at least to preserve his house . . . After the *juegos de villar*, the next most frequent inscription is that of *despacho de vino* (wine shop). There they sell Valdepeñas and other full-bodied wines. The displays are painted in striking colours, and are decorated with cloths and foliage. The confiterias and the pastelerias are also very numerous and fairly smartly decorated; the confitures of Spain deserve special mention; those known by the name *cabello de angel* (angel's hair) are exquisite. The pastry is as good as it can be in a country where there is no butter, or at least where it is so expensive and of such bad quality that one can hardly use it; it approaches what we call petit four. All these signs are written in small letters, which makes them at first diffcult for the foreigner to understand, expert reader of signs though he may be.

Another nineteenth-century visitor to Spain, the Englishman Henry Inglis, was so taken with the street life of the Madrileños, that he devoted over eight pages to the Prado *paseo* alone. Fortified with stew and a bottle of Valdepeñas, Inglis was warm and receptive to the scenes he enountered. He noted that without the street life, Madrileños would look upon life as a thing of very little value.

> Everybody – man, woman, and child – looks forward to the evening promenade with pleasure and impatience; everybody asks everybody the same question, shall you be on the *paseo* tonight?

3

FAÇADES AND REVOLUTION

Barcelona

For Don Quixote Barcelona was 'the seat of courtesy, the haven of strangers, the refuge of the distressed, the mother of the valiant, the champion of the wronged, the abode of true friendship, unique both in beauty and situation.' And it is perhaps no coincidence that the climactic blow to Don Quixote's illusion – his conclusive defeat at the hands of the Knight of the White Moon – ends here in Barcelona, a proud and transparent city where nothing is left to the imagination. At dawn, the sun rises 'bigger than a shield', while the sea 'appears very broad and spacious', and 'a good deal bigger' than the lagoons of Castile.

It was under moonlight that Joseph Baretti approached Barcelona in 1760. In the surrounding fields, he found Catalonian peasants still at work and loudly reciting their prayers as they harvested grapes and mulberries.

> Those who charge Spaniards with idleness, ought to make an exception in favour of the Catalonian rustics . . . although the peasantry of every country be in general very ready to get up betimes to their works, yet I never observed them anywhere to rise so early, as I find them to do in the neighbourhood of Piera. My good Canon assures me, that the Aragonians do not yield much to the Catalans in this particular; yet he owns that the Catalans are the most active people throughout

Spain, and assigns a good reason for it. The reason is, says he, that, from the age of fifteen to sixty, the poor Catalans are obliged to pay a capitation of forty-four reales annually, besides their quota of the taxes that are common on all subjects.

Baretti judged it the best built town he had yet seen in Spain, 'more than sufficiently decorated with palaces, churches, and other edifices, some of which would be considered as magnificent even in cities of the greatest name'. Industrial and commercial expansion meant that the city was beginning to spread beyond the medieval walls that had acted as backdrop to Don Quixote's jousting. The 'new town' in the port district was called Barceloneta. Baretti admired the 'pretty uniformity of what is already built'. No house had more than two storeys, and the streets were wide enough to 'admit of two and even three vehicles abreast.' Within the town, 'there is a large square called La Rambla, where on summer evenings people of both sexes resort to walk and confabulate until supper time, and often during the best part of the night, as is the general custom in all the hot parts of Spain.'

Economic prosperity was to bring with it its social cost, however. Within twenty years of Baretti's moonlit progress, a growing number of peasants had become the vagabond labour of the city, and an ever-present potential for riot and petty crime as this account of the *murris* or 'people with no fixed abode' by the local Bishop Climent in 1773 makes clear:

> They wander about in mixed bands of men, women, and children. They live more from robbery than beggary, for they thrust themselves on the households of priests and working men, who find themselves obliged to shelter them at night and give them what they demand. And when I asked some of the constables why they did not arrest people who by virtue of the mere fact of being vagabonds are obviously indictable, they replied that they did not dare, partly because they are so ferocious and partly because, when some of them had been brought to this city under arrest, they were soon back at liberty and burned down the homes and houses of those who had arrested them.

When Augustus Hare visited Barcelona in 1873, the city presented a colourful scene, if now clearly divided between those who had profited from the economic boom and those who had not. It was 14 January, a local feast day.

The life and animation of Barcelona are charming. As we drove into the town after leaving the solitudes of Montserrat, it seemed as if the whole of the gay, pleasure-loving population must be in the streets . . . The Rambla is the centre and axis of life in Barcelona. Here are the principal hotels, and hence all the best streets diverge. The lower division is the fashionable walk of the aristocracy, and is full of smart people, but at the upper extremity, where the peasants chiefly congregate, is the bird and flower market, where multitudes of canaries are sold daily amid the great bunches of heliotrope, and where the most wonderful mantas are to be seen, of scarlet, blue, and gold, flowing from the shoulders of rough looking men, who would be content with the common dress of ploughmen in England. At the lower end of the Rambla begins the Muralla del Mar, a delightful terrace, sheltered and sunny, overhanging the port and shipping, though raised high above them, and with views across the still reaches of water to the fortified hill of Montjuich, which raises abruptly above the sea, like Shakespeare's cliff at Dover. To ascend this hill towards sunset is quite a duty with visitors to Barcelona, for from thence, across a foreground of wild aloes, which are here frequently formed into hedges, the whole white town is seen like a map, lying in its brown, burnt-up plain, surrounded by mountains, the flat tops of the houses giving it a peculiarly eastern appearance, for there are no sloping roofs in Barcelona . . .

Hare found the heart of the town – today known as the old quarter or Barrio Gòtic – dull and unpicturesque by comparison with these hillside views. He felt somewhat oppressed by the 'high, drab coloured walls', although his mood changed when the dark streets led him through a Gothic arch and into a quadrangle bathed in sunlight, the Cathedral cloister. He marvelled at the ever-varying representations of life here – the solemn canons, with their breviaries, pacing up and down, and toiling through their appointed task of psalm-saying; the polite old beggars, the men in their bright mantas and scarlet barrettas, the women in their blue petticoats and white handkerchiefs over their heads; the children, who shout, and feed the canons' geese with bread . . .

In 1884 the traveller John Lomas could not hide his initial disappointment at encountering the urban sprawl of Barcelona which spread out over the hilly landscape. In *Sketches in Spain* he wrote that Barcelona revealed itself in a 'squalor and dreariness that sits but ill upon the boastedly First City of Spain.' Forty years later, the American Trowbridge Hall saw method in urban madness, identifying the tensions and ambitions of an industrial society, where hard work seemed to be the norm. This capitalist fervour set Barcelona apart from a Spain that he perceived as nearer to Africa than Europe, an exotic but backward land of mainly rural labourers. Barcelona sprawled on the shores of the Mediterranean with her feet in the water, but like some monster rising from its depths, she had 'stretched out her long, grasping tentacles and seized the far outlying villages' to fill her factories with immigrant labour.

> In a country whose national ideal of happiness is to do nothing, Barcelona would seem to me out of place. From way afar we heard the laboured breath of the great city moving and working in mighty travail and upon reaching the dingy outskirts we could see nothing save miles of ugly factories whose soaring chimneys belched forth clouds of smoke.

Barcelona's nineteenth-century commercial expansion rang alarm bells amongst the literary world. At the turn of the century, the most famous of Catalan poets Joan Maragall wrote:

> Oh, Barcelona, stop a moment: take a look
> At how the sea spreads blue towards the low horizon.
> Look at the little towns, sun-bleached, along the coast,
> That, gorged with sun, go out to sail along the blue.
> And you want to flee from the sea?

In fact Barcelona has never really ceased to be essentially a maritime city, with its most striking symbol the statue of Columbus, pointing not towards America but towards the Mediterranean, the sea in which the great discoverer's maritime vocation was formed, and from which Catalans have drawn their economic lifeblood for most of their history. The mood of Barcelona's 'Golden Age' of expansion is captured in *The City of Marvels*, a novel by Eduardo Mendoza. The narrator offers this explanation for the ease with which the central character, Onofre Bouvila, begins his pursuit of fortune not at the factory gates but down on the docks.

> That Barcelona went about its business 'turning its back on the sea' was already a well-worn phrase by the end of the nineteenth century, though in fact daily life in the city gave the lie to that cliché. Barcelona had always been and continued to be a maritime city: it had lived off and for the sea; it was nourished by the sea, and gave back the fruits of its endeavours to the sea; the streets of Barcelona guided the wanderer's steps down to the sea, and that sea linked the city with the outside world. From the sea came the wind and the weather, the smells, sometimes pleasant and sometimes not so pleasant, and the salt, which ate away at walls; sea noises lulled the people of Barcelona to sleep at *siesta* time, ship sirens marked the passing hours, and the sad squawking of seagulls was a constant reminder that the cheering sun-spangled shadows of trees along the city's avenues were a form of deception. The sea peopled the back alleys with twisted characters speaking foreign tongues and producing knives, pistols, or clubs at the drop of a hat; the sea covered the tracks of evildoers who fled to the open waters, leaving behind bloodcurdling cries in the night and crimes unpunished. The streets and squares of Barcelona were blinding sea-white in fair weather and dull sea-grey on stormy days.

And yet for all the city's maritime tradition, the obsessions of Catalans have been contained within the city, where to be European has been a question of style as much as of identity. Visiting Barcelona in 1830 at the end of a long tour of

Spain, Henry Inglis was struck by just how different the Catalan capital appeared from the rest of Spain both in architecture and population.

A glance at Barcelona is sufficient to show that we approach the frontier. We no longer see a purely Spanish population. Spanish hats are scarcely to be seen, nor is the mantilla altogether indispensable. In the buildings too we perceive a difference; the streets are wider, and few of the houses are adorned with balconies. I thought too, but this might be fancy, that I could perceive a different expression in the countenances of the people. Of one thing I am certain, that although the women of Barcelona have not perhaps the grace of the Andalusians, their claims to beauty are stronger: their features are more regular, their complexions are clearer, their hair less coarse, and their forms slighter: still it must be admitted, that there is more witchery hid in the eye of an Andalusian, than perhaps all the separate charms of a woman of Barcelona . . . I found another peculiarity in the aspect of the Barcelona population. No caps were to be seen: these as well as grey hats, were forbidden, immediately upon the revolution breaking out in France. For my own part, I continued to wear my grey hat while in Barcelona, without being challenged; but I have good reason to believe, that this forebearance arose from the authorities knowing that I had the honour of being acquainted with the Conde de Espana, the ruler and dictator of Catalunia. But the strange and gaudy dress of the Catalunian peasantry is the most striking peculiarity in the appearance of the Barcelona population: all wear their red caps, which hang at least a foot down their backs; and with their crimson girdles, and gaudy coloured woollen plaids, they give a peculiar grotesqueness to the appearance of the Rambla . . .

In 1992 the novelist Jonathan Keates remarked on the city's extrovertness.

Barcelona likes to flaunt itself as the city of prodigies, the place where the architecture is a nervous condition and every pastrycook is a poet. It is beautiful, not as Venice and Lisbon and Prague are beautiful, with their *grande tenue* and operatic gesture, but in the absent-minded half-digested fashion of a brilliant sketchbook, catching up dashes of Gothic, hints of antique Roman, lavish splurges of knobbly, warty art nouveau kitsch, of reactionary dandyism à la Gaudi and the self-conscious 'sincerity' espoused by the wideawake-hatted, floppy-collared show-men of Els Quatre Gats.

Els Quatre Gats is a café/bar founded in 1897. The young Picasso was one of the artists and writers who met here in an atmosphere of conscious bohemianism modelled on the beer-halls and cabarets of Montmartre. They were a mixed bag of people, united in their love of art nouveau, then sweeping southwards from France, England, and Germany and which in Barcelona came to be known as Modernismo.

In his travelogue, *Por Tierras de Portugal y De España*, Unamuno had reservations about what he perceived as the arrogance, persecution complex, and narrow-mindedness of the inhabitants of Barcelona, but he confessed to a more charitable respect for the city's physical attributes.

Undeniably Barcelona is a beautiful city, at least externally, in the ornateness of its attire . . . it has, undoubtedly, buildings which deservedly catch one's eye alongside some really absurd architecture and extravagance . . . there is no lack of façades in Barcelona, and one could almost describe it as the city of façades. Façades dominate everything.

Among the oldest surviving architectural styles that predominate in Barcelona none have been recorded with as much admiration as the Gothic. In what he referred to as a 'commercial history' of the city, published in 1761, the Catalan Antoni de Capmany judged Gothic to be superior to Greek in height and sense of space. Its buildings were best suited for meditation and 'secret reverence' and for conveying a sense of the past, 'a sort of delicious sorrow . . . best for the noble seriousness of a place of worship.'

A more domestic view of Barcelona's Gothic architecture

was provided by Lady Holland, an adventurous English woman, who together with her husband, two young sons, a tutor, and the family doctor, drove by diligence to Barcelona from Paris in the winter of 1802. Lady Holland's journal records how she and her family spent their first night in Barcelona in a private residence lent to them near the centre of the city.

It was a spacious, handsome mansion exactly in the centre of the city, built round a small square court into which the windows of the apartments looked. The streets which surrounded the house are at the widest 8 feet 8 inches, geometrically measured . . . Houses high, roof projecting, by which means a ray of sun never can nor never did penetrate into a single apartment. In this dreary dungeon I and my poor children were destined to remain, as it is utterly impracticable to hire a carriage, first because the Court had taken all horses, and, secondly, because it is never the custom to hire any in Barcelona. Walking the streets was also out of the question, not only from the danger of being exposed to meet a carriage in the streets but from the certainty of being insulted owing to dress.

The Holland entourage soon moved to a villa in Sarria, some three miles outside the city. Calm and composed, Lady Holland suggested she may have been unduly harsh on Barcelona; she now judged it to be a 'very fine city, full of magnificent public buildings and the handsomest promenade of any place I have yet seen.' On one of her final tours of the city, she went 'bien costumée à L'Espagne' to visit one of the centrepieces of Gothic architecture, the Cathedral.

It appears gloomy as it is not stuccoed or painted, but the masonry left unadorned as when just built and the stones being of dark colour the tinge is solemn. The sacristan took us behind the altar of a saint's chapel, and showed us the most venerated relic in the skeleton line, no less than the entire body of St Olegar; he reposes in a large glass coffin with very clean vestments, which the man with great gravity and perfect belief assured us were put on a century ago, and that the saint was so pleased with his new dress that, as a mark of approbation, he stood upright upon his feet whilst the priest passed the surplice over his raw bones.

In the early 1960s, Honor Tracy flew from Valencia to Barcelona, and put to the test the Catalans' boast that their capital was more French than Spanish, closer to Paris than Madrid. She found a great many things which reminded her of France, the crowded boulevards, the steaming fountains, side streets with shabby cafés and tall grey houses. The underground had 'a noticeably French smell'. Down by the port she found the Molino Rojo, a 'music hall of huge indecency . . . modelled on the Moulin Rouge although the indecency is wholly Spanish, being curiously child-like, and rather engaging.' She was less impressed by Barcelona's other eccentricities.

> Barcelona . . . looks forward and out, she does not drowse and cackle like an old hen on an empty nest. She busies herself with art and literature, she is willing to experiment and startle. Driving about the city you will now and again happen on a lunatic building by the 'tortured genius' Gaudi, if not on his masterpiece itself, the Church of the Holy Family, its spires thrusting skyward like so many dental drills. During the Civil War the anarchists very properly tried to burn it down, but the material used in building it would not catch fire. It stands there yet unfinished, hideous and indestructible. Gaudi's tragedy was to be born before his time: he would have been just the man for the Disney Island contract.

She had stumbled across Modernismo, the architecture that grew out of the Gothic tradition and linked Barcelona to the modern world. Antonio Gaudí (1852–1926), the architect who more than any other was allowed to scatter his ideas through the parks and streets of a major city, has been both venerated and reviled.

It was the mix of eccentricity and Catholicism in Gaudí's work which appealed to Evelyn Waugh. He visited Barcelona in 1929 as part of his travels through the Mediterranean with which he hoped to pull himself up from a nervous breakdown provoked by his failed marriage. Waugh judged Barcelona one of the loveliest cities he had ever seen. This was rare from a writer usually acerbic in his criticism. He reserved his best compliments for Gaudí, whose work 'apotheosized all the writhing, bubbling, convoluting, convulsing soul of Art Nouveau.' Waugh arrived in the city three years after Gaudí had been killed by a tram, barefoot and holding a bible in one hand. The architect's master work, the Sagrada Familia, the church which had sprung from his conversion to Catholicism, was incomplete; the argument about its future has continued to the present day. Waugh opined that it should not be allowed to decay. He too felt that Gaudí was a mad genius.

> I do not say that if I were rich I could not find a better way of devoting my fortune but I feel it would be a graceful action on the part of someone who was a little wrong in the head to pay for its completion.

While Waugh drank in the Sagrada Familia during a leisurely sojourn in the Mediterranean, George Orwell stumbled on the unfinished church, whilst on the run from the Communist police during the Spanish Civil War. The latter in fact mistook it for the Cathedral.

> A modern cathedral and one of the most hideous buildings in the world . . . Unlike most of the churches in Barcelona it was not damaged during the Revolution – it was spared because of its 'artistic' value, people said. I think the Anarchists showed bad taste in not blowing it up when they had the chance.

Salvador Dali was thrown into ecstatic revelries by Gaudí's work which he considered the 'sum-total conscience of our perversions'. In his autobiography, Dali describes Gaudí as 'Catholic apostolic, and Roman' and the Sagrada Familia as the 'most perfect iconography of folk Christianity and piety'. Gaudí had 'immobilized in the mineral a blade of grass, a flock of fowls, and even the sheep herder on whom he modelled Judas – in other words, the world and the people – with naive truthfulness.' Theological contortions notwithstanding, what Catalonia's most eccentric artist really enthused over was Gaudí's creative vitality.

His brain is at the tips of his fingers and tongue. He is gustative. His architecture aims to embody the sum of all gluttenous sensations. It strikes me as the idea of man's desire incarnate. The Sagrada Familia is a gigantic erogenous zone prickly with gooseflesh aching to be stroked by hand and by tongue.

I remember Lorca in front of the admirable façade of the Sagrada Familia claiming to hear a griterio – a cacophany of shouts – that rose stridently to the top of the cathedral, creating such tension in him that it became unbearable. There is the proof of Gaudí's genius. He appeals to all our senses and creates the imagination of the sense.

Sacheverell Sitwell visited Spain in 1947 and 1948 with his brother Osbert and sister Edith, but returned alone in 1949 to take a closer look at the buildings of Gaudí. He made a late mention of them in the introduction to his book *Spain*.

The church of the Sagrada Familia is well enough known, but I saw for the first time the apartment house in one of the main streets of Barcelona built by Gaudí in the shape of the mountain of Montserrat, with waving balconies to suggest its dolomitic formations. I saw the courtyard and some of the excessively curious interiors in this building and noted how Gaudí, long in advance of his day, made provision for lifts and not for staircases. A private house, opposite, was built by Gaudí to simulate a breaking wave. The walls surge wildly upwards, while the roof with its cresting of green tiles represents the foam and the spray. I suspect that Gaudí, like Debussy, admired Hokusai's woodcut of the Great Wave! After this, his bishop's palace at Astorga, among the Maragatos, is 'tame as tame'. The Parque Guell outside the town is fantastic; at once a fun fair, a petrified forest, and the great temple of Amun at Karnak, itself drunk, and reeling in an eccentric earthquake. Nevertheless, it is extremely interesting and Gaudí is, clearly, the genius of L'Art Nouveau. After it, Picasso's little scheme to buy a stretch of Mediterranean shore and erect apartment buildings in the shape of gigantic women's heads is sanity indeed. But both Picasso and Gaudí are Catalan fantasists; and so is Salvador Dali. As such, and always, they will be part of Spain.

On his earlier visit to Barcelona sponsored by Franco's Ministry of Tourism, Sitwell was shocked by the excesses committed by the Communists during the Civil War, but seduced by the 'conspicuous extravagance of the city's fashionable society', where the reward of beauty was boxes of chocolates and *marrons*.

> After a dinner party in fashionable society a young man has to set forth the next morning, and must find, in the first place, some suitable box, or glass vase, or basket, or all three, after which he goes to the florist for flowers to put in the bowl or basket, and to the chocolate shop for chocolates or *marrons glacés*, then finally, to another shop where they will arrange the flowers, wrap up the chocolates and mount and decorate the whole affair with silken ribbons.

Henry Swinburne visited Barcelona in 1775, when the city was only just recovering some of the ancient privileges which had been suppressed by the French Bourbon dynasty. He was as enthusiastic about Barcelona's mild climate as about the independent spirit of its inhabitants which tended to break out 'upon the least stretch of arbitrary power.' It was, he noted, the violent spirit of the Catalans, and their enthusiastic passion for liberty, which had often 'rendered their country the seat of civil war and bloodshed; insurrection has been more frequent than in any other part of Europe.'

The potential for insurrection has never been far from the area along and around the Ramblas, the city's pedestrian avenues. It was here that Orwell took up his observation post in 1937 during the Spanish Civil War, on the roof of a cinema called the Poliarama. He wrote this account in *Homage to Catalonia*:

> To the right of the Ramblas the working-class quarters were solidly Anarchist; to the left a confused fight was going on among the tortuous by-streets, but on that side the P.S.U.C. and the Civil Guards were more or less

in control. Up at our end of the Ramblas, round the
Plaza de Cataluna, the position was so complicated that
it would have been quite unintelligible if every building
had not flown a party flag. The principal landmark here
was the Hotel Colon, the headquarters of the P.S.U.C.,
dominating the Plaza de Cataluña. In a window near the
last O but one in the huge 'Hotel Colon' that sprawled
across its face they had a machine gun that could sweep
the square with deadly effect. A hundred yards to the
right of us, down the Ramblas, the J.S.U., the youth
league of the P.S.U.C. (corresponding to the Young
Communist League in England), were holding a big
department store whose sand-bagged side-windows
fronted our observatory. They had hauled down their red
flag and hoisted the Catalan national flag. On the
Telephone Exchange, the starting point of all the trouble, the Catalan national flag and the Anarchist flag were
flying side by side. Some kind of temporary compromise
had been arrived at there, the exchange was working
uninterruptedly and there was no firing from the
building.

   In our position it was strangely peaceful. The Civil
Guards in the Café Moka had drawn down the steel
curtains and piled up the café furniture to make
barricades . . .

The Hotel Colon has since been moved and today, after
renovation, stands by the Cathedral. The Poliarama no longer
exists although you can still see the twin domes from what
is now the Restaurant Moka across the Ramblas.

In Juan Goytisolo's novel, *Marks of Identity*, Alvaro, an exile
from the Civil War, returns to his native city Barcelona in
search of his past. The year is 1966. He longs to recreate the
creative tension of revolution, a city 'deserted by aristocrats
and businessmen, priests and playboys, ladies and fops.' But
he only finds a town that has been prostituted by tourism,
a 'prosperous, flourishing city of over a million pompous
corpses, satisfied with their condition.'

In his wanderings round the European underworld, Jean
Genet, like Picasso, immersed himself for a while in the Barrio
Chino, a few blocks of dark narrow streets to one side of the

Ramblas. It was the most miserable period of Genet's life but his hedonism flourished on the experience of the city and his rough and dirty homosexual lover Stilitano. The Ramblas in Genet's time were frequented by two young homosexuals who carried a tame little monkey on their shoulders.

> It was an easy pretext for approaching clients that the monkey would jump up on the man they pointed out to it. One of the *mariconas* was called Pepé. He was pale and thin. His waist was very supple, his step quick. His eyes in particular splendid, his lashes immense.
>
> I asked him, in fun, which was the monkey, he or the animal he carried on his shoulder. We started quarrelling. I punched him. His lashes remained stuck to my knuckles; they were false. I had just discovered the existence of fakes.

The *mariconas*, usually transvestites, still walk along the Ramblas. There are musicians and jugglers and emaciated whores, and, on a good day, the occasional monkey. As Robert Hughes has put it, 'no European capital in recent years has made such a point of reinventing itself as has Barcelona'.

Perhaps none have captured Barcelona's social and political pretensions with such wit as Manuel Vazquez Montalban. In *Murder in the Central Committee*, first published in 1981, his hero, the gourmet detective Pepe Carvalho, wanders the streets, and realizes that a city he once knew has been lost for ever.

> He started on the Calle de la Cera Ancha, walking between gypsies who had brought their stools and brandy-laced coffee to the bars of the Ronda and the corner of Calle Salvadors. In the nineteen-forties he had watched the gypsies, or their parents, dancing and generally surviving around the doors of the Bar Moderno or the Alujas – watched them from the balcony of a house constructed in 1846, two years before the Communist Manifesto, in a clear gesture of historic optimism on the builder's part. The street divided into the Calle de la Botella and the Calle de la Cera Estrecha, where the Pardo cinema had ceased to cater for old people, gypsies and boisterous children and become a

film club. How you have changed, Pardo of Barcelona! Repopulated with cosmopolitan immigrants, Guineans, Chileans, Uruguayans; boys and girls in flower and marijuana, trying out post-marital, pre-marital and anti-marital relations; counter-cultural bookshops where the Nazi Hermann Hesse lies next to a manual of some yogi from Freguenal de la Sierra. Denuded ever since the disappearance of the shady street traders and Pepa the lottery queen, the district has no heroic remnants other than the Pardo fountain; the Romanesque chapel half-hidden between a local school and a tailor's shop, its apse formerly shared by the alcohol merchant and a blacksmith; and the condom shop – La Pajarita – which may be declared a historical monument or building of national interest if Jordi Pujol, president of the Generalitat of Catalonia, grants the request that Carvalho had been thinking of sending one day.

Kenneth Tynan, who visited Barcelona in 1959, remarked that Barcelona was not just one city but several. One of them was the 'city of cosmopolitan pleasure', but what appealed to Tynan was the sheer variety of the city, and its distinctiveness from the rest of Spain.

You do not go to Barcelona for the Spain of the travel brochure, all fans and flamenco: these attributes are an Andalusian monopoly, with head offices in Seville. Nor will you find in Barcelona that other traditional face of Spain, sombre, ascetic and God-bitten; for this you must go to Old Castile, where physical saintliness is as common as undernourishment, of which it is a by-product. The face of Barcelona is a Catalan face, busy and clever, button-holing you with with news and noise and argument. It emphatically belongs to the individual . . . the energy of Barcelona is not only, or even mainly, political. What excites me about it is the way in which all its aspects – politics, art, history, commerce, even tourism – seem intermixed and interrelated, all of a tumultuous piece. Barcelona is several cities and an accretion of civilisations, but they all belong together, living in a state of turbulent coexistence.

4

MISTRESS, PAMPERED AND ADORED

Seville

Seville has stirred the romantic imagination for so long that
it is difficult to separate illusion from reality. As the popular
Spanish proverb has insisted for more than 400 years, 'He who
has not seen Seville, has not seen a marvel.' Few Spanish cities
have managed to perpetuate such legends about themselves.
Camilo José Cela wrote in *A First Andalusian Journey*,
published in 1959, that 'about Seville one could speak all one's
life, without reaching a definite conclusion. Seville like the
blue of the sky and the green of the olive trees is ever changing
. . . It inspires even the dullest of poets.'

'Seville', concluded the Spanish essayist Azorín, after
spending the first half of the twentieth century touring the
whole of Spain, 'is silence, elegance, the majesty of words and
deeds, the profound spirituality created by a long tradition
of art, poetry, and riches. Spirituality which is everywhere;
spirituality which floats in the atmosphere and manifests itself
in a thousand details.'

Seville was one of the great Moorish cities of the Middle
Ages, the most important of Spain's *taifa* or city states which
enjoyed enormous prosperity in the twelfth and thirteenth
centuries under the Almohads. Ibn Abdun, a chronicler who
lived in the city at the beginning of the twelfth century and

whose manuscripts were discovered by Spanish arabists in the 1930s, wrote:

> Agriculture is the basis of our civilisation, and from it life can be lived to its full advantage. Whole riches are lost through bad harvests, entire cities change . . . when there is no production, fortunes are lost, and a whole social organisation falls apart . . .

Equally important in preserving Seville's position in the Moorish kingdom was its transport, with the River Guadalquivir a particular focus of social and commercial life. Ibn Abdun, whose series of admonitions were meant to bring the inhabitants closer to the spirit of the Koran, said this of the river:

> We must protect that part of the river where the port lies, no property must be sold, no new construction must be permitted. This area, is in effect, the heart of the city, through which merchants export their wares; it is also a haven for foreigners, and a repair yard for boats, it belongs to no one but the State . . . We must put every effort into protecting this meeting point of merchants, travellers, and others . . .

When the Christians conquered Seville, ousting the Moors in 1248, they were astonished by what they found. The city was not the work of barbarians but of a great civilising race. King Ferdinand III's chronicler recorded that 'No place so wealthy or so beautifully adorned had ever been seen before, nor any so populous, or so powerful, or so filled with noble and marvellous sights.'

It was in the sixteenth century that Seville reached its zenith as the centre of the Spanish seaborne empire, becoming in the words of the poet Luis Gongora 'the great Babylon, map of the nations.'

Cervantes was a witness of Seville's heyday. He visited it as a student in 1564 and later as an agent for Antonio de Guevara, royal commissioner for the American fleets, and tax collector. It is surely one of the tragic ironies of Spanish literary history that its greatest genius found misfortune rather than glory in Seville. He was imprisoned after being charged

with swindling one of his clients. And yet suffering can produce art and so it proved in the case of Cervantes. From his
experiences in Seville, Cervantes gained his raw material for
the 'exemplary' novel or short story on picaresque life,
Rinconete y Cortadillo. Passages like the following provide a
lasting image of the duality of existence in Imperial Spain.

> They had taken their leave of the party who had
> supported them so far on the journey before performing
> the robbery, and the next day they sold their shirts in
> the second-hand shop near the Arenal Gate, and made
> twenty reales out of them. After this they went to look
> at the city, and were amazed at the size and splendour
> of its cathedral and the vast number of people by the river
> because it was at the time when they were loading up
> the fleet. There were six galleys there, the sight of which
> made them sigh and dread the day when a mistake on
> their part would lead them to spend the rest of their lives
> in them.

By the time Henry Swinburne visited Seville in April 1776,
Seville was no longer the heart of the Spanish Empire and the
River Guadalquivir had long ceased to be the jewelled water-
way of Spain. Swinburne recalled the days when the city's
'court was the most splendid in Europe . . . its streets
thronged with people . . . its river crowded with ships . . .
its ports covered with bales of merchandise . . . Great were
the buildings begun, and still vaster the projects for future
ones. Its prosperity seemed proof against the fickleness of
fortune . . .' By contrast Seville, losing out to the 'superior
excellence of the port of Cadiz' appeared to have fallen from
the 'highest pitch of grandeur to solitude and poverty'.
Swinburne went on to comment:

> The streets of Seville are crooked, dirty, and so
> narrow, that in most of them two coaches find it difficult
> to pass a-breast. The widest and handsomest place is the
> Alameda, or great walk of old elms, in the heart of the
> city; it is six hundred yards by one hundred and fifty,
> decorated with three fountains, and the statues of
> Hercules, the reputed founder, and Julius Caesar, the
> restorer of Seville.

Most of the churches are built and ornamented in so barbarous a style, that I had not the patience to examine them; the cathedral, the capuchins, and the Caridad, are the only sacred edifices really interesting; the first by its antiquity, size, and reputation; the two latter by the chef-d'oevres of Murillo.

The cathedral is more cried up than I think it deserves; it is by no means equal to York Minster for lightness, elegance, and Gothic delicacy. The cluttered pillars are too thick, the aisles too narrow, and their choir, by being placed in the centre, spoils the whole *coup d'oeil*, and renders the rest of the church little better than a heap of long passages. The ornamental parts, commonly laid to be after the Gothic manner, seem rather to be clumsy imitations of the models left by the Moors. Not one of the great entrances or porches is finished; and to disfigure the whole pile, a long range of buildings, in the modern style, had been added to the old part.

Seville has been loved, however, rather more than rejected through the centuries. The town has lived so immersed in its own aura of mystery and beauty not even the most cynical of pens has managed to diminish it. Close on the heels of Swinburne came another Anglican, the Reverend Joseph Townsend. The rector of Pewsey, Wiltshire travelled widely in Europe in pursuit of his main interests, conchology, palaeontology, and geology. Touring Spain in 1787, Townsend came to Seville with a letter of introduction to the local archbishop whose librarian he was offered as a guide to the city. Townsend was full of praise for Seville's artistic treasures, in particular the paintings of Murillo who was born in the city in 1618.

In Seville, the eye covets only pictures, and amidst the profusion of these, it overlooks works, which, in other situations, would rivet the attention, and everywhere fixes on the pencil of Murillo. His most famous performances are in the Hospital de Caridad, and, suited to the institution, express some sort of charity . . . In my opinion the most masterly of all his works is the refectory of an hospital designed for the reception of superannuated priests. It represents an angel holding a basket to the infant Jesus, who, standing on his mother's lap, takes bread from it to feed three venerable priests. No representation ever approached nearer to real life, nor is possible to see more expression, than glows upon that canvas. In the parochial church of Santa Cruz, are two pictures in a superior style, a Stabat Mater dolorosa, which excels in grace and softness; and the famous Descent from the Cross, of Pedro de Campana, which Murillo was accustomed daily to admire, and opposite to which, by his own directions, he was buried.

Compared to the austerity of Castile, southern Spain and its capital city provided a striking contrast. It was in Andalusia that the image of Spain as different from the rest of Europe, soft as Murillo's paintings, exotic and oriental, became a source of constant fascination for romantic minds. The delights of Seville in spring immediately won over Washington Irving, who arrived in the city on 14 April 1828, after taking the steam boat up the Guadalquivir from Cadiz. He booked into the Fonda de la Reyna, a small hotel in the Barrio de Santa Cruz, and within a day of his arrival was so taken by what he saw, in the company of the painter David Wilkie, that he felt compelled to express his enthusiasm in a letter to his friend Alexander Everett.

There appears much to be seen in this city, and the whole character of the place is peculiar, retaining a strong infusion of the old *Moresco*. I am apprehensive it will be close and sultry in summer, though I am assured that the mode of living in the lower stories, with patios covered with awnings, and deep in the interior of the houses, guarantees one against the heat of the sun. The houses have certainly a cool and delicious appearance, the inner courts, shady, decorated with fountains and set out with citrons, oranges, and flowers. If I find them as comfortable in hot weather as they are described, I shall probably remain some time here.

Irving planned to stay for just a few weeks in Seville. His love affair with the town was of such intensity however that

he stayed for over a year. One of his favourite buildings was
the Cathedral.

> Visit it in the evening when the last rays of the sun, or
> rather the last glimmer of the daylight, is shining
> through its painted windows. Visit it at night, when its
> various chapels are partially lighted up, its immense aisles
> are dimly illuminated by their rows of silver lamps, and
> when Mass is preparing amidst gleams of gold and clouds
> of incense at its high altar . . . I do not think altogether
> I have ever been equally delighted with any building
> of the kind. It is so majestic, ample and complete; so
> sumptuous in all its appointments, and noble and august
> in its ceremonies.

It was on 15 September 1830 that Ford had written from
his London home to his friend Addington, announcing his
intention of spending the winter in Seville. Ford gave as his
main reason the poor health of his wife which necessitated a
warm climate. Subsequent letters to Addington were from the
Plazuela San Isidro No 11, Seville. The house belonged to Hall
Standish, an English expatriate art collector who was taking
advantage of the latest wave of officially sponsored anti-
clericalism to get his hands on as much religious art as he
could. In his *Handbook for Travellers in Spain*, Ford provides
a detailed anatomy of the contents of Seville's cathedral. No
treasure, no painting, no secret altar is left undiscovered by
Ford's inquisitive eye. And yet Ford's originality shines
through not so much in his somewhat self-consciously
'educated' judgements as in his description of the human
atmosphere, still recognizable today.

> The Cathedral is always thronged, not only by the
> devout, but by idlers and beggars. The sexes were
> formerly not allowed to walk about or talk together; the
> ancient Silenliati, in the form of *celadores*, and *perliqueros*,
> beadles, and vergers, kept guard, and papal excom-
> munications are suspended in *terrorem*; nor are women
> even now allowed to enter after *oraciones*, when the
> shades of evening come on, and the pretext of 'going to
> church' reminds the scholar of Ovid. The Cathedral of

Seville is a chosen rendezvous; lovers care little for the presence of the *Imagenes Sagradas* – they are, say they, *Santon muy callados*, and never tell tales.

When Lorca, in his poem named after the city, noted that 'Seville is a tower full of fine arches . . . A city that lies in wait for rhythms and coils them like labyrinths . . . like the stems of a burning vine', he was capturing the predominant profile of the Cathedral tower, La Giralda, so evocative of Spain's Moorish past. Ford wrote in his *Handbook* of La Giralda as 'the great tower from whence the mueddin summoned the faithful to prayers; and here still hang his substitutes, the bells, for they are almost treated as persons, being all duly baptized, before they are suspended, with a peculiar oil, and they are christened after saints.'

In *Don Quixote*, the Knight of the Wood tells Quixote and Sancho that his courtly adventures on behalf of Dona Casildea of Vandalia, included challenging to a duel 'that famous Seville giantress, the Giralda, who is as valiant and strong as if she were of brass, and without stirring from one place, is the most changeable and volatile woman in the world.'

Seville's Moorish past, and its absorption by Christian culture, is also to be found in the Alcazar and its gardens, another source of wonder for romantic travellers. On the palace Eugene Poitou wrote in 1873:

One thinks oneself in a palace of fairies. One is astonished, charmed, dazzled. The walls seemed clothed in a guipure of gold and silk. I do not think the Moors have ever been equalled in the art of internal decoration. In spite of the profusion of ornament which covers the halls up to the very roof, and even the roof itself, there is neither heaviness, nor overloading, nor a gaudy abundance of richness in the marvellous whole, so varied and so elegant are the forms.

Only, in its present condition, and after its recent restoration, the Alcazar has, perhaps, a single defect: the paintings are too gorgeous, the colours are too vivid, the tones too hard. Is this the fault of the modern artists, who have not possessed the faculty of communicating to their work that harmony so noticeable in the work

wrought by Moorish hands? Or is it simply that Time
has not yet given to the too vivid colours that subdued
tint which he gives to everything?

Visiting Seville in the early 1950s, H.V. Morton thought
the gardens of the Alcazar the most beautiful place in the
whole city.

> Here was the Seville one reads about: the orange trees,
> the roses, the hedge of box and myrtle, the cypresses and
> the fish-ponds. There was a delightfully juvenile water-
> trap in a little garden, where the king could drench his
> guests with jets of water from the paving beneath his
> feet, a typical Arab jest . . . centuries of gardening are
> to be imagined on this site, and many monarchs have
> impatiently waited for winter so that they could dig up,
> alter and transform; for gardening is not the peaceful
> occupation it is imagined to be, but a perpetually restless
> search for perfection. Charles V and Philip II dug,
> planted, and improved, made pavilions, reservoirs, and
> even a maze; and in later times other kings introduced
> baroque novelties such as dripping grottoes, garden
> gates, wall fountains, and rusticated stonework. There
> is a beautiful fish-pond with a little bronze Mercury
> rising in the centre as if he were in Italy. The flower
> beds were gay with cannas and agapanthus, plumbago
> was in flower, so was jasmine; and I sat on a seat covered
> with Moorish tiles beneath one of the largest Magnolia
> grandiflora I have ever seen . . .

The scent of fruit and flowers, the play of light on
buildings, the very special oriental atmosphere of Seville enraptured George Borrow as he walked through the park of Las
Delicias and glimpsed the Torre de Oro at sundown. The missionary was in Seville between 1838 and 1840 in the last of
a succession of attempts to propagate the Bible among the
Spaniards. Borrow's elderly fiancée, the prim Mrs Clarke, did
not take kindly to the city: she was appalled by the heat, the
flies, the food, and the general bohemianism of Borrow's
rented apartments in the Plazuela de la Pila Seca. But Borrow
himself was enchanted with the place.

Oh, how pleasant it is, especially in springtide to stray along the shores of the Guadalquivir! Not far from the city, down the river, lies a grove called Las Delicias, or the Delights. It consists of trees of various kinds, but more especially of poplars and elms, and is traversed by long shady walks. This walk is the favourite promenade of the Sevillians, and there one occasionally sees assembled whatever the town produces of beauty or gallantry. There wander the black-eyed Andalucian dames and damsels, clad in their graceful silken mantillas; and there gallops the Andalucian cavalier on his long-tailed thick-maned steed of Moorish ancestry. As the sun is descending, it is enchanting to glance back from this place in the direction of the city; the prospect is inexpressibly beautiful. Yonder in the distance, high and enormous, stands the Golden Tower, now used as a toll-house, but the principal bulwark of the city in the time of the Moors. It stands on the shore of the river, like a giant keeping watch, and is the first edifice which attracts the eye of the voyager as he moves up the stream to Seville. On the other side, opposite the tower, stands the noble Augustine convent, the ornament of the faubourg of Triana, whilst between the two edifices rolls the river Guadalquivir, bearing on its bosom a flotilla of barks from Catalonia and Valencia. Farther up is seen the bridge of boats which traverses the water. The principal object of this prospect, however, is the Golden Tower where the beams of the setting sun seem to be concentrated as in the focus, so that it appears built of pure gold, and probably from that circumstance received the name which it now bears. Cold, cold, must the heart be which can remain insensible to the beauties of this magic scene, to do justice to which the pencil of Claude himself were barely equal. Often have I shed tears of rapture whilst I beheld it, and listened to the thrush and the nightingale piping forth their melodious songs in the woods, and inhaled the breeze laden with the perfume of the thousand orange gardens of Seville.

Since childhood, Laurie Lee had imagined himself 'walking

down a white dusty road through groves of orange trees'. The poet put this fantasy down to his upbringing in the Cotswold damp or something his mother had told him. But it was nonetheless one of several 'clichés' that had brought him to Spain in the late summer of 1936 on the eve of the Spanish Civil War. As he approached Seville, he felt he was following some 'old direction'. He was dazzled by the 'creamy crustation of flower-baked houses fanning out from each bank of the river.' But he noted too the 'fact of belonging' of those who lived in poverty, the 'children and beggars sleeping out in the gutters under a coating of disease and filth.' He lodged in Triana, one of the oldest surviving suburbs, on the eastern side of the Guadalquivir River.

> In my day it still had a seedy vigour full of tile-makers and free-rund pottery, of medieval shambles bursting with panniered donkeys, squabbling wives and working pots. Stately cockerels with brilliant combs and feathers strutted like Aztecs about the rooftops, while from my yard I could hear the incessant throb of guitars being practiced in shuttered rooms.

For a nineteenth-century visitor to Seville, John Lomas, the most 'delicious of all Sevillian bits' was the chance to peep into the patios of the houses in the quieter barrios.

> Anything more exquisite after its kind – more perfectly ordered, delicately arranged, and beautifully kept up than the court of a Sevillian gentleman's residence cannot be imagined, and the poorer classes follow suit with marvellous success and unanimity. There is no greater outer door as in Toledo, but cunningly wrought and fairy-like iron gates, which only serve to set off an enticing picture of marble pavement, colonnade, and fountain, in a farming of *palmitos*, bananas, and lemon trees, with here and there a coquettishly-perched cage of singing birds. In no other place is there a greater temptation to become the inquisitive pryer into the domestic ways of one's fellows.

The most famous of Seville's quieter barrios, the old Jewish quarter of Santa Cruz, struck V.S. Pritchett as quintessentially

Spanish in its striking contrasts. He wrote in *The Spanish Temper*:

> In the Barrio Santa Cruz, where each street bears its name in large, simple letters that have been there since the seventeenth century, one seems to be walking on cobbled porcelain, and by the weak yellow light of the tiled courtyards, one sees the gloss of the evergreens and the ferns, the hard leaves of the orange tree, and hears the gurgle of a small fountain. Darkness, jasmine, water, and white walls. One passes the sedate small baroque churches, which are like the ornate little drawing rooms of God, and there one may see the pearled Virgins or the carved Christs that are borne by the brotherhoods in the processions of Holy Week. Again, the continuous play of contrast in Spanish life strikes the traveller. The plain, frugal, simple life matched by the passion for some crystallization of ornament or decoration.

If Seville has its inner sanctums, its quieter barrios, it has also been described by the poet Antonio Machado as an 'open palm in the valley of the Guadalquivir', a city without secrets where the spirit of the place is manifested in the streets and public squares with that gaiety or *alegria* of which Sevillanos are particularly proud.

Havelock Ellis, a sociologist who visited Seville at the turn of the century, comments in his book *The Soul of Spain*:

> The Sevillians may be said to be the last Parisians of Spain. They possess a certain well-poised gaiety – *alegria*, as they themselves call it – a fine sense of temperance and harmony. They have that wit which is the sign of an alert intelligence; they are sufficient to themselves, and they are a people of artists. In most of these respects they differ from their fellow-countrymen in temperament. Spaniards generally are a grave and silent people, tending to run to extremes, by no means artists, with fine moral qualities indeed but, while very honest, also, it must be said, sometimes lacking in quick intelligence. The Sevillians, and especially the women of Seville, possess a quality which, like the ancient Romans, the Spaniards

call 'salt', a sapid and antiseptic quality of bright intelligence which permeates all that they are and all that they
do. They do nothing quite in the same way as other
people, and are thus placed, perhaps a little consciously,
apart from other people.

The Parisian dandy, Théophile Gautier, visited Seville in
1840 at the age of twenty-nine as part of a lengthy Spanish
adventure. He strolled Seville's main commercial street, the
Calle Sierpes, dressed in frills and velvet. He was offered
'respectable girls' and paintings by Murillo. The Spanish
painter was then just a little too popular for a refined lover
of arts such as Gautier. A Murillo painting was available to
the 'commonest burgher, the slenderest abbot.' Gautier was
struck, however, by the beauty and apparent abundance of
Sevillian women.

> There is something nimble, lovely, vivacious about
> them, and they prance along rather than walk. The
> rapidity with which their fans open and close beneath
> their fingers, the flash of their glance, the self-assurance
> of their movements, the undulating suppleness of their
> figures – all this makes them unique. In England, France,
> and Italy you may find women with a more perfect and
> regular beauty, but surely you won't see prettier or
> saucier ones.

For George Borrow, the most singular of all Sevillanas were
the gypsies, a people he was to devote particular attention to
during his missionary exploits. In *The Zincali*, his account of
the gypsies of Spain, he devoted a whole chapter to the Gitana
of Seville.

> There is no female eye in Seville can support the glance
> of hers, – so fierce and penetrating, and yet so artful and
> sly is the expression of their dark orbs; her mouth is fine
> and delicate, and there is not a queen on the proudest
> throne between Madrid and Moscow who might not and
> would not envy the white and even rows of teeth which
> adorn it, which seem not of pearl but of the purest
> elephant's bone of Multan. She comes not alone; a
> swarthy two-year-old bantling clasps her neck with one

arm, its naked body half extant from the coarse blanket, which, drawn round her shoulders, is secured at her bosom by a skewer. Though tender of age, it looks wicked and sly, like a veritable imp of Roma. Huge rings of false gold dangle from wide slits in the lobes of her ears; her nether garments are rags, her feet are cased in hempen sandals.

It was in Seville that the poet Byron took lodgings with two unmarried ladies, Josepha Beltram and her sister, in the Calle de las Cruzes No 19. The year was 1809. Byron had sailed from Falmouth to Lisbon, and after spending two weeks in Portugal had travelled on horseback across the border with his friend John Hobhouse, covering seventy miles a day under the scorching sun. Spain was then engulfed in the Peninsular War, with Seville the headquarters of the Spanish revolutionary Grand Junta and their English allies. While in the city however, politics was not of primary concern to one of Europe's Romantic heroes. After he and Hobhouse had shared a bedroom for the night with the Beltram sisters, Byron wrote to his mother:

> The eldest honoured your worthy son with very particular attention, embracing him with great tenderness at parting (I was there but three days), after cutting off a lock of his hair, and presenting him with one of her own, about three feet in length, which I send, and beg you to retain till my return. Her last words were, Adios, tu hermoso! Me gustas mucho – 'Adieu, you pretty fellow! You please me much.' She offered me a share of her apartment, which my virtue induced me to decline . . .

Byron left Seville on 28 July, the day of the Battle of Talavera. For a moment he was tempted to drop in on Wellington, but he felt he must hurry on, reserving till later his grim lines on the three armies which combined 'To feed the crow on Talavera's plain.' Instead Byron rode to Cadiz, a city in which his enthusiasm for Andalusian women bubbled over – 'the first spot in the creation . . . London is filthy by comparison.' His flirtation with a local admiral's daughter, – 'a little made and apt to fall in love' according to Hobhouse's decription – inspired his subsequent poem to 'The Girl of Cadiz'.

> Our English maids are long to woo,
> And frigid even in possession;
> And if their charms be fair to view,
> Their lips are slow to love's confession;
> But, born beneath a brighter sun,
> For love ordained the Spanish maid is . . .

The image of the Sevillana, particularly one of gypsy blood, as temptress, has its most famous literary location in the tobacco factory which is today a university. In 1776, Henry Swinburne described the factory thus:

> One hundred and eighty mules work twenty-eight mills or machines for grinding and mixing the tobacco with the red earth of the *Almazarron*; the excessive adulteration with this earth practised of late years by the directors, has occasioned a prodigious falling off in the exploitation of this commodity, and unless they alter the method, the trade will soon be confined to Spain and its dominions; the northern markets have long refused to take any off their hands.

Swinburne's comments preceeded the first performance of Bizet's *Carmen* by one hundred years. The intervening years saw the tobacco factories of Seville transformed in the romantic imagination. Gautier felt himself assailed by the noise of the factory no sooner had he entered it, but it was the noise of women not of machines.

> Most of them were young, and some were very pretty. The extreme carelessness of their dress enables us to appreciate their charms at ease. Some with the swagger of a cavalry officer, had the stump of a cigar stuck resolutely in the corner of their mouths, while others – Oh, muse come to my aid! – were chewing away like old sailors, for they are allowed to use as much tobacco as they can consume on the premises . . .

One of the few visitors to Seville who showed himself concerned about the morality of the workings of these factories was Willis Bexley, author of *Art-Remains and Art-Realities, Painters, Priests, and Princes*, published in 1875.

> In this pest house the women smell as if they breathed the deadly malaria of the Pontine marshes and were becoming prematurely mummified. Sallow, shrunken, shrivelled specimens of humanity, life seems to have but little hold upon the older of the operatives.

Bexley noted the long hours the women were forced to work, and the poor ventilation of the nicotine-filled atmosphere. Long before any government had issued its first health warning, Bexley had concluded that nicotine was 'among the deadliest of poisons.'

If Carmen, or at least her tobacco factory, is one key *mise-en-scene* of romantic Seville, another are the adventures of Don Juan which literature has located amongst jasmine-scented balconies and dimly lit streets ripe for seduction and deceit. The backdrop is of a religion as baroque as parts of Seville's Cathedral. Don Juan, as portrayed by the sixteenth-century dramatist Tirso de Molina and, later, by José Zorrilla in the nineteenth century is not a very complex character. He defies institutions and pursues women with a callous disregard for the right of either. In the words of V.S. Pritchett, the Don Juan of Tirso de Molina is an Andalusian in his 'love of the preposterous fantasy, of laughing at his enemies, and of succeeding by boast and effrontery and trick.'

In one of numerous scenes of seduction, (he has just intercepted a love note which he plans to trick into bed) Tirso's Don Juan boasts in an aside, 'Seville loudly proclaims me a seducer, and the greatest pleasure that I have is in seducing a woman and leaving her without honour . . .'

Pritchett suggests a reason for the collective identification with a figure who in colder Anglo-Saxon climes would be dismissed as a coldly calculating chauvinist.

> Don Juan is an act which, in some form or other, every Spaniard dreams of performing, and in fact in his inner life is doing all the time. He is asserting the exclusive, dramatic right of the human ego, myself before all other selves, unrepentedly.

The character of Don Juan, created in fiction, has survived as a historical figure in the person of a seventeenth-century Sevillano Don Miguel Mañara. It was Mañara that inspired Mérimée to write one of his earlier Andalusian tales. Mañara was a consumate womaniser who became a charitable benefactor after surviving a duel or, according to another version, the death of his long suffering wife. Still another version has Mañara stumbling across a funeral cortège and seeing his own body.

Whatever the myths surrounding his conversion, Mañara certainly existed. He founded a religious order called the Very Humble Brotherhood whose job it was to look after the city's poor and criminal fraternity. It is the church in Seville beneath which Mañara is buried which provides the most astonishing allegory of the obsession with decay that marked the Baroque period. It contains works by the Sevillian painter, Valdes Leal, showing earthly goods and rotting flesh to serve as a reminder of the fickleness and transient nature of human life.

The commentary of the Reverend Richard Roberts, in 1859, exemplifies their impact.

> At the Caridad, a kind of alms-house on a large scale, I was greatly struck with a picture of Juan Valdes Leal, the enemy and rival of Murillo. It represents a bishop in his coffin with owls and the creeping things man inherits after death, around him in the dark vault, while above the heavens are opened and a pierced hand comes forth holding a pair of scales, one of them containing emblems of earthly pleasure, the other a cross, and a heart burning with Divine Love.

It is in Seville's famous Feria that the images of Don Juan and Carmen multiply amidst the strutting riders and the swaying hips of the women as they parade between the *casetas*. Sacheverell Sitwell gives us this description of the Feria in the early 1950s:

> We are on the outer side of our avenue and can see in every detail the splendid cavaliers and their ladies as they ride towards us and pass by. Taking the young women first, there are the two sorts, those who go pillion and

those who ride alone. The pillion riders, perched precariously with an arm round their rider's waist or holding to the horse's tail, wear the flounced skirt of the pedestrians. Their brothers, or lovers, ride generally one arm akimbo, which accentuates their thin waists. Many are wearing elaborate and fanciful leather trousers . . . the young women ride pillion with an amazing grace, the beauty of their bare heads and arms in that violent sunlight being as animal as the steeds they share. Every young woman is beautiful to look at, some of the young girls being real visions of Spanish beauty with their camellia skins and black hair and eyes. But not all are dark, and there are young girls riding pillion, in green or white crinolines, with fair hair, bareheaded like the rest, and glowing in the midday sun. It is wonderful to watch a cavalier, arms akimbo, riding towards us, Spanish-fashion, and then to wait and admire the young woman upon the crupper holding lightly to his waist . . .

At the heart of the Feria is its ability to embrace people of all backgrounds and to touch them with colour and warmth. The atmosphere of communal celebration as lived in the *casetas*, or small huts, that make up the fair's temporary village, is identified in this piece written by the poet Manuel Machado in 1920:

A caseta in the Feria is the traditional luxury of many Sevillian families. Its a luxury of the finest quality, far superior to a box at the Opera, or a season ticket for the bullfight; it may be notably more expensive, but it's infinitely more enjoyable. At the same time the caseta is an extension of the home, a continuation of family life, both intimate and personal . . . the caseta is the home itself – conjugal, paternal, fraternal – which for a few days conveys all the pleasure and charm of the Feria, whether in the morning with the neighing of the horses from Jerez, in the afternoon, basking in a gentle breeze, or in the fantasy of the evening, full of enchanted songs and dances.

Eight years after this portrait was written, Seville was visited by Gertrude Bone and her painter husband. It was 1928, the year before the Great Crash but also of Seville's great Ibero-American exhibition. At the time the dictatorship of Primo de Rivera 'like a tottering wall, was leaning to collapse.'

> Against the daffodil sky of a December sunset, the fronds of the tropical palms in the Plaza de San Fernando move like the state fairs of an emperor. The rows of orange trees growing in the streets are decorated with ripe fruit. And a waterseller is still seated by the front of a tree, her clay pitchers and vases in a pyramid beneath the shade. On the quayside beneath the Golden Tower, groups of seafaring men, pilots, and small skippers sit at tables in the open air, drinking beer and eating olives and shrimps. The wharf is lined with timber and pighead. Donkeys, small in stature and resplendent in ornament, pass in train, carrying stone and sand for the highways and buildings of the great exhibition now mustered among the historical monuments.

When Laurie Lee returned to Seville in the early 1950s for the first time since the Spanish Civil War, Seville had fallen prey to an ebullient commercialism of hotels, packed bus stations, plastic flamenco dolls and cheap holy images. And yet, in the presence of Lee's young wife, he saw it in the light of a new found romanticism which touched everything he looked on.

> It is all part of the special femininity of Seville, a mixture of gaiety and languor. For among so much that is harsh and puritan in this country, Seville is set apart like a mistress, pampered and adored. It is the heart of Andalusia and of the Andalusians. It is the first charge on their purse and passions. In spite of war, hunger, decay and cruelty, ways are still found to preserve the softer bloom of this city, the charm and professional *alegria*. Not only in its own province but throughout Spain, men turn to Seville as a symbol . . . So Seville remains favoured and sensual exuding from the banks of

its golden river a miasma of perpetual excitement compounded of those appetites that are most particularly Spanish: chivalry, bloodshed, poetry, and religious mortification.

Seville's particular charm has survived the centuries. When Columbus approached Guanahani Island (later Watling Island) off South America on 8 October 1492, after his historic voyage of discovery, he thought first of Paradise, and second of Seville. 'Thanks be to God', wrote Columbus in his diary, 'the sea was as calm as the Guadalquivir' and the air 'sweet smelling, like an April in Seville.'

5

THE PILGRIM'S WAY

The Road to Santiago

The pilgrim leaves France behind him at Saint Jean-Pied-De-Port, crossing the River Nive over the Roman bridge and travelling up through the Ibaneta pass beyond the small border post of Arneguy. Of the summit, one of Spain's earliest travel guides, a twelfth-century French monk called Aimery Picaud, wrote:

> This mountain is so high that in truth it seems almost to touch the sky, and when you climb it you believe that you can do the same.

It was Picaud, author of the *Codex Calixtinus*, who also recounted that from this same summit Charlemagne knelt and prayed. The spot where the Emperor planted his crucifix is today marked by a small monument, facing towards Santiago de Compostela, the greatest shrine in the Christian world after Jerusalem and Rome, and the traditional focal point of Catholic Spain.

According to the Acts of the Apostles, Santiago, or St James as he is translated into English, was the elder of two sons of Salome and her husband Zebedee, a fisherman living on the banks of Lake Galilee. It is also said that in AD 44 King Herod Agrippa I killed James with a sword. The rest is legend.

In *The Way of St James*, James Bentley, the theologian and travel writer, describes how James the apostle was trans-

formed into Santiago, patron saint of Spain, and how his name
was given to a town in north-west Galicia to where thousands
of pilgrims have made their way through the centuries.

Why anyone should suppose that the body of St James
the Great should be found in Spain is a tricky question.
Nothing in the Bible, which is our only authentic
source of information about him, indicates this . . .
the decapitated body of the apostle lay entombed in
Jerusalem. Then around the year 810, Bishop Theodimir
of Irinese, whose see lay in the north-west corner of
Spain, claimed that, guided by a star, a hermit named
Pelayo had discovered St James's corpse in the wild countryside of the diocese, buried alongside two of his
disciples . . . The place became known as St James of the
Field of the Star, or Santiago de Compostela (though
dusty philologists sometimes contest the derivation from
the Latin campus stellae and insist the Compostela
derives from the word for a place of burial, compositum).
    Legends blossomed in order to support the authen-
ticity of the relics . . . after his burial in Jerusalem his
relics had been exhumed, placed in an unmanned ship and
sailed of their own accord to Spain, landing in the realms
of a pagan queen called Lupa . . . then the tale became
all the more complex and marvellous because of the
Muslim conquest of Spain and its gradual reconquest by
the Christians . . . In 844 at the Battle of Clavijo in the
Ebro valley he was said to have appeared at the side of
King Ramiro I on a white charger, brandishing his
sword and rallying the Christian troops as they defeated
the Moors. Estimates vary as to the number of Muslims
the saint decapitated . . .

Thus did the son of Zebedee grow from a disciple of
Jesus to a pilgrim saint and slayer of Moors or 'Santiago
Matamoros'. Travellers took the pilgrim road through
Roncesvalles from the ninth century onwards, although it was
not until the twelfth century that the route to Santiago
became the busiest trunk road in Christendom, a testing
ground for the eventual arrival of mass tourism. Another
'tourist' guide, written in 1150, was the *Book of St James*,

attributed to Pope Calixtus II. Although the authorship is probably apocryphal, the account, reproduced in T.A. Layton's *The Way of Saint James*, is thought to be an authentic enough portrait of the volume and diversity of pilgrims at the time.

> They come from all climates and nations of the world and even further away, French, Normans, Scots, Irish, Welsh, Teutons, Gascons, those from Navarre, Basques, Provincials, Anglo-Saxons, Britons, those from Cornwall, Flamands, Frisians, Italians, those from Poitiers, Danes, Norwegians, Russians, Sicilians, Asians, Indians, Cretans, Jerusalemers, Antiochans, Arabs, Moors, Lybians, and many others of all tongues, who came in companies or phalanxes and they all sing in unison to the Apostle. One cannot contemplate without marvelling the spectacle of the cohorts of pilgrims walking around the altar of this venerable saint. In one corner will be found Teutons, in another the French, in another Italians, all with lighted candles is lit up as resplendently as on one of the lightest of summer days. And they keep vigil and chant songs to the accompaniment of a multitude of musical instruments. Here some will be lamenting their sins, others will be giving alms to the blind, while others will be reading psalms. Here will be heard all kinds of languages and the various voices and songs of strangers.

A more contemporary account shows how the themes of devotion and universality have survived the advent of modern times. In *Spanish Pilgrimage* (1990), Robin Hanbury-Tenison describes his arrival at the Chapel of Roncesvalles, on the Spanish side of the Pyrenean pass that so enraptured Belloc (see p. 21).

> The bell from the Royal Collegiate College tolled and we hurried across the hillside for the pilgrim mass at 8 o'clock. Before entering the jumble of buildings we looked back to see our two white steeds grazing contentedly beside our two tents, set in an idyllic grassy meadow below the great wooded Pyrenees. It was a good

moment. There was a congregation of about fifty contrasting sharply between the mostly elderly locals in sober, repectable clothes and the young pilgrims in anoraks, shorts and trainers. The singing was excellent, led by the priests who moved along with consummate dignity to deliver prayers and homilies appropriate to those setting out on a long journey, to give us all communion and to bless us. Looking up at the candlelight glinting on the golden columns and illuminating the red hangings behind, while the robed figures changed places, their arms folded in front of them, a sense of timelessness and history swept over me. I began to feel a strength and conviction that what we were doing was right whatever our motives.

Northern Spain is a landscape of meadows thick with hazel trees, ancient woods of oak and beach blanketing the higher hills, strange rock formations, changing in appearance and colour beneath shifting skies where, in the words of Jan Morris, 'the Celtic strain is strong, and where wee folk, poltergeists, and the smell of brimstone are all familiar.' The atmosphere of the pilgrims' way, in which land, people and buildings take on a quasi-biblical character, is captured in an early twentieth-century novel *Flor de Santidad*, by Galician-born Ramón de Valle Inclán.

It began to get dark, and the twilight gave the wild and rugged place a hermit-like intonation which outlined in a sombre light the dark figure of the pilgrim. Icy gusts of wind, like the howls of a wolf, lashed incessantly against his long and dirty hair, and blew from one shoulder to the other his beard, which whenever the wind calmed down, fell shaken and twisted across his chest. He was covered in rosaries and crosses. The rain began to fall in big thick drops, and there were dust clouds along the path, and up in the hills a black goat was bleating. The clouds were congregating on the horizon, a horizon of water. The sheep were returning to the sheds, and only the sound of cowbells disturbed the cold, numb winter countryside; at the far end of a green and shaded gully, stood the shrine of San Clodio the Martyr, surrounded by centennial cypresses which swayed sadly. The pilgrim stopped, and with his two hands leaning on his staff, looked at the hamlet in the fold of the mountain, between the pine trees. Without the energy to reach it, he closed his eyes clouded with tiredness, breathed in some air and walked on.

The pilgrim journeys through Navarra with its villages of solid stone and houses displaying coats of arms; Rioja with its vineyards; León with its parched fields in summer, and Galicia, with its mist and rain where, in the words of the Galicia's most loved poetess, Rosalia de Castro, 'the dark night falls, falls little by little over the green mountains.'

For Picaud, journeying through such pastoral scenes had its down side. In his *Codex*, the eleventh-century cleric issued a dire warning for pilgrims concerning their diet.

> Whether it be the fish which is so vulgarly called the barbel or that which the Poitvins call the Alose (shad) and the Italians the slipia or eel or tench, in no part of Spain nor in Galicia should you eat them, for without any doubt you will die soon afterwards or fall ill. If by some chance you eat them and you are not ill that is because you have more health in you than others. All the fish and meat of beef and pork in Spain and Galicia makes foreigners ill.

Among the English pilgrims of the sixteenth century was Andrew Boorde. His advice to fellow travellers was that they should wash their faces only once a week to clear away spots, or otherwise wipe themselves with a scarlet cloth or soft brown paper. Walter Starkie in *The Road to Santiago*, describes Boorde as 'by far the most light-hearted and kindly of the pilgrims whose accounts have descended on us'. Boorde was often exasperated by the folly of the pilgrims who ignored Picaud's advice and grew terribly ill.

> I had rather they should die in England through my industry, than they should kill themselves along the way [to Santiago] . . . I assure all the world that I had rather go five times to Rome out of England, than one to Compostella: by water it is no pain, but by land it is the greatest journey that one Englishman can go on.

Sea journeys were not always painless. According to one who went by sea in the reign of Henry VI, the pilgrims were often horribly sick; they were mocked and taunted by the sailors and had to lie out on deck often without straw. 'Men may leave all games, that sail to St James', went the popular axiom.

Those who had obtained the necessary licence from King Henry included Willam Wey, a fellow of Eton College, whose crossing to Corunna from Weymouth took eight days. Wey advised future pilgrims to take with them such essentials as a 'lytel cawldron', a frying pan, dishes, and cups, all of which seemed to be in scarce supply in Santiago.

George Borrow felt, somewhat unwittingly, a sense of anticipation in the final approach to Santiago de Compostela, interspersed with a horror at Galician poverty. He was following part of the Camino de Santiago, more out of curiosity than from any sense of spiritual duty. Here he writes vividly of the Galician landscape.

> Small villages are at first continually seen, with low walls, and roofs formed of inmense slates, the eaves nearly touching the ground; these hamlets, however, gradually become less frequent as the path grows more steep and narrow, until they finally cease at a short distance before the spot is attained where the rivulet is abandoned, and is no more seen, though its tributaries may yet be heard in many a gully, or decried in tiny rills dashing down the steeps. Everything here is wild, strange, and beautiful . . .

In Villafranca de Bierzo, Borrow struck unusual bad fortune by knocking at the door of two or three houses only to be 'either disregarded or not heard'. He was later shown hospitality by a woman who mistook Borrow in the dark for a German watchmaker from Pontevedra and offered him a room for the night. Nearing Santiago de Compostela, Borrow was joined by a large group of pilgrims who like refugees made their way along the road flanked by soldiers. The missionary had chosen to make his pilgrimage in 1833, in the midst of the Carlist War, the civil war between the supporters of the Regent María Cristina, and Don Carlos the brother of King Ferdinand VII.

. . . I found myself amidst a train of two or three hundred people, some on foot, but the greater part mounted either on mules or the pony mares: I could not distinguish a single horse except my own and Antonio's [his servant]. A few soldiers were thinly scattered along the road. The country was hilly, but less mountainous and picturesque than the one which we had traversed the preceding day; it was for the most partitioned into small fields, which were planted with maize. At the distance of every two or three leagues we changed our escort, at some village where was stationed a detachment. The villages were mostly an assemblage of wretched cabins; the roofs were thatched, dark and moist, and not infrequently covered with rank vegetation. There were dunghills before the doors, and no lack of pools and puddles. Immense swine were stalking about, intermingled with naked children. The interior of the cabins corresponded with their external appearance: they were filled with filth and misery.

By contrast, the city of Santiago de Compostela stood 'on a pleasant level amidst mountains', and its Cathedral was, thought Borrow, a 'majestic venerable pile, in every respect calculated to excite awe and admiration'. An American scholar of the Romanesque, A. Kingsley Porter, in the 1920s paid tribute to the special atmosphere of Santiago de Compostela where one feels 'as nowhere else, wrapped about by the beauty of the Middle Ages.'

The Mexican writer Carlos Fuentes has described in *The Buried Mirror* the Cathedral's main entrance, the Puerta de la Gloria, or Gate of Glory: 'undoubtedly one of the greatest pieces of architectural sculpture in Christian Europe'. Down the centuries it has ushered in pilgrims to the main shrine through its extraordinary display of religious self-assurance and celebration.

On each side of the 'gate', four prophets and four apostles seem to be talking to each other. A particular humane and sympathetic figure stands out: the prophet Daniel. He is the Mona Lisa of the Middle Ages, and his enigmatic smile tells us that the world is well ordered, secure, and truthful under God's architecture. In conversation, the saints and the prophets seem to be in the midst of some heavenly cocktail party. What is their small talk about? Surely about the admirable symmetry of the medieval Christian order, where everything and everyone knew their rightful place and where collective wisdom had vanquished individual pride.

On 25 July, the feast of St James, the Cathedral is packed with worshippers beneath the *botafumeiro*, the huge censer, which guided by human hands and an almost supernatural rhythm, swings above the central nave, adding to the *olor de santidad*, the smell of holiness, for which the Cathedral of Santiago is famed. The saint has in different periods of Spanish history been transformed not just into a warrior but into the image of the Church triumphant inseparable from the nation-state as extolled in the militant cry 'Santiago o Cierra España' (Santiago or a Spain that is closed to its enemies). The political exploitation of the cult of Santiago and the popular submission to it was particularly pronounced during the Franco regime. It was witnessed by the novelist Honor Tracy in 1954, the Marian and Jubilee Year. The account comes from her book *Silk Hats and No Breakfast*.

It was a gorgeous and protracted ceremony. At the high altar, where in dazzling light the Apostle sat enthroned, were the Archbishop and the Canons, mitred like Bishops themselves, as here their privilege is, dressed in crimson and gold, and the Knights of Santiago in their long white robes with the red cross and the square white hats. On the two benches facing inwards to the long approach to the altar sat the Army in a blaze of medals, swords, gold, and purple sashes and plumed helmets and the Falange, never to be outdone, in their gold and white; while from a gallery high above the nave peeped and nodded the white-winged caps of nuns as they scrutinised and discussed the assembly. The robing of the Archbishop took up a good deal of time, as, either from etiquette or sheer helplessness, he gave no assistance whatever; and then he had to receive the silver shell in which the town's offering to St James was formerly

given, but which today is a mere symbol, the grant of
the secular power being made in a more prosaic fashion.
It was brought to him by the Civil Governor, who
delivered with it a tedious harangue with a highly
political flavour; and his courteous reply, purely religious
in tone, had the air of a snub. Then the great folk set
out in procession to bring in the head of the martyred
Apostle, and in the absence the *Botafumeiro*, or giant
censer, was lashed to an immense cable by ropes and
swung from one side of the Cathedral to the other. Five
young men in red robes stood and pulled, each time with
greater force, until at last the silver monster, with flames
shooting from it, swung up to the very roof and down
with a terrifying sweep to the other side narrowly clear-
ing the heads of the faithful in its path. Through the
kindness of Don Vicente's cousin, I had been given a
place immediately under it and when at last it came to
a stop I found myself trembling and sweating like a
frightened animal. Now the great ones solemnly
returned, bearing the head; from a gallery the young
novices of choristers broke out; and the Sacrifice of the
Mass began. In the shadowy background of the
Cathedral, meanwhile, the common folk were huddled
in their thousands – workmen, tourists, old peasant
women in their black shawls, old men with faces seemingly carved from wood – gazing at the brilliant spectacle
in awe.

An earlier English visitor, the Protestant Major William
Dalrymple, travelled to Galicia as part of five-month's leave
from his garrison at Gibraltar in 1774. In a letter dated
10 September 1774, he recognized the smell of religious
exploitation.

This town is situated amidst uncultivated hills, is large,
and swarms with priests, who enjoying great incomes,
live in luxury and every kind of dissipation; still preying
upon the weakness, folly, and even rascality of their
fellow creatures, who came on pilgrimage to the shrine
of the sacred apostle. Here Hypocricy has raised a most
stupendous temple, wherein Delusion officiates as high

priest, and Ignorance daily crowds in superstitious multitudes for its votaries; the credulous and virtuous to obtain and further merit heaven, and the vicious to expiate their crimes, are alike received; and equally made to contribute to the ease and pleasures of the sacerdotal tribe: the Bishop, supreme emperor, heals the minds, and cures the consciences of all by the same prescription.

In Santiago de Compostela in 1954, Walter Starkie was dazzled by the 'apotheosis of baroque ornamentation with its twisted lamps, Salomic columns, chubby angels, scrolls, escutcheons and riding high above the Churrigueresque extravaganza the 'Moor slayer' in full panoply'. He started dreaming of what the pilgrimage must have been like in the twelfth century, the golden age of Christianity, when the doors of the Cathedral stayed open day and night during feast days.

They would stay in their thousands all night jostling and struggling perpetually to watch as near as possible to the entrance to the crypt containing the body of the Apostle, and many a time fierce battles raged and so much blood was spilt that the basilica had to be re-consecrated. Every part of the cathedral, even the galleries above, were thronged with people who bivouaked there for days and nights, and so foul did the atmosphere become that braziers of incense were lit in the corners . . . Today the solemn pontifical Mass, the singing of the antiphonal choirs and the glowing colours of the scene reminded me of the pictures of Bellini I had seen in the Academia in Venice.

In all probability St James never came to Spain at all; he most certainly never fought in a battle against the Moors because he lived several centuries before they set foot on Spanish soil. Yet Santiago, notes Jan Morris, has been so ensconced in the Spanish mind, that 'long ago, in the way of all the best hallucinations, it achieved a kind of truth.'

6

SOUL AND FIESTA

Spanish Religion

'Spain', wrote the Spanish essayist Angel Ganivet in *Idearium Español*, a collection of notes and aphorisms regarding the character of his people, published in 1897, 'was probably Christian before Christ. Christianity fitted us like a ring to the finger and it took us over to never leave us.' The history of Spain has been more affected by religion than any other factor. Religion has determined state, war, and conquest, and proved a pervading influence on the culture of the Spanish people in all its manifestations. Professor E. Allison Peers explains in *Spain, the Church and the Orders*, published in 1939, why the Catholic Church in Spain is the Church of the Spanish people.

Whether or not we can accept its dogmas and join in its services, acquaintance with the country will at once lead us to that conclusion. It is confirmed by the universally acknowledged fact that no other religious body can describe itself as the Church's serious rival. With the rarest exceptions, individuals who have left it, instead of transferring their allegiance elsewhere, have cut themselves off from institutional Christianity altogether. 'The whole nation,' wrote Richard Ford in his *Handbook to Spain*, 'is divided into two classes – bigoted Romanists or Infidels; there is no via media.' Not as a result of logical reasoning, but from temperament and according

to century-old tradition, the attitude of the Spaniard to
the Church is 'all or none'. In religion, as in politics, he
sees everything as either black or white; the pendulum
swings relentlessly; and the man who can no longer
accept Catholic dogma makes no attempt to find a
religion less exacting and less unyielding, but goes
straight to the other extreme, and either becomes
fanatically opposed to all forms of religion (whence
perhaps the success of the Anarchist movement and
whence undoubtedly the anti-Christian outrages to be
chronicled hereafter) or cherishes within his own breast
a strictly individual form of personal religion – how far
satisfying to him none but he can tell.

It is in her mystics that Spanish religion fires itself. The
belief in the possibility of union with God on earth and the
striving to achieve it has produced some of the great figures
of Spanish Catholicism and some of the most inspiring
religious writing the world has ever known.

Among Spain's numerous mystics, few perhaps have proved
as controversial as St Ignatius of Loyola, the founder of the
Jesuit order, the Society of Jesus. Ignatius was born near
Azpeitia, in the Basque country, in 1491, a few years before
the Catholic Church declared its counter-reformation against
Protestantism. The son of a nobleman, Ignatius was brought
up in the Spanish court, and fought in the service of the Duke
of Najera. According to Polanco, his biographer, at the age
of twenty-six Ignatius was 'attached to the faith' but nevertheless was 'much addicted to gambling and dissolute in his
dealings with women, contentious about using his sword.'
Gerard Hughes, a modern Jesuit writer, tells the story of the
conversion of Ignatius at Loyola. While recovering from an
injury incurred in defending the city of Pamplona against
French troops it is said that he read a collection of saints lives.

While reading these he began on a second series of
daydreams, and now he was imagining himself outdoing
the saints in their austerities. One saint, Humphrey of
the desert, who seemed able to live on herbs, fresh air
and prayer, particularly fascinated him. Inigo was now
saying to himself, 'If Humphrey can do it, so can I. If

Dominic and Francis can do it, so can I.' For weeks he
alternated between the two kinds of daydream, until suddenly he noticed something which was to change not
only his own life but millions of other people as well.

While both kinds of daydream were enjoyable at the
time, he discovered that after he had dreamed of his great
deeds and of the lady whose love he would win, he felt
bored, empty and sad, but after dreaming of outdoing
the saints he felt happy, hopeful and enouraged. He
reflected on this difference and so learned his first lesson
in what later he would call 'Discernment of Spirits',
which we might term 'Distinguishing between our
creative inner moods and feelings.' This story of Inigo
gives the beginnings of an answer to the question 'Where
is our treasure?' The treasure lies hidden in our inner
moods and feelings.

Once recovered from his injuries, Ignatius made a
pilgrimage to the Virgin of Montserrat, where he vowed
himself forever a soldier of Christ. He then exchanged his
soldier's clothes for those of a hermit and limped down the
road to the town of Manresa. There he lived in a cell, fasted,
and scourged himself at regular intervals in an act of self-denial
that was to form the three guiding principles of the Jesuit
order: chastity, obedience and poverty.

It was in Manresa that Ignatius wrote the first draft of the
Spiritual Exercises, a series of meditations on the life of Christ
intended to exert a cumulative and lasting effect on the will
of the exercitant. The rules were written 'for overcoming
oneself and for regulating one's life without being swayed by
any inordinate attachment.'

Somerset Maugham followed in the steps of St Ignatius
while on a tour of Spain in 1920. In *Don Fernando* he describes
the marble altar at Loyola as 'very magnificent and extremely
ugly'. But his poetic imagination was captured as he made his
way up into the sunny country of the Catalan hills, towards
Manresa, where the 'colour has not the pastel lightness of
French landscape, but is deeper and richer.' And where the
sky is bright blue 'with small stationary clouds very white
against it.' He found the cave in which the saint composed

his mystical tract on the side of a rocky hill which afforded
a splendid prospect of Montserrat, 'sharp-eyed on a clear day,
but in the mist incredibly mysterious.' The cave was guarded
by an enormous iron grille, and the Jesuit college and church
built over it were locked up, as the priests had been expelled
(it was a period when the Jesuits were subjected to persecution
by the State). Maugham records:

> I had the curiosity on one occasion to attempt to do one
> of the exercises myself. It was a singular experience. I
> began with the composition of place. It seems simple
> enough, but I found it none too easy, and I am not sur-
> prised that the commentators have seen the necessity of
> providing the exercitant with particulars circumstantial
> enough to eke out a halting fancy. But I found this
> child's play compared with the meditation. It is true that
> I had not prepared myself by fasting or corporal penance,
> and grace was certainly not vouchsafed me. To me it was
> incredibly difficult to fix my mind on a subject and con-
> centrate on it without distraction. I was forever wander-
> ing along by-paths and down crooked ways.

In *Handbook for Travellers in Spain*, Richard Ford describes
St Ignatius as an enthusiastic, somewhat naïve, if sincere
dreamer who during his illness 'went mad, as did Don
Quixote by perusing chivalrous romances' only to subse-
quently become a tool in the hands of 'crafty' fellow Jesuits.
Ford was uncomplimentary about the Jesuits generally.

> Their object was to uphold Popery, not Christianity, and
> thus to govern mankind through religion; they purposed
> to revive the crusades, to restore to the tiara in the new
> world what it was losing in the old. They created
> unscrupulous agents; their education was teaching men
> *not* to think; they required a slavish obedience of the
> intellect, and left the understanding without freedom,
> the heart without virtue. As printing, which gave wings
> to the Bible, was shattering the fabric of the Vatican,
> the Jesuits, monopolising the lever of *education*, became
> missionaries abroad, tutors, and teachers of the rising
> youth at home, and thus not only disarmed knowledge

of its power, but made it minister to its own suicidal destruction, and became a tool for the carrying on of that implacable, exterminating contest, which Rome has ever warred, wars, and will war against all civil and religious liberty. Accordingly the active, intellectual Jesuits infused a new life into the fat indolence of the monastic system. They raised cheerful, gorgeous temples, and abjured the gloomy cowl and routine of the cloister now getting obsolete. Men of this world rather than the next, they adopted a purely mundane policy, of the earth, earthly. They professed to secure the salvation of all who would only implicitly trust to them, and thus removed heavy responsibility, which depresses the soul, and placed it on velvet: their redeeming merit, according to Brillat Savarin, was (after colonizing and civilizing the new world) the discovery of the turkey and its introduction to the truffle; but gastronomy owes everything to the church.

In the writings of Father James Brodrick, author of a biography of St Ignatius published in 1956, we have a more sympathetic view. The starting point here is not the Jesuits, but the Basques among whom Ignatius was born and brought up.

Men and their habitat are bound together by a thousand subtle influences, visible in so far as they control nature but only to be guessed at in so far as nature controls them. The skies over their heads, the hills that limit their horizon, the prevailing winds, their food and drink, must all, over long ages, affect them physically and mentally. And then there is the powerful cohesive force of language and common traditions. All in all, the influences in Euskalerria have produced a magnificent kind of human being, full of dignity and self-respect, with an equal respect for the dignity of others, hard working, frugal, nobly independent, brave to the point of rashness, profoundly conservative, and at the time gay and venturesome, lovers of difficult sports on which they gamble enthusiastically, born to sing and to dance . . . religion is at the root of their very existence . . .

St Ignatius told his followers to go outside the monastery walls, and set down new roots in foreign lands and cultures, making a virtue of worldliness. St Ignatius was a Basque, and his order became more European than Spanish, even if its original military form and its periods of crisis and intensity seem part and parcel of the Hispanic soul. In contrast, St Teresa, another great pillar of the counter-reformation, spent much of her life in the heart of Spain, Castile. Shirley du Boulay, her biographer, writes:

> Its wind-swept plains, its granite boulders, its bitter winters and sun-scorched summers were the womb that nourished the 'undaunted daughter of desires' of Richard Crashaw's poem. A gentler landscape would not have produced a woman of such courage and determination.
> Apart from its famous towns – Madrid, Toledo, Valladolid and Segovia – Castille is a bleak and desolate region. It is monotonous, the barren landscape seldom softened by mist or rain. Yet this very monotony, this quality of endlessness, is curiously exciting. It speaks of hardship and danger, of struggle and tenacity, of time and eternity, of life and death. The light is diamond bright, the climate at the mercy of violent changes in temperature. So dry is the land that much of it is still uncultivated; today, even where it has been watered, sunflowers struggle to reach a pathetic two feet in height. This is central Spain, a land not of patios, fountains, and orange blossom, but harsh, ascetic, extreme. *Todo o nada* (all or nothing). Castille does not compromise.

It is this geographical background that provided St Teresa with the symbols descriptive of her inner journey towards mystical union and her conversion to the contemplative life.

In her autobiography, *The Life*, which in its complete form first passed from hand to hand in 1565, the unwatered and untended garden symbolizes the human at the beginning of a life of prayer.

> A beginner must look on himself as one setting out to make a garden for his Lord's pleasure, on most unfruitful soil which abounds in weeds. His Majesty roots up the

weeds and will put in good plants instead. Let us reckon that this is already done when a soul decides to practice prayer and had begun to do so. We have then, as good gardeners, with God's help to make these plants grow, and to water them carefully so that they do not die, but also to produce flowers, which give out a good smell, to delight this Lord of ours. Then He will often come to take his pleasure in this garden and enjoy the virtues.

The walled town of Avila where St Teresa spent most of her life embodies another symbol of inner life: the castle. In *The Interior Castle*, she describes her spiritual journey as a passage through a series of rooms or 'mansions' (*moradas*). In the first mansion, the person is too obsessed with self-knowledge to see the spiritual light at the centre of the castle. By the time he has arrived at the second mansion, a conversion experience is under way. On entering the seventh mansion, union is complete and the soul lives on in a permanently altered state.

It is like rain falling from the heavens into a river or spring; there is nothing but water there and it is impossible to divide or separate the water belonging to the river from that which falls from the heavens.

In *The Eagle and the Dove*, published in 1943, Vita Sackville-West wrote about the paradox she saw as the key to understanding St Teresa, 'the oddest mixture between the most abstruse mystical life and rough common sense in trying to deal with it.' It was, Sackville-West noted, typical of the saint to 'cling to iron railings to prevent herself from being supernaturally lifted into the air.' She concluded:

In addition to this factual, often of-the-soil vividness of expression, she possessed also something of the poet's vision, when her imagery flamed more splendid; and then, God became like to a burning furnace, or to a most brilliant diamond much larger than the whole world, in which all our actions were reflected, or the soul suddenly became bright as a mirror, clear behind, sideways, upwards, and downwards, a sculptured mirror, with Christ in the centre, and the lustre dimmed only as by a vapour when the soul was in mortal sin . . . Both *The Interior Castle* and *The Way of Perfection*, apart from their other qualities of profundity, enlightenment, and sagacity both human and spiritual, possess a kind of shimmering beauty made up of water and of light. They are as nacreous as oyster shells, with a prismatic transparency surely reflected from the incandescent certainty at the centre of her soul.

Richard Ford on the other hand did not warm to St Teresa's intense spirituality and self-denying qualities. In his entry on Avila in the *Handbook*, he dismissed her as a 'mere tool of the Jesuits', whose writings were edited by 'two crafty Dominicans.' Her miracles were mere superstitions, of 'pagan and oriental origin.'

Another nineteenth-century traveller, John Lomas, was caught up in the liberalism of the day and its rabid anti-clericalism. 'Roman Catholicism,' he noted, 'at its best affects the dangerous extreme of form and ceremony – dangerous as tending to choke all the devotional feeling, and inner life.' And yet he distinguished between the Catholic Church's outer forms and its inner substance. In the mystic Teresa he recognized a true saint. Visiting the celebrated Convent of the Encarnación, where Teresa took the veil in 1534, Lomas discovered a 'wretched pile of buildings now, the chapel decked out with all that gilt and stucco can do, and the adjoining courtyard – a wilderness of untidy gravel and weed.' He was no more impressed by the 'vilely decorated' chapel marking her birthplace. He lingered however at the place, thinking on the memory of 'a woman who, in a ceaseless fight of forty-seven years, conquered self, conquered suffering, conquered persecution, and conquered time.'

Half a century later St Teresa drew Kate O'Brien to Avila. The Irish writer found there not the 'lifeless provincial place' mourned by V.S. Pritchett, but a point for reflection on the spirit of an early feminist.

Her legend is scattered over all the town, though with a certain carelessness and non-sentimentality. Spanish crudity too. One does not like to see her index finger in a bottle – though that represents a mere nothing, as one discovers from her biographers, of the mutilations perpetrated on her remains by rapacious lunatics and votaries of the seventeenth century. But her leather girdle, the hazel-tree she planted, a drum she had when she was a child, her little drinking jug . . . these relics touch imagination gently and make us less afraid of the strange, impassioned mystic, of whom presently we find, taking some trouble to approach, there is no need on earth to be afraid.

St John of the Cross, while less approachable in biographical detail, has nevertheless also drawn a succession of observers of Spain into the country's religious culture. While on a riding tour of southern Spain in 1962, John Betjeman's wife Penelope Chetwode made a pilgrimage to Ubeda where the saint died. After enjoying a breakfast of Russian tea, toast, and peach jam at the local parador, she found herself sufficiently prepared to tackle the full gamut of religious ceremony. High Mass at the Carmelite Church of San Miguel had a full choir of friars singing in four parts, but the trebles singing with *cante jondo* voices made the harmony sound odd. She wondered what an English choir master would have thought of it.

> The liturgical feast of St John of the Cross (he actually died of erysipelas in the Carmelite Monastery of Ubeda on December 12, 1591) is evidently a highbrow as opposed to a popular fiesta. No fireworks were let off at the elevation and the big congregation was obviously drawn largely from the professional class, most people being well-dressed and following the Mass in their Missals. The moving sermon on the Divine Doctrine of St John was preached by a friar from Granada and lasted for thirty-five minutes.

St John of the Cross never matched the extrovert nature of his mentor St Teresa. His four treatises, or *Divine Doctrine*, on the paths of mystical prayer, take the form of letters and jottings to friends and patrons, such as the following to a benefactress, Dona Ana de Penalosa. It is taken from a commentary on his 'semi-ecstatic love poem', 'Living Flame of Love'.

... Even so, when a log of wood has been set upon the fire, it is transformed into fire and united with it; yet as the fire grows hotter and the wood remains upon it for a longer time, it glows much more and becomes more completely enkindled, until it gives out sparks of fire and flame.

Prejudice as much as admiration has coloured views of Spanish religious life. Few English children are probably aware that the popular and seemingly harmless nursery rhyme, 'Mary, Mary quite contrary, how does your garden grow? With jingle bells and cockle shells and pretty maids all in a row', derives from Protestant revulsion at Mary Tudor's flirtation with Catholic Spain (the cockle shells being one of the symbols of the pilgrimage to Santiago de Compostela).

The Black Legend about Spain which Protestants in particular perpetrated from the time of the Reformation challenged the comfortable notion that Spanish Catholicism was the spiritual expression of a people with a peculiarly individualistic and mystical temperament. The legend asserted that the intense spirituality and self-denying qualities of the mystics gloss over the doctrine of discipline and the teaching by austerity, whereby the taking of physical and other punishments was elevated to a virtue among Spaniards generally.

Among the more colourful early literary portraits of the Spaniards' alleged propensity for blood and suffering was that of a Holy Week procession by a seventeenth-century Frenchwoman, the writer and Countess Mme d'Aulnoy. In her *Relation du Voyage d'Espagne*, published in 1691, she gives an account of the admiration that male flagellation aroused among women. Whenever a male penitent passed someone of the opposite sex he would purposely increase the intensity of his strokes so that she would be sprinkled with his blood. Mme d'Aulnoy herself confessed that her mild disgust was mixed with a tinge of excitement.

I thought I would swoon away . . . Fancy a man coming so near that he'll cover you all over with blood . . . There are certain rules by which to discipline themselves elegantly, and masters to teach the art, just as to dance and fence . . . On the back of their waistcoats they have two great holes, and a ribbon tied to their whip. Commonly 'tis their mistress which honours them with this favour.

D'Aulnoy's account of Spain was immensely popular and was widely translated over the next 150 years. The lady herself, whose works include the fairytale *Goldilocks*, is thought to have never set foot in Spain.

Giacomo Casanova spent a 'miserable year' in Spain from 1767–8 after being expelled from Vienna and Paris in quick succession. Part of his unhappiness was caused by the all-pervasive influence of the Church. Observing women pilgrims wearing nun's habits, he reflected that the 'the idea of pleasing God by wearing monkish garb seems very odd indeed'. He also remarked on the superstition of a Spanish whore who denounced as an atheist a client who had laughed at the absurdity of covering religious pictures while business took place.

Casanova himself appears to have been impotent when it came to challenging the influence of the priesthood: 'a band of knaves, but one has to treat them with more respect than one would pay to honest men elsewhere.' Of the Inquisition, which remained fairly active at the time, Casanova was terrified, although on one occasion he was surprised.

A few days before, I had met a Frenchman named Segur, who had just come out of the prisons of the Inquisition. He had been shut up for three years for committing the following crime: in the hall of his house there was a fountain, composed of a marble basin and the statue of a naked child, who discharged the water in the same way as the well known statue of Brussels, that is to say, by his virile member. The child might be a Cupid or an Infant Jesus, as you pleased, but the sculptor had adorned the head with a kind of aureole; and so the fanatics declared that it was mocking God.

Poor Segur was accused of impiety, and the Inquisition dealt with him accordingly. I felt that my fault might be adjudged as great as Segur's, and not caring to run the risk of a like punishment I called on the bishop, who held the office of Grand Inquisitor, and told him word for word the conversation I had had with the iconoclast chaplain. I ended by craving pardon, if I had offended the chaplain, as I was a good Christian, and orthodox on all points. I had never expected to find the Grand Inquisitor of Madrid a kindly and intelligent, though ill-favoured, prelate; but so it was, and he did nothing but laugh from the beginning to the end of my story, for he would not let me call it a confession.

The confession Casanova had made concerned his criticism of a young priest who had been so scandalized by the exposed breast of a Madonna with Child in a chapel in Madrid's Calle St Jeronimo that he had painted over it a handkerchief.

Writing early in the twentieth century, Havelock Ellis drew his conclusions about the repressive side to Spanish religion less from contemporary evidence than from the Baroque art which decorates many Spanish churches.

I recall, for instance, a most sorrowful Christ which I came across not long since over an altar in an aisle of Palencia Cathedral. It was a large wooden image on a crucifix, carved in the Spanish realistic muscular style, and around the waist there was a charming little embroidered skirt, very short, and below it peeped out a delicate lace petticoat, a coquettish disguise made to suggest and not conceal, for there was nothing to suggest and not conceal, for there was nothing to conceal. Such is the piquant figure that Spanish religion devises for the adoration of Spanish women, and the bent dolorous face looks more dolorous than ever with eyes turned to this ballet-girl's costume.

Of the many religious ceremonies witnessed by William Jacob while on his travels through Spain, none seemed to him so ludicrous as the processions he witnessed while walking the streets of Seville in 1809.

A priest, seated in a sedan chair, with the holy elements in a gold case on his lap, escorted by a guard of soldiers, and preceded by a bellman, is literally denominated by the people 'His Majesty down the street.' To increase the singularity of the spectacle, the bellman strikes three strokes, in allusion to the three persons of the Trinity, and then ceases. At this well known sound, whatever be the state of the weather, or the condition of the streets, every one drops on his knees, and continues in this devout posture till the object of adoration is out of sight. If this procession should pass through the street, containing a theatre or a ballroom, the actors on this stage, and the dancers at the assembly, alike drop on their knees till the sound is lost, when they resume their thoughtless dissipation.

There are nightly processions through the streets of this city . . . The different wards conduct the processions by turns, so that it is every night parading in some parts of the town; being more or less splendid, according to the revenues of the church or the convent whence it proceeds. The Rosario is complimented by the inhabitants of the streets through which it passes, by illuminations, that have a splendid effect, but which is in a great measure counteracted by the horrid noise of the singers and the chanters.

The young V.S. Pritchett cast a cynical look – subsequently revised – on Spanish religious life during a walk from one end of the country to the other in 1928. In *Marching Spain*, Pritchett discovered a Salamanca seemingly populated only by priests and nuns. The town was 'glutted with convents, monasteries, churches, seminaries, their little businesses and intrigues, and theological glooms, the friction between the Orders, the suspicions of the laity, all the jealousies of an over-developed and inbred ecclesiasticism'.

Sixty-one kilometres away is the town of Zamora, where the eleventh-century crusader El Cid received his knightly arms, and here Pritchett found local religious life expressed in a quite different way. There were fewer priests and nuns, but more bells, the ringing of which had a fanatical rhythm.

In the early morning I was awakened by the clamour and banging of bells, as though all the cans and pails of the city were being whacked into challenge by the faithful. When one outburst had tired itself, another bombardment began in a further parish, and was taken up turn by turn in the lower parishes by the river. Bang, bang, banging good iron and copper religion that cuffed you on the head and the ears and knocked you into a state of sanctity. I do not blame those Spanish bells, for the Spaniard hears none but the harshest noises, nothing but violence ever penetrates him. Nothing but force ever convinces him. The cruelty of the Inquisition convinced him as it stirred the English to resist. We must be persuaded by quietness and privacy. Our bells must be sentimental, sweet, milky. Bang us and we bang back. Bang bells and we have them stopped.

By contrast George Borrow felt a sense of awe in 1836 when visiting St Alban's College in Valladolid. It remains the sole survivor of the many English Catholic institutions established in the Iberian Peninsula during the Reformation.

This is by far the most remarkable establishment of the kind in the Peninsula, and I believe the most prosperous . . . I could not however fail to be struck with the order, neatness, and system which pervaded it. There was however an air of monastic discipline, though I am far from asserting that such actually existed . . . Of all the curiosities of this College, the most remarkable is the picture gallery, which contains neither more or less than the portraits of a variety of scholars of this house who eventually suffered martyrdom in England, in the exercise of their vocation in the angry times of the Sixth Edward and the fierce Elizabeth. Yes, in this very house were many of those pale smiling half-foreign priests educated, who, like stealthy grimalkins, traversed green England in all directions; crept into old halls beneath umbrageous rookeries, fanning the dying embers of popery, with either no hope nor perhaps wish than to perish disembowelled by the bloody hands of the executioner, amongst the yells of a rabble as bigoted as themselves . . .

The social dimension to pilgrimage was witnessed by an early English traveller, Terence Mason Hughes, who lived in Spain in 1846. Hughes writes in *Revelations of Spain*:

No church is without its favoured shrine or image, and each in turn attracts the homage of the faithful. The pilgrimage to distant pueblos consumes, at the least, an entire day: and it's astonishing to see the assiduity with which women and children (for the men, here, as in France, excepting the peasantry alone, have to a considerable extent been alienated from these tiresome manifestations of piety) plod on through the intolerable summer heat to distances extending for leagues . . . Even in the views of those who promote these spectacles, and in the interest of sound religion, it would be well to confine them to the churches. It is impossible to deny that the effect is entirely theatrical, and that from long custom they do not impress one soul amongst a thousand of the population. In fact, they repair to it as to a play. Every one chats and laughs as if nothing particular were going on; the very persons who take part in the procession sometimes laugh with the rest; and I have seen youths whistling merry tunes in chorus, while the padres and pious women who accompanied them were chanting Latin hymns in praise of Nuestra Señora del Calvario, behind her weeping image with its bosom transpierced by the sword . . . [In the romeria or rural pilgrimage] religion, a business or a pretence, is combined with the pleasures of a gypsying party, the pent-up town's-folk can both save their souls and enjoy a mouthful of country air; and after hailing each other with a *Buenas Fiestas!* reciting the accustomed rosary, and witnessing the internal splendours of a church all glittering with waxlights and festooned with silken hangings, and gold or silver embroidery, can ruralise at will, and unite corporeal to spiritual exercise . . .

Nicholas Wollaston was in Zaragoza in 1987 during the annual festivities of the Virgin of Pilar, said to have first appeared in AD 40. In *Tilting at Don Quixote*, he describes the scene in the city's huge basilica which is one of Spain's most important religious shrines.

Outside the immense, astonishing cathedral a pop singer yells his thumping message; and inside, also into a microphone, a priest intones his eternal words. Children are led or carried by choirboys to Our Lady of the Pilar – a doll standing on something like a mauve lampshade, dazzled by spotlights – and allowed to kiss her pedestal; then they turn and smile, hands in prayer, for a photograph – a flash, a nod, a ticket – and the next child is brought. Round the back a line of worshippers shuffles past a brass porthole to press their lips on a tiny corner of the Pilar's pillar. Nearby is a vast bank of candles under a metal canopy; the heat is enough to roast any of the bulls they killed this afternoon.

There is non-stop mass all evening, a continuous celebration. The cathedral, full of the same ornamentation, plastered loops, encrusted garlands that fill the confectionery shops, is packed; and the people, who earlier were parading through the streets, eating ices and fantastic cakes, are rejoicing in the palace of God, the temple of Pilar. It's a total occasion, the flummery of worship, a triumph of reverence and wonder, absorbing for anyone susceptible to religious vehemence: the gaudy prelates and surpliced choir, the chanting and preaching, bobbing and crossing, the deaf woman pressing her ear to a loudspeaker to catch the word of God, the silent figures in the chapels and busy confessionals, the men and women of all ages lining up at the altar steps, the vast congregation assembled to praise and pray, a little dog among them and a Velazquez dwarf in a smart suit and red fiesta scarf waiting for the sacrament – all the more moving for my own faithfulness.

The element of collective catharsis and the drama of Spain's most famous religious festival – the Holy Week in Seville – were exhaustively observed by Eric Newby in 1983. From Palm Sunday through to Holy Saturday he witnessed some fifty-one processions escorting one hundred and three separate *pasos* or religious images. The longest, that of the Virgin of the Macarena, lasted for twelve and a half hours.

Night and day, except for an hour or so after midday, the great floats, all of them enormously heavy, embellished with silver, some decorated with flowers and bearing sumptuously dressed figures of the Virgin, costing thousands of pounds each year to decorate (the floats and figures are of inestimable worth, a Virgin's

clothing and accessories alone valued at £100,000),
other effigies depicting events in the last six days of
the life of Christ, had swayed through the streets, those
of the Virgins like great ships illuminated by masses of
candles, all borne on the backs of sweating porters invisi-
ble beneath the velvet draperies, some macabre, some
beautiful, some very old, some made as late as the 1970s.

Another witness to a Seville procession, Gertrude Bone,
captured in *Days in Old Spain* (1938) the memorable
atmosphere of the darkened streets 'when the pasos issue from
the church in silence, save for the strange Oriental wailing of
the saetas ('arrows' of song) which greet their appearance,
when the penitents in grotesque black habits with lighted
candles walk in two wavering lines, the skipping and jerking
of their narrow trains on the pavements, the inclination of the
peaked eyeless hood distributing strange shadows like bats in
the moonlight . . .'
In a remote unnamed mountain village in Andalusia Bone
came upon a procession that in its spontaneity seemed to
express the uncluttered Christianity of the Gospels.

The pasos were wedged in the crowd. The balconies
were filled with spectators, and barely lifted above the
heads of the people stood the figure of Christ mocked,
hands tied, head drooping and wounded, torn garments,
a roughly carved figure of some tragic intensity. Excited
by the jostling crowd, a drunken gipsy began to sing a
ribald song. The people, from rebukes, passed to jeering.
Jests and protests were shouted from one to another.
Suddenly an old woman whose fierce profile was cut, as
it were, from her black shawl, began to sing a saeta of
devotion in a piercing voice. The gipsy refused to stop
and sang louder, taking it as a challenge. The people
laughed aloud at both, and in the middle of the swaying,
noisy crowd stood the tragic and abandoned figure,
taking on in circumstance something of the fickleness and
triviality which had brought about its Passion.

An adventurous woman of high social standing, Matilda
Betham-Edwards visited Burgos Cathedral as she made her

way through Spain to the Sahara, a century earlier. In her
diary published in 1868, Betham Edwards wrote:

> . . . though there was plenty of worshippers, except for
> the sombreros and brown capas or cloaks of the men,
> and the silk and lace mantillas of the women, there was
> no costume at all. People seem to enjoy going to church
> in Spain. The ladies come in with their little dogs, drop
> on their knees on a mat, adjust their fans and fall into
> a sort of quiet ecstasy of prayer, the dogs sitting
> demurely by. The men are equally devout; and every one,
> caballero or beggar, soldier or priest, comes in his turn,
> week-day and Sunday. The churches are beautifully kept,
> warm in cold weather, cool in summer, clean and dusky
> and quiet always. No wonder they are never empty.

7

TEMPLE OF THE INTELLECT

Roman Spain

Merida is the former capital of the Roman province of Lusitania, which stretched from the Costa Brava to Portugal. It was originally founded as a military settlement by the Emperor Augustus but gradually grew into the administrative centre of an invading force that was to have a formative affect on Spanish culture. In 218 BC Romans landed – led by the Scipios – at the Mediterranean port of Ampurias. They were to remain on Iberian soil for 700 years, until defeated and expelled by the Visigoths. They left behind brilliant feats of engineering, a language, and a philosophy of life, elements of which have survived to the present day.

Trowbridge Hall in 1923 approached Merida across the 'harsh, savage province of Extremadura'. He wrote in *Spain in Silhouette*:

> The welcome that awaits us at the low-rafted, stuffy inn of Merida, the celebrated capital of Lusitania, is one of cold indifference, a moldering chill, and an overpowering odor of the past – a past largely of strong oil and stronger garlic. However, all of Merida lives among strong odors of antiquity bequeathed to her by Rome – Roman aqueducts, Roman bridges, Roman forums, Roman coliseums – crumbling masses of reddish brown, colored by the rain and winds of time.

On Merida, Gertrude Bone wrote in *Days of Old Spain*:

The Romans have won Merida for good. True, for everyone who ever left an imprint on the Spanish race has passed through the once magnificent capital of Lusitania, but of Visigoth and Moor hardly any traces remain, of the Renaissance nothing, of the Templars 'a mountain of ruins'. So that one now leaves Spain, becoming no longer a traveller in the Iberian Peninsula, but in Ancient Rome, treading the quiet paths of the archaeologists, pensive with other memories, of Palatine and Pincian Hills, of Capital and Forum, of the roomy and sovereign empires of Augustus, Trajan, and Hadrian. I have my own strong conviction that the Spaniard more than any other Latin nation continues the features and ideal of the Roman, but the familiar quiet of the grass-grown and sunny Circus, the Stadium, the theatre, that elaborate architectural housing for the human voice, the heavy solemnity of the aqueduct, these dominations of an empire whose emperors were gods belong to an older world than Spain. Perhaps the very decay and unimportance of Merida in the time of Spain's great building epoch after the Reconquest saved the Roman monuments from being despoiled. No considerable palace seems to have been erected on the spot. Visigoth and Moor have taken all they wanted of column and moulding. The earth lay lightly on Eternal Rome. Beside the ruins, at which the learned are now busy, the town lies like an Arab town, unable to open out into views, its chimneyless house roofs lying close and almost overlapping, one narrow street disclosing nothing until one turns into the next, its whitewashed house fronts striking an Oriental dazzle to the eyes. How relentless is the Roman bridge which led to the splendours of Merida! Its half-mile of narrow deviating level lies over the Guadiana like an ordeal by sunlight. Before one has gone half-way one has the feeling of being unable to turn back. One must go on, caught in the forced march across, or die in the returning. Once in that formidable narrow alley, horses, oxen, carts, donkeys, as men, are all under the lash of necessity. Fortitude wavers. One is no longer an individual. Legions march with one to an imperial command – I want more room.

Merida drew fulsome praise from Richard Ford when he visited it in 1832. With his eye for meticulous detail, he informs us in the *Handbook* that

> 36 different coins were struck here . . . The common reverse is a 'turreted gate' with the words 'Augusta Emirata' as an inscription, which constitute the city arms. This unique city is the Rome of Spain, in some points rivalling the eternal city itself; stupendous monuments of antiquity meet the eye at every step . . . Merida rises on the right bank of the Guadiana, which is crossed by a Roman bridge of 81 arches, 2575 feet long, 26 feet broad, and 33 feet above the level of the bed of the river; it is indeed a bridge and worthy of its builder – Trajan, a true Pontifex Maximus.

Gerald Brenan walked across the same bridge in 1949, towards sunset. He found it crowded with people, mules, and donkeys returning from the farther bank.

> The water of the river was a pale, ethereal blue and on the broad expanse of yellow gravel on either side of it were women washing clothes in basins and spreading them out to dry, cattle standing idle with only their tails moving, and horsemen and mulateers giving their mounts to drink. Then behind these rose low green hills, almost crystalline in the clear light, and behind them diminutive rock-crowned mountains, as blue and as high in tone as the mountains of a Patinir landscape. One never grows tired of Spanish light and scenery.

It was on 6 November 1859 that the Vicar of Milton Abbas, Dorset, Reverend Richard Roberts, consciously following in Ford's footsteps, finally arrived in Merida after taking one week to ride 140 miles across part of Castile and most of Extremadura. Roberts, like other visitors to Spain, regarded the remains he came across as monuments to the ambition, power, and intellect of the Romans in Spain.

> The finest view . . . is commanded by a terrace at the back of the Posada de las Animas, close to the great Roman bridge. Below flows the river, spanned by the

eighty-one arches, which ensure a safe passage during the widest-spread innundation. A square tower of the same date, but pierced in Moorish days by a horse-shoe arch, stands at its townward extremity, and serves as a *tête de pont*; while a noble wall rising directly out of the water, and terminating in a broad quay, flanks the bridge to the south. The salient points of view as you turn towards the town, are distinctively Roman, a solitary palm-tree, the pride of some burgher's garden . . .

Italica, an odd collection of ruins a few miles from Seville, started as a military camp in the third century and turned into an important town with an amphitheatre and forum. It was the birthplace of the emperors Trajan and Hadrian. Alas, no detailed record exists of its heyday, so that most of the accounts that have been written of it focus on the state of abandonment that it had fallen into by the eighteenth century.

When Swinburne went looking for Italica in 1776 he had difficulty in finding it. Suffering under the impact of a sweltering sun, Swinburne stumbled on a monastery where the monks sold lemons through a gap in the wall. Clearly hallucinating, he next mistook a collection of vast towers and bulwarks built of cement and pebbles for the amphitheatre. It was in fact the remains of a partly restored Moorish castle.

> From the knowledge I had acquired of the different modes of building, since I came into the south of Spain, I ventured to pronounce, that if this was Italica, the Moors had built on the site, and antiquaries were grossly mistaken when they talked of Roman edifices and amphitheatres; not that I thought the situation such, as the judicious Romans might have preferred it to that of Hispalis, the present Seville, for beauty and strength. The view from it over that city, the course of that river, and the rich plain, are worth more than the labour it cost us to get so high: at this blooming season of the year, when everything is in full vegetation, green and fresh, I don't remember to have seen a finer country . . .

His eventual discovery of the real Italica proved something of an anticlimax, but Swinburne had the wit to turn his disappointment into a mocking analogy of the search for El Dorado.

> Of the ancient colony of Italica . . . scarce the least vestige remains . . . the peasants that were here at work in the olive yards told us that underneath there had formerly been found columns of silver and brass, but as they were bewitched by some magician, nobody was ever able to draw them up; and nowadays, not a soul has the courage even to dig for them as they have all the reason in the world to believe that the conjurer would twist their heads off for attempting it.

An examination of the bullrings around Spain in 1849 enlightened William Clark as to the uses of the Roman amphitheatres, about which he had 'puzzled in vain with conjectures at Verona and Nîmes.' His interest in the cultural undercurrent linking different periods of Spanish history led him to Italica by a more direct route than Swinburne's.

> I accordingly made an expedition thither in a kind of cabriolet peculiar to the country – gaudily painted, studded with brass nails, and attached to the horse by the most complicated system of harness. The driver sat upon my toes, his legs dangling over the side, and urged, scolded, or soothed his beast with a rich and varied vocabulary. By dint of all this we executed the four miles in about an hour and a half, coming to a final halt at the wretched hamlet of Santiponce. I was immediately pounced upon by a crowd of women and children offering Roman coins, first, at a dollar a-piece, and finally letting me have a dozen for a shilling. At intervals among the olive-clad slopes, fragments of solid rock-like masonry are visible just above the ground, evidencing the extent and grandeur of this second-rate Roman colony. I question whether, a thousand years hence, such traces of Manchester will be seen among the corn-fields . . .
> Half a mile from the hamlet is the Amphitheatre . . . It has evidently been destroyed by some violent means, perhaps gunpowder. Vast masses of cement and stone lie rent and shattered round the oval. The arena itself is

raised much above its old level, and is now a corn field.
It is still possible, in despite of the brambles, to work
one's way into some under-ground chambers – without
much profit, I confess. However, having come on purpose, I persisted in taking some rude measurements,
while my companion, an artillery-man, yawned fearfully,
and complained of having been brought to the ancient
Italica under false pretences. 'What was Trajan to him,
or he to Trajan?'

By contrast Borrow in 1836 proved more enthusiastic about
Italica by simply reinventing ancient Rome among the dusty
ruins.

On all sides are to be seen the time-worn broken granite
benches, from whence myriads of human beings once
gazed down on the area below, where the gladiator
shouted, and the lion and the leopard yelled: all around
beneath these flights of benches, are vaulted excavations
from whence the combatants, part human, part bestial,
darted forth by their several doors. I spent many hours
in this singular place, forcing my way through the wild
fennel and brushwood into the caverns, now the haunt
of adders and other reptiles, whose hissing I heard.
Having sated my curiosity I left the ruins, and, returning
by another way, reached a place where lay the carcass of
a horse half devoured; upon it with lustrous eyes, stood
an enormous vulture, who, as I approached, slowly
soared aloft till he alighted on the eastern gate of the
amphitheatre, from whence he uttered a hoarse cry, as
in anger that I had disturbed him from his feast of
carrion.

The imposing architectural legacy of the Roman era
impressed the young Laurie Lee as he walked across Spain in
the 1930s, its longevity contrasting with the human frailty he
encountered along the way. He paid only a brief visit to the
town of Segovia but it was enough to imprint on his memory
a lasting image of endurance.

Here were churches, castles, and medieval walls standing
sharp in the evening light, but all dwarfed by that

extraordinary phenomenon of masonry, the Roman aqueduct, which overshadowed the whole. It came looping from the hills in a series of arches, some rising to over a hundred feet, and composed of blocks of granite weighing several tons and held together by their weight alone. This imperial gesture, built to carry water from a spring ten miles away, still strode across the valley with massive grace, a hundred vistas framed by its soaring arches, to enter the city at last high above the rooftops, stepping like a mammoth among the houses . . .

At close quarters, the aqueduct seemed both benevolent and mad, its jets of masonry vaulting the sky, and the huge blocked feet coming down on the side of the town and throwing everything out of scale.

It took the Romans 200 years to complete their conquest of the Iberian Peninsula. On their arrival Spain was a land of recalcitrant tribes, including the wild Basques in the North. The Celt-Iberians put up a particularly fierce resistance around their city Numantia, which is near the town of Soria. For six years the guerillas of Iberia held out against the Roman invaders. For writers like Carlos Fuentes, this 'sort of Vietnam for Rome' came to symbolize the tradition of resistance, 'which is not particular to Spain but peculiarly coloured, concentrated, and heightened by the events of her history and culture, as well as by the experience of the Hispanic world in the Americas.'

The vivid description given by the Latin chronicler Appian of the last days of Numantia resonates through Hispanic history, from the conquest of Peru to the bombing of Guernica.

The majority of the inhabitants having killed themselves, the rest came out offering a strange and horrible sight, their bodies dirty, squalid, and stinking, their nails long, their hair unkempt and their dress repugnant. If they seemed worthy of pity because of their misery, they also inflicted sorrow because on their faces were written rage, and pain and exhaustion.

And yet amidst the violence of tribal wars and conquest,

there were Romans resident in Spain who brought sophistication and a more peaceful perception of life. The poet Martial was born north of Salamanca in the province of Aragon. He returned there after spending forty years of his bachelor life in Rome and to escape 'the togas stinking of purple dye and the conversations of haughty widows.' He lived on a farm near Bilbilis, a small town on a bend of the River Jalon. The town was to be eventually rebuilt by the Moors and is today known as Catalayud. One can still see the remains of the Roman settlement, and although there is no trace of Martial's house the surrounding landscape is virtually unchanged in aspect from the time the poet lived there between AD 82–104.

In a letter to Juvenal, Martial describes the poplar grove and meadow, the natural spring, the rose trees and vines, and the tepid water of the river near to his farm where he would swim.

> Here we live hazily and work pleasantly. I enjoy a vast unconscionable sleep which often lasts till ten and so make up for all I've lost these thirty years. You'll find no togas here; if you ask for one, they'll give you the nearest rug off a broken chair. When I get up I find a fire heaped with splendid logs from the oak forest, which the bailiff's wife has crowned with her pots and pans.

Tarragona, or Tarraco as it was known in Roman times, was the most important depot for the Mediterranean fleet. In *Many Cities*, a personal search for the underlying unities of European civilisation, Hilaire Belloc describes Tarragona as the 'most orderly, most compact' of all the living cities of Spain.

> Tarragona, which gave its name to all these coasts of Spain when the Roman imperial power was at its height, stands now still marked with all the impress of a capital – but not too large; exact, dignified, and with no touch of mourning, of death, or even of decay. The port, which seems so small to our modern eyes, and which was yet the making of this centre over against the coasts of Italy, lies at its foot with a modern quarter around it. From this flat arises the hill of the city, which you

mount by a main street, or better, by a fine flight of steps
upon the seaward side, which climb right up to the broad
parapet-way and garden, overhanging the Mediterranean
upon the height; and there it is, upon the very summit
of the hill, that you find the heart of the city and its
memories. There you will see, built by chance into the
walls of private houses, the stones of fifteen hundred and
two thousand years.

On Salamanca, where the Romans built a bridge across the
River Tormes, Belloc wrote:

Here, as in a hundred other cases, it is from the Roman
approach that one sees the European meaning. The road,
thus coming upon Salamanca northward from the
mountains, was, and is, Roman. The bridge over which
that road reaches the city (coming in at the foot of its
low cliff) is the bridge over which the Roman armies
marched – which the Roman armies made. Its stones are
still Roman, and the strength of them.

8

A CALAMITY FROM THE SKIES

Jewish Spain

Among the many enthusiastic visitors to Spain in the first half of the nineteenth century was Benjamin Disraeli. 'Oh wonderful Spain!' he wrote in a letter in the summer of 1830. 'Think of this romantic land covered with Moorish ruins and full of Murillo! Ah, that I could describe to you the wonders of the painted temples of Seville; ah, that I could wander with you amid the fantastic and imaginative walls of delicate Alhambra! . . . I thought that enthusiasm wax dead within me and nothing could be new . . . I dare to say that I am better. It is all the Sun.'

Disraeli was twenty-six years old, recovering from a near breakdown brought on by financial worries. Spain proved a cathartic experience for the Anglicized Jew. Yet this was the same land from which his Sephardic ancestors had been expelled four centuries earlier.

The plight of the Jews in Spain was of particular interest to George Borrow who arrived on the Iberian Peninsula in 1835 determined to share some biblical truths with the native population. Borrow's first port of call was Lisbon to which many Jews had fled after being banished from Spain in 1492 during the Reconquest. He found them 'gathered in small clusters about the pillars at lower extremities of the gold and

silver streets' around noon every day. They spoke in broken
Spanish or Portuguese or in a 'harsh guttural language' which
Borrow thought was Arabic. Their dress generally consisted
of a 'red cap, with a blue silken tassel at the top of it, a blue
tunic girded at the waist with a red sash, and wide linen
pantaloons or trousers.'

The Jews Borrow encountered in Spain were less conspicuous, and appeared to harbour a deep sense of insecurity.
These were the crypto-Jews who lived in an atmosphere of
suspicion and deceit. Staying overnight in a posada in Talavera
on the main road to Madrid, Borrow struck up a conversation
with a Jew he refered to as Abarbenel after one of the great
Rabinical commentators.

> *Myself*: You say you are wealthy. In what does your
> wealth consist?
> *Abarbenel*: In gold and silver, and stones of price; for I
> have inherited all the hoards of my forefathers. The
> greater part is buried underground; indeed, I have never
> examined the tenth part of it. I have coins of silver and
> gold older than the times of Ferdinand the Accursed and
> Jezebel; I have also large sums employed in usury. We
> keep ourselves close, however, and pretend to be poor,
> miserably so; but on certain occasions, at our festivals,
> when our gates are barred, and our savage dogs are let
> loose in the court, we eat our food off services such as
> the Queen of Spain cannot boast of, and wash our feet
> in ewers of silver, fashioned and wrought before the
> Americas were discovered, though our garments are at
> all times coarse and our food for the most part of the
> plainest description . . .
> *Myself*: Are you known for what you are? Do the
> authorities molest you?
> *Abarbenel*: People of course suspect me to be what I am;
> but as I conform outwardly in most respects to their
> ways, they do not interfere with me. True it is that
> sometimes, when I enter the church to hear the mass,
> they glare at me over the left shoulder, as much as to
> say – 'what do you do here?' And sometimes they cross
> themselves as they pass by; but as they go no further,

I do not trouble myself on that account. With respect to the authorities, they are not bad friends of mine. Many of the higher class have borrowed money from me for usury, so that I have them to a certain extent in my power . . . The truth is that our family has always known how to guide itself wonderfully. I must say there is much of the wisdom of the snake amongst us.

Avarice, promiscuity, deceit and corruption combine in this caricature of the errant Jew. According to Gregorio Marañón, Borrow's account fascinated the philosopher Unamuno who spent his life attempting to unravel the cultural complexities behind the Spanish soul. Marañón himself was less convinced by Jorgito el Ingles, as the missionary came to be known in Madrid. He thought Borrow's account of the Jews was the product of fantasy and probably apocryphal. Borrow nonetheless was regarded as something of an authority on all matters racial by his contemporaries, not least by Richard Ford who pulled few punches on the religious intolerance of Catholic Spain. In *Gatherings*, Ford commented that 'the term Jew, it must be remembered, is the acme of Spanish loathing and vituperation,' a theme on which he expanded with numerous historical references in his *Handbook*.

The name Jew, *Judio*, is still the *maledictio Pessima*, the *Nimreseth*, the insult never to be forgiven, *anathema maranatha*. Sancho Panza, the type of the lower classes, glories in hating a Jew, as proof of his being a true Christian. Spaniards, even in this century, were taught to think all foreigners to be heretics and Jews. The cry of *Judiada* is still a prelude to certain murder. 'I hate oppression in every shape,' said a Valencian Liberal to Lord Carnarvon, 'I am a friend to the human race: if indeed there be a Jew among us, burn him, I say, burn him, alive.'

Such a cry echoed around the Church of Santiago in Toledo when John Lomas visited it in 1884 while researching his book, *The Nature, Art and Life of Spain*. Lomas' attention was particularly drawn to a pulpit from which the inquisitorial preacher Vicente Ferrer preached his virulent sermons of damnation against the Jewish race in the early fifteenth century.

His theme was the well-worn one of how the accursed Israelite had dared to put sacrilegious hands upon God Himself, had tortured him, and had brought desolation upon our Blessed Mother. Then there was the lament that such a race, whom God had cursed and driven away, and upon whom He could only look with abhorrence, should be tolerated, and allowed to grow fat and proud, in so sacred a spot as Toledo – a city beloved of the Virgin and where she had deigned to set her feet – with the inevitable sequitur that whoever smote a Jew in person of possessions did a God-service. It was an old tale, and an enticing one, in as much as it opened up an easy road not only to the favour of Heaven but also to the enjoyment of rapine, and murder, and lust, and divers other equally religious impulses and emotions. And so the plea that the Jews of Toledo were descended from a tribe which had refused to vote for the death of Christ was lost sight of. That was only a belief to be cherished when Christians wanted money, and felt obliged to resort to moral persuasion in order to get it. And Toledo's streets ran once more with Jewish blood, the holy emissary of the Prince of Peace himself directing the crusade, while, greatest desolation of all to Jewish hearts, their beloved sanctuary was taken away from them, and converted into a house for the Nazarene imposter.

In his book on Toledo published in 1907, Albert Calvert writes with bitter irony about the final ruin of the Jewish community in Toledo as encouraged by 'Saint' Vicente Ferrer.

Visiting the city in 1391 he so inflamed the devout populace with apostolic zeal that they burst into the larger of two Juderias or Ghettos, put practically the whole of its inhabitants – including the venerable rabbis, Judah ben Asher and Israel Alnaqua – to the sword, sacked the quarter from end to end, and demolished most of the synagogues. The saintly Ferrer reappeared at Toledo twenty years later, but there were nominally no

Jews left to massacre. The Hebrews that remained had been 'converted'. The good friar did what he could, and induced the Toledans to confiscate the Synagogue built in Alfonso X's reign and convert it into the Christian Church of Santa María la Blanca. We suggest that it should have been renamed San Vicente del Sangre.

Prior to their persecution, Jews had played a conspicuous part in Toledan society, enjoying one of their most prosperous periods after the Moorish-occupied city fell to the Christian King Alfonso of Castile in 1085. It is thought that the very name Toledo has its roots in the Hebraic word Toledoth, meaning generations. Between the eleventh and thirteenth centuries it became the Jerusalem of the West, the unchallenged capital of the Hispanic Jews, with ten synagogues and five *madrisas* (schools adjacent to the synagogues). Trowbridge Hall in *Spain in Silhouette* writes:

> In the days of its glory the synagogue was ceiled with the cedar of Lebanon, the floor covered with the sacred soil of Palestine, and the walls enriched by the genius of the Moorish builders whose splendid art speaks with the same eloquence whether in mosque, synagogue, or cathedral. While Santa María La Blanca has suffered sorely, nothing can rob beauty of its innate sweetness.

Santa María was one of only two synagogues that survived destruction through conversion (nine existed in the thirteenth century). The other, situated in the same quarter, was El Transito (so called after the Transit of the Virgin Mary or the Assumption). This, in the words of Hall, is

> located where the dwellings were of the meanest appearance, hiding their luxury behind sordid exteriors, feigning poverty so as to save their stores of wealth from taxation. This was built by the wealthy Samuel Levy, the Rothschild of those times, the friend and treasurer of Pedro the Cruel, until that bloody monarch relieved him at once of his money and his head. It was erected in the days of ʹthe Jew's greatest prosperity, and is superbly trellised with honeycombed carvings that in delicacy and richness are in no way inferior to the best

in the Alhambra. Above the holy of holies, where the rabbis expounded the law, and shrouded by an Eastern veil of stucco, is a twining arabesque singing in Kufic letters a paean of joy: 'Now hath God delivered us from the power of our enemies and since the days of our captivity never had we a safer refuge. But nothing endures mutability.'

From the synagogue a narrow street, named after Samuel Levy, leads to the palace built by him in the early fourteenth century and now known as the house of El Greco. Although the painter never lived there, his name stands as another symbol of forced conversion. Hall saw it not as a treasurer's palace, but as an artist's home.

> . . . a garden beautiful, within hearing of the voice of the Tagus, with ivy-coloured walls, masses of blossom, a tiny courtyard with quaint walls, and a rambling wooden gallery that leads to a museum of painted treasure more precious than gold.

In *El Greco y Toledo* Marañón examines in detail the Jewish characteristics of El Greco's figures and his landscapes, demonstrating the historical realities that lay behind the painter's mystical brush strokes:

> The traces of the oriental soul that have survived in Toledo represent the most striking aspect of this venerable town. I've always criticised those who claim that Toledo is a Castilian town. It is an oriental town, located in Western Europe, which wanted to reach out across the mysterious Atlantic, the ambition of all the great dreams of yesterday, but which settled its foundations on the rocks of the Tagus; and it has stayed that way for ever, petrified, in the midst of a kind of suburban oriental life which remains its most charming characteristic.
>   And its not just the town, but the countryside on the left bank of the river, that so closely resembles the Holy Land. Here the olives seem sacred, the flocks of sheep have a biblical air about them, and the footprints in the

earth, smelling of rosemary, could belong to the feet of
a prophet.

It was in Toledo during the thirteenth century that the
School of Translators flourished, to the great benefit of the
development of European culture. Jewish, Muslim, and
Christian scholars worked side by side under the patronage of
King Alfonso the Wise, exchanging theses and translations of
a variety of works ranging from the first book on chess to
the Bible. 'The purpose of this extraordinary feat of medieval
intelligence,' writes Carlos Fuentes, 'was to put down all the
knowledge of the times . . . the result was a sort of
encyclopedia, before encyclopedias came into vogue in the
eighteenth century.'

Joseph Baretti had mixed feelings about Toledo when he
visited it in October 1760. Most of its houses, he noted, 'are
meanly built, the squares irregular, the streets narrow, badly
paved, and not very clean.' But two monuments caught his
fancy. The first was the Christian Cathedral, 'a gothic edifice
which can almost vie for amplitude with that of Milan . . .';
the second, which remarkably he never actually saw, was the
converted synagogue of Santa María la Blanca.

> I am told that here is a synagogue that had once many
> Hebrew sayings and scripture-passages written on its
> walls within, according to the practice of the Jews in all
> their places of public worship. When that synagogue was
> some centuries ago turned into a church, its walls were
> plastered over and whitewashed, so that the inscriptions
> remained lost for a long time to the world. But in process
> of time some of the plaster fell down; and a learned canon
> of this cathedral observing Hebrew characters left there
> undiscovered, has lately found means to read several of
> those passages and sayings, which he intends soon to
> publish with notes. The Jews that were formerly in
> possession of the synagogue, if they were not African by
> birth were at least so by descent; and it appears by the
> characters read by the canon on those walls, that their
> manner of writing their tongue was partly different from
> that which is generally used by the modern European

Jews. An account of that African manner of writing it, will render the work of the canon very interesting to the studious of the tongue.

The Toledo which Gerald Brenan visited just after the Second World War struck him as a 'strange, dark, almost ominous city' where the most 'menacing religious power the world has seen' held its state and 'from tortuous lanes and gloomy palaces stretched out its tentacles – sometimes for good, sometimes for evil.' He was impressed by the Transito, one of two surviving synagogues which filled him with an intense and peculiar emotion.

> These arabesque patterns . . . have a hypnotic effect on the mind which on second thoughts could well be called mystical. I have often asked myself why this should be so. Sitting in this synagogue today it occurred to me that it might be because, while the general design was too complex for the eye to follow out in detail, it gave one a feeling of certainty that a pattern was there and that the same leaf or scroll that one saw in front of one would reappear a little farther on in the same context, and then a little farther on again, and so again and again. The surface of the wall had the apparent complexity of nature, yet everything in it – even the Hebrew writing which affirmed its purpose – was under the law of order and eternal recurrence. This gave a deep feeling of satisfaction and reassurance.

Sacheverell Sitwell delivered a romantic accolade to the 'tangible memorial of the Jews in Spain' as he motored across the plain of Castile following a visit to Toledo in the 1950s. His focus was on the oriental and exotic, the Jewish Spain that had once existed.

> . . . both synagogues seem to be haunted by ghosts of the Sephardim; and we can imagine Samuel Levi with his red beard and long gown or caftan, looking like an astrologer, or the same race as the red bearded Nostradamus who was a Spanish Jew of Salon, near Avignon. May not Gil de Siloee, the Jew of Nuremberg, and one of the greatest sculptors of the Middle Ages, have been red bearded too? And we begin to fill the

galleries of El Transito with Jewesses in their curious and elaborate headdresses and costumes, styles of dresses which have not been seen in Spain for four centuries and more, but their traces still exist scattered far and wide with the Sephardim, and in Sarajevo the Sephardim women wore, till lately, a headdress of peculiar shape supposed to be in reminiscence of sailing ships that took them off from Spain.

The cultural tolerance that existed in Toledo during the Reconquest was also to be found in the tenth and early eleventh century in Cordoba. Under the caliphs, it became the capital of the Muslim Spanish kingdom of Al-Andalus, which covered the greater part of what is today the Iberian Peninsula. The spirit of the age was exemplified by Hasdai ibn Shaprut, a Jew who served as physician and translator in the Muslim court in the first half of the tenth century. Of the many testimonies which survive of the period of cultural tolerance and interchange, one of the most eloquent was written as a tribute to Hasdai in Al-Harizi's book *Tahkemoni*, written shortly after the physician's death.

> All the wise men of his generation gathered round him, shining like brilliant lights, to pass on their wisdom to all who seek God. He filled them with God's spirit, with wisdom and intelligence, with prodigal knowledge, with the art of shaping ideas and kindling fire in their hearts . . . His generosity made the tongues of the dumb sing forth and closed hearts opened up to compose delightful poems that shone like the stars on high. Then their eyes beheld poetic art, the skies opened wide and divine visions appeared. In his times wisdom spread throughout Israel, for he was the redeemer and supporter of science. After those times the light of brilliant minds went out.

Religious persecution of the Jewish people in Spain took hold from the late eleventh century onwards, intensifying after the fall of Granada in 1492. However the idea that purity of race and religious orthodoxy was inseparable from the very notion of Spain neither began nor ended with 'Saint' Vicente Ferrer. The saddest aspect of John Lomas' visit to the Church

of Santiago in Toledo was the realization that 'one is compelled to speak of these matters as an old tale and a drama
enacted once more.' The persecution of the Jews in Spain was
pursued with varying degrees of intensity throughout the
Roman and Visigothic periods. The extreme measures taken
by the Catholic monarchs had a trial period in the early
seventh century when King Sisebut decreed that all Jews
should convert to Christianity. At the end of the eleventh
century, thousands of Jews living in Andalusia were forced
to flee into exile into Christian-occupied Spain following the
arrival of fanatical Muslim tribes from North Africa. The
expulsions were only a prelude to far greater horrors. The
persecution brutally interrupted a period of Spanish history
that had produced an outpouring of Jewish poetic talent. The
following passage is taken from the anthology, *The Jews in
Cordoba*, which was published in 1985 to mark the 850th
anniversary of the birth in the city of Maimonides, the Jewish
philosopher and theologian. Written by the poet Abraham ibn
Ezra, it vividly captures the sense of collective vertigo provoked by the Almohad invasion of Spain in the first half of
the twelfth century.

> My head will grow bald and I will wait bitterly for
> the 'aljama' in Seville, for her wounded princes and her
> captured sons; for her daughters, so fair, handed over to
> a strange religion.
>
> How was Cordoba abandoned and turned into a sea
> of ruin? There, the wise men and the great died of
> hunger and of thirst.
>
> No Jew, not a single one, survived in Jaen, nor in
> Almeria, nor in Mallorca, nor in Malaga did any comfort
> remain, the Jews who fled were cruelly wounded. So I
> lament bitterly and wail so much. My cries flow like
> waters because of my grief. Ay! Sepharad has been
> overwhelmed by a calamity from the skies: My eyes, my
> eyes shed tears.

Cordoba was conquered by the Christian armies of King
Ferdinand III, another 'saint', in 1236. The days of Jewish
glory in the city were over and would never return. By the
time Henry Inglis visited the birth place of Maimonides in
1830, Cordoba had shrunk in size and cultural aspiration.

. . . Situation is the only glory of Cordoba that remains. Science has found other sanctuaries, and riches new channels; and modern Cordoba is one of the most decayed, most deserted, and most miserable cities of Spain. Cordoba, when metropolis of the kingdom of Abdoulraman, in 759, is said to have contained three hundred thousand persons; forty years ago it contained thirty-four thousand; and since then, twelve thousand more must be deducted from the number of its inhabitants; and of the twenty-two thousand yet remaining, upwards of three thousand are shut in by convent walls.

Attacks on Jewish quarters became particularly pronounced following the Black Death of 1348 when the plague was interpreted by Christians as divine punishment. The anti-semitic fanaticism which was unleashed with renewed vigour in the fifteenth century has been described by Paul Johnson in his *History of the Jews* as 'the most momentous event in Jewish history since the mid-second century AD.' In all some 150,000 Jews were forced to leave Spain. Hundreds of others were tortured or burnt at the stake. 'What Spain lost others gained,' comments Johnson, 'and in the long run the Sephardic diaspora was to prove exceedingly creative and of critical importance in Jewish development.'

With the persecution of the Jewish race, Spain lost a sense of her own history which she is only just beginning to recover. Jan Morris has described the Jewish legacy, drawing attention to that terrible moment in Spanish history when the Catholic monarchs, at a moment of great national opportunity, 'threw out of their domain several hundred thousand of their most talented, efficient, and necessary subjects'.

They left their shades in the Jewish quarters of the cities, from the hill-top ghetto of Toledo to the lovely labyrinth called Santa Cruz in Seville . . . there was indeed a time when most men of culture were Jewish, and such a hegemony cannot easily be expunged; the Jews have left behind them a strain of blood, a look in the eye, that is apparent everywhere in the cities of Spain, and subtly contributes to her grandeur.

9

SUBLIME IS THIS MANSION

Moorish Spain

'The peculiar charm of this old dreamy palace,' wrote Washington Irving of the Alhambra in 1833, 'is its power of calling up vague reveries and picturings of the past, and thus clothing naked realities with the illusions of the memory and the imagination.'

It was from the Alhambra Palace in Granada that Boabdil, the last Moorish King, descended into the valley to surrender the keys of the city to the Catholic monarchs in 1492. The act represented the end of more than 700 years of Moorish occupation, the official severing of links with an empire that straddled the Mediterranean from Baghdad to Cordoba. And yet the Moorish influence on Spain has persisted in the country's architecture, in her language, in her cuisine, her agriculture, and in the imagination of successive visitors to Spain. As she made her way through Spain towards the Sahara in 1866, Matilda Betham-Edwards meditated at length on Spain's Moorish legacy which she feared would waste away because of the Spaniards' indifference towards it.

I don't know which phase of Spanish history is most generally interesting – the Mahomedan, the Catholic, or the Aristocratic: the former being typified in the Alhambra, the second in the paintings of Murillo and Zurbarán, and the third in the splendid courts of the Philips. I confess that for me the Mahomedan phase, so graceful, so artistic, so beneficent as it was, surpasses in interest every other. Look a little into the history of Spain, and what do facts tell you? To whom is she indebted for her most sumptuous monuments, her most elegant arts, her most picturesque costumes, her most precious products? To the Moors. Who bought down the cool waters from rocky prisons, turning whole wastes into sunny vineyards and gardens? The Moors. Who made the Spanish language what it is now, the most sonorous and picturesque of any in Europe? The Moors. Who planted the orange tree and the palm, the fig and the olive? The Moors.

The Alhambra comes from the Arabic word *qualat alhamra* which means red castle, although it was conceived as much more than a fortress. Described as the 'last and fairest flower of Muslim civilization in Western Europe' by the great hispanist Professor J.B. Trend, it was to be a seat of pleasure as well as government. King al-Ahmar authorized the first buildings and transferred his court there in 1238, following the fall of Cordoba. The building was completed in the fourteenth century during the reigns of Yusuf I and his son Mohammad V. Ford, in the *Handbook*, notes how the building, from its origins, was a source of pride.

The founder, like Edward III at Windsor, has everywhere introduced his motto, his 'Honi soit qui mal y pense.' The words *'Wa la ghaliba illa Allah'* – 'there is no conqueror but Allah', are to be seen in every portion of the Tarkish and Azelajo. The origin is this: when he returned from the surrender of Seville, his subjects saluted him as galib – the conqueror – and he replied – adopting the Tahlil, or true Mussulman war-cry – 'There is no conqueror but God' . . . The greatest decorator of the Alhambra was Yusuf I, who although unsuccessful in war was eminent in the arts of peace: so vast were his revenues, that he was imagined to possess the philosopher's stone; but his secret was quiet and industry, 'et magnum vectigal parsimonia'. He regilt and repainted the palace, which then must have been a thing of the Tales of the Genii . . .

An Arab visitor to Granada in 1465, in a comment reproduced by Michael Jacobs in his recent book on Andalusia, compared the town in its cultural splendour to Damascus: 'it is a meeting place of illustrious people, poets, scientists, artists, there are here some of the finest men of our time, grandiose monuments, charming little corners . . . with its Alhambra it is one of the great cities of Islam.' One of the most detailed portraits of the Moorish presence in Spain in the fifteenth century was written by a German traveller, Hieronymus Munzer, who rode through Spain on his way to Portugal with some letters for King John II from the Emperor Maximilian. Munzer arrived in Granada on the afternoon of 22 October 1494, two years, nine months and twenty days after the fall of the town to the Catholic monarchs.

> We entered the great and glorious city of Granada, following a long street through which were passing a great number of Moors. We put up at a good inn, but immediately went out again, as we wished to visit the great Mosque, which is the most ample and sumptuous in the city. This stood on the site now occupied by the Cathedral. We had to take off our shoes before we went in although the weather was wet and the ground muddy. The entire pavement of the mosque was covered with mats woven with reeds; in the middle was a courtyard with a fountain for ablutions. There were nine rows of columns and a hundred and thirty arches. We saw a number of lamps burning, and holy men, who chanted the Hours after their own fashion, although to us it seemed a most melancholy clamour . . .

As he rode through the city, Munzer counted many smaller mosques, 'more than two hundred', each occupied by Moors praying, and later that evening heard 'such crying from the towers of the mosques as can scarcely be imagined.' Sometimes the muezzin's call, which he could hear from the inn he was staying at, sounded like a 'groan rather than a song'. The bulk of the Moorish population was concentrated in the Albaicin, the quarter which runs adjacent to the River Darro.

The Moorish houses are almost all of them small, with tiny rooms and grimy outer walls; but they are all very clean inside. It is the exception to find any which are not provided with cisterns and two pipes: one for drinking-water and the other for sewage, for the Moors pay much attention to these necessities. Besides, all the streets have a gutter; and thus when there are no drains in a house, the inhabitants empty the slops into the gutter at night. Yes the people are clean beyond all imagination, and this in spite of the fact that a Christian house occupies more space than five or six Moorish ones, which are such intricate labyrinths that they are like swallows' nests . . .

Elsewhere he noted the infinity of gardens and orchards that graced the city, 'for the Moors are great lovers of gardening, and are extremely ingenious both in planting and watering . . . a people contented with very little.' The principal sustenance never wanting all the year round was fruit: 'they drink no wine, but on the contrary they make from the grapes an enormous quantity of raisins.'

After two days of observing the social habits of the population, Munzer was ready to visit the Alhambra. His host was the newly installed Mayor of Granada, Don Iñigo Lopez, the Count of Tendilla, who addressed him in Latin before taking him on a tour of the palace.

We saw halls with pavements of the whitest marble, delightful gardens with lemons and myrtle, pools with marble sides, four rooms full of arms, such as lances, cross-bows, swords, cuirasses and arrows; dormitories and dressing-rooms. Many of the rooms had marble basins with fountains . . . there was a bathroom, marvellously vaulted, and adjacent to it, a room with couches. There were lofty, slender columns, a courtyard which had in the middle a great marble fountain . . . I do not believe that anything like it is to be found in Europe, seeing that everything is so magnificent, so majestic, so exquisitely worked; that [none] who contemplates it can free himself of the idea that he is not in a paradise . . .

The Count proved an excellent if somewhat irreverent tour guide never short on amusing anecdotes with which to shock the German. At one point he described what went on in the great marble basin where the ladies of the King's harem used to take their baths.

> They came into the room naked; and the King from an adjoining room could see them without being seen, by looking through a window with wooden shutters which opened above. To her who pleased him he threw an orange, which was the signal that she should lie with him that night.

After Munzer's visit the Alhambra entered a long period of neglect. Betham-Edwards, in her book *Through Spain to the Sahara*, blamed it on the ingratitude of the Spaniards, 'who not only disclaim the good things thus inherited, but do their best to defile them'.

The Alhambra remained in a piteous state for much of the nineteenth century. As documented in the engravings of the time, the precinct of the palace became a place of temporary residence for gypsies and other poor nomads. In 1810, the Alhambra filled William Jacob with wonder and delight because it was quite unlike anything he had ever experienced. The peace of the fountains and gardens contrasted with the brutal realities of the Peninsular War.

> This noble palace . . . is hastening to decay, and, without repairs, to which the finances of Spain are inadequate, it will in a few years be a pile of ruins; its voluptuous apartments, its stately columns, and its lofty walls, will be mingled together, and no memorial be left in Spain of a people who once governed the Peninsula. The whole fortress of the Alhambra is very extensive, and contains a considerable number of inhabitants. One part has been converted into a prison for the French troops, in which I saw General Boyard, and some other officers, who complained bitterly of the treatment they received from the Spaniards. Within the inclosure of the walls stands a Mahomedan mosque, now converted into a Christian church, the absurd ornaments of which form

a striking contrast to the simple columns of the original
structure.

On evacuating the Alhambra, Sept 17, 1812, the
French mined the towers and blew up 8 in number . . .

And yet the Alhambra, like so many of Spain's monuments,
endured the vicissitudes of politics and war, a tribute to the
sturdiness of Moorish architecture. Among the early British
visitors to the Alhambra who came armed not just with
notebook but with sketchpad was Henry Swinburne. He and
his companion Thomas Gascoine were so impressed by what
they saw that they inscribed their names in one of the rooms
with the date 'January, 1775.'

The Alhambra's future was officially safeguarded in 1870
when the palace and its grounds were declared a national
monument. But the recovery of its oriental past, and its pro-
clamation as one of the great wonders of the world, took place
in the imagination of the Romantic travellers that began to
gather there in the first half of the nineteenth century.

Among the Romantics who went in search of oriental
Spain, it was the French who led the way. The Alhambra was
'discovered' after the publication in 1826 of Chateaubriand's
Le Dernier des Abencèrages. In it the hero Aben-Hamet
(Chateaubriand) writes the name of Blanche (Natalie de
Noailles) on the marble of the Hall of the Two Sisters, as
the two lovers wander through the galleries under the
moonlight.

> The moon, as it rose, spread its fitful light through the
> abandoned sanctuaries and the deserted courts of the
> Alhambra. Its pale beams patterned the grassy lawn and
> the walls of the great chambers with the tracery of an
> early architecture, with the arches of the cloisters, the
> moving shadow of the leaping waters and the shrubs
> swaying in the breeze. A nightingale was singing from
> amidst a cypress that pierced the domes of a ruined
> mosque, and the echoes gave back the lament. By
> moonlight Aben-Hamet wrote the name of Blanche on
> the marble in the hall of the Two Sisters, tracing it in
> Arab characters so that the traveller might come upon
> one mystery the more in this place of mysteries.

Three years later Victor Hugo included in *Les Orientales* the poem 'Grenade', which further fuelled the curiosity of Europeans for all matters concerning Moorish Spain. This is an extract:

> The Alhambra! The Alhambra! Palace that the Genies
> Gilded like a dream and filled with harmony,
> Fortress of festooned and crumbling battlements
> Where at night magic syllables resound
> When the moon, shining through a thousand Arab arches
> Spangles the walls with white clover!

Washington Irving was neither the first nor the last enthusiast who in his quest for Spain's Moorish past set off in 1829 from his downtown posada, traversed the streets and squares of Granada and footed it up the narrow, winding street of Gomeras that leads to the Alhambra through an avenue of elm trees. Ford who followed him within two years described these woody slopes 'kept green by watercourses, and tenanted by nightingales . . . Although everything looks the work of nature, it is the creation of man, as the Moor changed the barren rock into an Eden.'

Irving glimpsed the half-finished palace constructed by the Emperor Charles V which 'although inclined to eclipse the residence of the Muslim Kings,' appeared an 'arrogant intrusion'. Then he crossed the unostentatious portal that leads into the Alhambra. For Irving, whose childhood in Boston had been spent reading romantic history books on Moorish Spain, the encounter represented a climactic moment in which his fantasy became reality: like Don Quixote stepping down into the Cave of Montesinos with his books of chivalry under his arm.

> The translation was almost magical; it seemed as if we were at once transported into other times and another realm, and were treading the scenes of Arabian story. We found ourselves in a great court, paved with white marble and decorated at each end with light Moorish peristyles; it is called the Court of the Alberca. In the centre was an immense basin of fishpond, a hundred and

—

thirty feet in length by thirty in breadth, stocked with
gold-fish and bordered by hedges of roses. At the upper
end of this court rose the great Tower of Comares. From
the lower end we passed through a Moorish archway into
the renowned Court of Lions. There is no part of the
edifice that gives us a more complete idea of its original
beauty and magnificence than this, for none has suffered
so little from the ravages of time. In the centre stands
the fountain famous in song and story. The alabaster
basins still shed their diamond drops, and the twelve
lions which support them cast forth their crystal as in
the days of Boabdil. The court is laid out in flower-beds
and surrounded by light Arabian arcades of open filigree-
work, supported by slender pillars of white marble. The
architecture, like that of all the other parts of the palace,
is characterised by elegance rather than grandeur,
bespeaking a delicate and graceful taste and a disposition
to indolent enjoyment. When one looks upon the fairy
tracery of the peristyles and the apparently fragile fret-
work of the walls, it is difficult to believe that so much
has survived the wear and tear of centuries, the shock
of earthquakes, the violence of war and the quiet, though
no less baneful, pilferings of the tasteful traveller. It is
almost sufficient to excuse the popular tradition that the
whole is protected by a magic charm.

Ford arrived in the Alhambra in 1831 with his family and
servants. His entourage, he confessed in a letter to his friend
Addington, had 'no taste for the Moorish picturesque, but a
great notion of the more humble gratifications proceeding
from a confortable home and well appointed kitchen.' In the
end though, Ford's biographer Roland Prothero notes, 'poetry
conquered prose, confort gave way to romance.' Ford and his
family were put up where Irving had also stayed: in the apartments previously occupied by a peasant woman, Francisca de
Molina, or 'Tia Antonia' as she was immortalized in the *Tales
of the Alhambra* by Washington Irving.
   'No previous idea can come up to the exquisite beauty of
the Alhambra,' Ford wrote in a further letter to Addington.
'Here we are, with the most delicious breezes from the snowy

mountain above us, perfumed by a thousand groves and gardens of vine, orange, and pomegranate, carolled by nightingales, who daily and nightly sing in the dark grove . . . all by the side of gushing streams and never-failing fountains.'

At night time, the Alhambra took on a special magic. Ford wrote in the *Handbook*:

> To understand the Alhambra, it must be often visited, and beheld, in the semi-obscure evening, so beautiful of itself in the South. Then, when the moon, Diana's bark of pearl, floats above it in the air like his crescent symbol, the tender beam tips the filigree arches; a depth is given to the shadows, and a misty undefined magnitude to the saloons beyond. Granada, with its busy hum, lies below us, and its lights sparkle like stars on the obscure Albaicin, as if we were looking down on the cielo bajo, or reversed firmament. The baying of a dog and the tinkling of a guitar, indicating life there, increase the fascination of the Alhambra. Then in proportion to the silence around does the fancy and the imagination become alive; the shadows of the cypresses on the walls assume the forms of the dusky Moor as, dressed in his silken robes, he comes to lament over the profanation by the infidel, and the defilement by the unclean destroyer.

In the judgement of Spanish Arabic scholars, the inscription which encircles the Hall of the Two Sisters is the most noteworthy of those which adorn the Alhambra. It was written by Ibn Zamrak, the 'poet of the Alhambra' (1333–93). Ibn Zamrak was born in Granada into a Moorish family that had fled from the Christian military advance on Valencia. He served the court of King Mohammad V, rising to the rank of prime-minister, but was assassinated in Almeria while reading the Koran with his sons.

> I am the garden which beauty adorns: just look at me, and you'll understand me.

> Sublime is this mansion, because Fortune made it greater than any home.

1. Posada de Trinidad: 'I have not been in a single inn where the lower storey was not a stable and the upper one so full of fleas as it were an Egyptian course.' George Ticknor, 1818

2. Don Quixote: 'What giants?' asked Sancho Panza. 'Those you see there,' replied his master, 'with their long arms. Some giants have them about six miles long.'

3. Puerta del Sol, Madrid: 'the great place of assemblage for the idlers of the capital, poor or rich . . .' George Borrow, 1837

4. The *paseo* in Madrid: 'Everybody . . . looks forward to the evening promenade with pleasure and impatience; everybody asks the same question, shall you be on the *paseo* tonight?' Henry Inglis, 1837

5. The *tertulia*, Madrid (*c.* 1920). The philosopher Miguel de Unamuno (bearded) seated among friends and admirers

6. La Sagrada Familia (left) and Casa Batlló, Barcelona, by Antonio Gaudí: 'His brain is at the tip of his fingers and tongue . . . His architecture aims to embody the sum of all gluttonous sensations . . .' Salvador Dali, 1977

7. The Feria, Seville: ' Every young woman was beautiful to look at, some of the young girls being real visions of Spanish beauty.' Sacheverell Sitwell, 1950

8. The Giralda, Seville: 'He who has not seen Seville, has not seen a marvel.' Spanish proverb.

9. The Holy Inquisition: 'Ay! Sepharad has been overwhelmed by a calamity from the skies: my eyes, my eyes, shed tears . . .' Abraham ibn Ezra, early twelfth century

10. Cathedral of Santiago: '. . . as nowhere else, wrapped about by the beauty of the Middle Ages.' A. Kingsley Porter, 1920s

11. The aqueduct at Segovia: 'This imperial gesture ... still strode across the valley with massive grace, a hundred vistas framed by its soaring arches ...' Laurie Lee, *c*.1930

12. Richard Ford in Spanish dress: 'Spain is Spain ... and in being Spanish consists its originality, its raciness, its novelty, its idiosyncracy.'

13. Patio de los Leones, Alhambra palace: 'What delight it offers our eyes,
continually renewing the desires of the noble one . . .'
Inscribed on a wall of the palace.

14. Alhambra palace: 'Sublime is this mansion, because fortune makes it
greater than any home . . .'

15. *The Third of May, 1808,* Francisco de Goya. The populace of Madrid rose against the Napoleonic army only to be crushed. The uprising later led to the War of Independence

16. A scene from the Peninsular War: 'They cry *Viva,* and are very fond of us, and hate the French.' Duke of Wellington, August 1812

17. The siege of the Alcazar during the Civil War, Toledo, 1936: 'So now there was to spread over Spain a cloud of violence, in which the quarrels of several generations would find outlet.' Hugh Thomas, 1977

18. Ernest Hemingway observing Civil War dead outside Madrid, 1937: 'The hot weather makes all dead look alike . . .'

19. Sixteenth–century flamenco singer: the *duende* is 'not a question of power or ability, but of a truly living style; that is to say of blood, of living culture, of instant creation.' Anon.

20. *Woman Frying Eggs*, Diego Velazquez: 'The eggs were soon emptied into an earthen dish, where they floated at large in a sea of oil . . .'
Nineteenth–century American

21. *Bullfight, Suerte de Varas,* Francisco de Goya: 'He runs up to the mounted picador, who defends himself with his spear, while the magnanimous bull gores his horns into the entrails of the horse . . .' Marquess of Londonderry, 1833

22. The running of the bulls: 'Pamplona is no place to bring your wife . . .' Ernest Hemingway, 1959

23. Gerald Brenan and his wife, Gamel Woolsey, with Ralph Partridge (*right*), 1933: 'Yegen was a place of light and air and it was also a place of water.'

24. Robert Graves in Majorca, 1934: 'I wanted to go where town was still town, and country, country, and where the horse plough was not yet an anachronism.'

What delight it offers our eyes, continually renewing the
desires of the noble one.

They have no equal, these radiant columns, hidden and
magical they are.

To here the brilliant stars descend, tired of circling the
celestial limits, they rest in the patios, awaiting like slaves
the royal orders.

The smooth transparent marble illuminates the corners
and their shadows, reflecting pearls.

There can be no garden as green as this, nor with such
a sweet harvest or as much scent.

In 1976, the Argentine writer Jorge Luis Borges visited the
Alhambra. Borges was blind, but he drew on memory, history
and his sense of smell and touch to evoke the palace. In his
poem 'Alhambra' Borges lets his hand feel its way over the
smooth surfaces of the marble, he listens to the murmuring
of the streams, smells the sweetness of the lemon blossom,
before recalling with sadness King Boabdil's final defeat.

> Your gentle ways now depart,
> your keys will be denied you,
> the faithless cross will wipe out the moon,
> and the evening you gaze upon
> will be the last.

Oriental Spain was considered by Théophile Gautier to
be the source of 'all light and wisdom'. With some friends
he spent the 'most delightful' four days and nights in the
Alhambra, setting up a temporary camp with mattresses, a
copper lamp and bottles of sherry which he cooled in the
fountains. He slept two nights in the Court of the Lions,
the third in the Hall of the Two Sisters, and the fourth in
the Hall of the Abencerrages. While he was inevitably drawn
to the Alhambra as the greatest symbol of Moorish civilisation
in Spain, he was no less captivated by other places, not so well
known but equally evocative of legend and romance. In
Toledo, Gautier crossed the Bridge of the Alcantara and drove
for about a quarter of an hour through the fields lining the

Tagus to visit an ancient Moorish pleasure-house, the Palace of Galiana. What Gautier found was an enormous pile of red brick and, living among the ruins, a family of peasants: 'one could not possibly imagine anything blacker, smokier, more cavernous and more filthy . . . the dwellings of the Troglodytes were princely by comparison . . .'

And yet, once again the romantic sensibility touched the crude reality of Spain as Gautier imagined 'charming Galiana, the lovely Moor with her long eyes stained with henna, and her brocaded robe starred with pearls . . . leant over this window-sill, gazing far out over the Vega at the Moorish horsemen as they practiced hurling the djered.'

The palace was named after the beautiful daughter of the local sultan, King Galafar. It has since been restored to its former splendour, but in Gautier's day the legend of Galiana had worn better than her palace.

> Her most painful task was to evade the gallant attentions and adorations of her suitors. The most assiduous and determined of them all was a certain petty King of Guadalajara, named Bradamant, a Moorish giant, valiant and fierce; Galiana could not endure him, and, as the chronicler says: 'What matters it that the knight be of fire if the lady be of ice?' None the less, the Moor was undaunted, and his passionate desire to see Galiana and speak to her was so keen that he had a covered way hollowed out between Guadalajara and Toledo, by which he came to visit her every day . . .

Gautier had entered Toledo 'panting with curiosity and thirst' through the Puerta del Sol, 'a magnificent Arab gate with an elegantly curved arch and granite pillars with balls on top of them, richly bedizined with texts from the Koran'. He was led, together with his friend, 'in single file like the geese in the ballad' through an 'inextricable network of little alleys'. But it was the city of Cordoba which Gautier ultimately judged to have the most African appearance of any other in Spain.

> Its streets, or rather alleys, have a wildly irregular pave-ment like a dried-up watercourse, all strewn with the

chopped straw dropped from the asses' loads, and
nothing about them recalls the manners and customs of
Europe. One walks between interminable chalk-coloured
walls, with occasional windows trellised with bars and
gratings, meeting nobody but a few evil-looking beggars, pious women muffled in black veils, or majos who
ride past like lightning on their brown horses with
white harness, striking showers of sparks from the
cobblestones. If the Moors could return, they would not
have to make any changes in order to settle here again.

And yet as Gautier himself recognized, Cordoba in spite of
its Moorish airs has had Christianity grafted on to it, no more
so than in the Mezquita, its cathedral-mosque.

Thus three religions have performed their rites on this
spot. Of these, one has disappeared into the gulf of the
past, never to return, together with the civilization it
represented; another has been cast out of Europe, where
it barely maintains a foothold, into the depths of the
barbarous East; the third has reached its apogee, and
now, undermined by the spirit of criticism, is growing
daily weaker, even in countries where it reigned as
absolute sovereign; and perhaps the ancient mosque of
Abderrahman may yet last long enough to see a fourth
creed established beneath the shadow of its arches,
celebrating with other forms and other hymns the new
god, or rather the new prophet, for God is always the
same.

Cordoba in the tenth century was the capital of the Muslim
kingdom of Al-Andalus and the home of philosophers,
scientists and poets. The usually dry observer Swinburne in
1776 wrote at some length about this golden age of Arabian
gallantry and magnificence. The zenith of Muslim civilization
'rendered the Moors of Spain superior to all other contemporaries in arts and arms and made Cordoba one of the most
splendid cities of the world.'
The city in the following century was the home of Ibn
Hazm, among the most famous of Arab poets, who wrote an
incisive treatise on love, and of Ibn Zaydun whose impassioned

love poem to the Princess Wallada from prison recalls the biographies of the French troubadours. The Mezqita has for centuries aspired to rival the Alhambra as the most important architectural legacy of the Muslim presence in Spain, and yet Cordoba has never generated the same romantic appeal as Granada. Its identification with the Moorish past is blurred by its assimilation of other cultures; and the observations of visitors have tended to be more academic than sensual and emotional.

Emerging from his hotel at sunset in the middle of Cordoba in 1949, Gerald Brenan let himself be led like a blind man down one of the winding narrow streets that leads down to the river. There near the Roman bridge he watched the 'brownish-yellow current spotted with white bubbles', not at all the 'great river, King of Andalusia' evoked by the great sixteenth-century poet Luis Gongora. He was no less disillusioned by the mosque. Entering the courtyard planted with orange trees he was at first impressed by the feeling of peace and harmony he encountered, 'quite different from the mood of religious holiness and austerity imparted by Christian cloisters.' Once inside the building, however, he was less convinced by the forced merging of architectural styles resulting from the Christian Reconquest of Spain.

No two modes of architecture could well be more different from one another than the Muslim and the West Christian. West Christian architecture in its early phase is filled with the carving for weight and massiveness; and in its second phase, the Gothic, in a spectacular liberation from that weight in a skyward ascent. In both cases there is an emphasis on the tremendousness of the force of gravity, either in the form of great masses of stone weighing downwards, or of lofty columns springing up like trees in defiance of the down-pull. The load of original sin that oppresses the human conscience and seeks to drag the world back into the savagery of the Dark Ages is expressed in a load of stone. The sense of duration, too, the confidence in man's firm establishment on the earth, is emphasized: the Universal Church has been built on a rock and will last forever, and, while it lasts, it will interpret history in terms of moral profit and loss, as the Old Testament has taught it to do.

Moorish architecture is quite the opposite. A mosque is to be a court, a square, a market-place, lightly built to hold a large concourse of people. Allah is so great that nothing human can vie with Him in strength or endurance, and in a society where the harem system complicates the line of descent, the pride or *orgullo* of the feudal ages – which comes from the association of land tenure with family and from the vista of the long line of descendants – is out of place. Even the Moslem castles, large though they are, give the effect of being light and insubstantial. But a mosque is also a place for the contemplation of the Oneness of Allah. How can this better be done than by giving the eyes a maze of geometric patterns to brood over? The state aimed at is of semi-trance. The mind contemplates the patterns, knows that they can be unravelled and yet does not unravel them. It rests therefore on what it sees, and the delicate colour, the variations of light and shade add a sensuous tinge to the pleasure of certainty made visible.

Matilda Betham-Edwards was horrified by how the 'once exquisite' Maksura or Caliph's seat had been turned into an altar piece. It was a desecration in her view. And yet she still considered the Mezquita 'the temple of temples', in her imagination capturing the grand religious conception which the Moors had of it.

To have seen the Mosque of Cordoba forms an era in one's life. It is so vast, so solemn, so beautiful. You seem to be wandering at sunset time in a large and dusky forest, intersected by regular alleys of tall, stately palms. No matter in what direction you turn your face, northward, southward, eastward, westward, the same beautiful perspective meets your eye, file after file of marble and jasper columns supporting the double horse-shoe arch. Nothing can be more imposing, and at the same time graceful than this arrangement of transverse aisles; and the interlaced arches, being delicately coloured in red and white, may not inaptly be compared to foliage of a palmforest, flushed with the rays of the setting sun.

The destructiveness of the Reconquest is depicted in the epic twelfth-century *Poema de Mio Cid* dedicated to the Christian warlord. As Carlos Fuentes has remarked, 'El Cid is the embodiment of the politics that was at times secularly opportunistic, at times fervently religious, spurred by the rise of the army and of army leaders.' El Cid's rallying cries were intensely pugilistic.

Thou shalt see . . . so many white banners turn red with blood and so many good horses, riderless, roam, while the Moors call 'Mahomet!' and the Christians, 'Santiago' respond.

Spaniards have spent much of their history at war, fighting invaders and fighting themselves. 'We win our bread fighting against the infidel,' declared El Cid. The Holy War or *jihad* of Islam found its exact counterpoint in a militant Catholic Church during the Reconquest. Cross and sword followed each other across the Atlantic and back again. The majority of the early conquistadores were born and bred in the province of Extremadura and took their fighting spirit with them in campaigns of plunder and suppression. Miguel de Unamuno in 1909 travelled across Extremadura to the town of Trujillo, the birthplace of Francisco Pizarro, conqueror of Peru. Unamuno wrote in *Through the Lands of Portugal and Spain*:

It was the wild and harsh landscape of Extremadura which strengthened the ranks of those legendary adventurers who from the depth of these hills and fields, without having ever seen the sea which is far from here, set out to cross the ocean to conquer Eldorado, thirsty for gold and adventures. Extremeños have been called the wild indians of Spain, a reference to their bravery. And brave and fanatical they are, in effect . . . I have come to the conclusion that malaria, which is the curse of this Extremeño land, is what has moulded the character of these people. It's made them irritable as well as listless; they can move from drowsiness to feverish activity, but they are incapable of slow, steady work. Summers are terrible in this region . . . hell.

Unamuno found that the real spirit of the conquistador, the hidden key to his motivation, was to be found in the card rooms of the dancing halls of Trujillo.

Gambling is the terrible scourge of these towns and cities of Extremadura: games of chance is the principle occupation of these inhabitants of Trujillo. And it is in this passion for gambling, so terribly absorbing for the Extremeños, that one finds much of the explanation of the epic of the conquista. Peru was the great card table on which the Pizarro brothers threw their bloody cards. The spirit which drove into those great adventures in the Americas was the same spirit that led their descendants to gather round the card table. It is the anxiety to enrich oneself without working . . . its the love felt not only for material gain, but for adventure, for violent emotions, and all the feelings generated by the game of chance. Who can deny that in the soul of those conquistadores, as in that of those card players, there is nothing more than the thirst for gold, the obsession with profit? But there is too a love for adventure, for the unexpected . . .

It has taken eight centuries for Spaniards to come to terms with their militant past. In his novels, the Catalan Juan Goytisolo has turned to Moorish Spain as a point of creative reference. He writes from the perspective of an exile who can only reconcile himself with his country by celebrating the Arab contribution to it. In the first part of his autobiography, *Realms of Strife*, the author, exiled in France, confesses to 'hating' Spain and yet reconciles himself to his native country when he meets with an immigrant Moor.

The expatriate has found a friend. Their eyes had met the day before on a café terrace in the main square, and he bumped into him again crossing the road on the way to the post office. The stranger said hello without more ado in his garbled Moorish Spanish: he's wearing a blue woollen hat, and trousers and overcoat in the same colour. He looks like a fisherman or a sailor, but isn't; he has worked for several years in the port with Spaniards, he explains; there he learned to get about in the language of Cantinflas and Joselito. After drinking tea together, they went to buy wine in the Jewish shop and quietly closed themselves off in the flat on the Rue Molière.

This encounter between the exile and the immigrant captures the sense of cultural loss arising from the expulsion of the Moors from Spain in the sixteenth century. In the nineteenth century, a young anonymous American travelled on a boat from Cadiz and left a moving account of the feelings of a fellow traveller, an Arab whom he met looking across the Straits of Gibraltar to southern Spain.

His ancestors were of Granadian origin, and his name of Muhamed-Bueno . . . had certainly as much of Spanish in it as of Arabic. He seemed, too, to have a strong feeling of pride for Andalusia, and boasted much of its luxuriance and beauty. He spoke of its mild temperature, its pleasant sky, of the regularity of the seasons, of the valuable mines contained in its mountains, the fertility of the soil, and the variety and abundance of its productions; its excellent wheat, delicious fruits, the beauty and perfumes of its flowers . . . but above all, he seemed to remember the freshness and abundance of the waters which trickle everywhere down the side of its mountains . . . Though Mohamad seemed a familiar, amusing fellow, he was yet a strict observer of the tenets and prescriptions of his faith. After making a sparing meal of some fried fish which he bought with him in a straw pannier, he washed his hands carefully over the side of the vessel, and at sunset, turning his back upon the west, he bent forward in a reverential posture, and seemed busy in his devotions.

10

VIVA WELLINGTON

Peninsular and Carlist Wars

Spain has been the victim of many an arrogant and autocratic war leader. She has also bred revolutionaries. Spaniards have fought off invaders and yet looked on quite impotent as foreigners have trampled all over their land. Any visitor to the Prado Museum in Madrid cannot but be struck by the vividness with which Spanish painters depict physical cruelty. The British journalist Robert Graham in 1983 remarked after one such visit that he could think of no other major picture gallery in the world that housed so many dead bodies and violent scenes. In *Spain: Change of a Nation*, Graham attempted to reach an understanding of the country through observing the brushstrokes of its painters. He lingered in particular on Goya's *Executions of May 3 1808*.

The populace of Madrid had risen heroically against the Napoleonic army the day before. Though crushed, the uprising led to what became Spain's War of Independence. Goya portrays the brutal aftermath by focusing on the victim of a firing squad in the fraction of a second before execution. The victim is already on his knees. But his trunk is erect, his arms splayed wide above his head. Is he triumphantly baring his breast before the executioners? Or is he merely afraid and confused as to how to die? Two details emphasise the imminence of his fate. The corpses of those already executed are close by, and the muskets of the execution squad are levelled anew, their bayonets almost touching the victim. The drama is heightened by the use of light. The huge canvas is oppressively coloured, save for a lantern on the ground which throws a brilliant light on the man about to die, who is wearing yellow breeches and a white shirt. The whiteness of the shirt highlights the wantoness of the killing, while the background of night stresses the murkiness of the act – an impression reinforced by the anonymity of the executioners, whose faces are turned slightly away, and whose lethal weapons appear almost as an extension of their bodies. Goya is unsparingly direct.

Goya's savage protest was given literary expression during his time in the prose sketches of Blanco White, theologian, poet, novelist, critic and political journalist. In 1808 White was in Madrid in the midst of one of the most turbulent periods of Spanish history. A palace coup orchestrated by sections of the aristocracy and the army led to the removal of the unpopular royal favourite Manuel de Godoy and the abdication of the Bourbon King Charles IV in favour of his son Ferdinand. The entrance of the new King into the Spanish capital had been preceded by French troops led by General Murat. The French had enjoyed the support of the majority of the population until it was realized that Napoleon was behind a plot to remove the Bourbon dynasty completely and replace it with Bonapartes. When Ferdinand was exiled from Madrid and Joseph Bonaparte installed as King, the mood of the population changed from collaboration to savage rebellion. White witnessed the fanatical mob as it gathered at the royal palace to try and prevent the French from removing the remaining members of the Spanish royal family.

A rush of people crying 'To arms' conveyed to us the first notice of the tumult. I heard that the French troops were firing on the people, but the outrage appeared to me both so impolitic and so enormous that I could not rest until I went out to ascertain the truth. I had just arrived at an opening named Plazuela de Santo Domingo, the meeting of four large streets, one of which leads to the Palace, when, hearing the sound of a French drum in that direction, I stopped with a considerable number of decent and quiet people, whom curiosity kept riveted to the spot. Though a strong piquet of infantry was fast advancing upon us, we could not imagine that we stood in any kind of danger. Under this mistaken notion we awaited their approach. But, seeing the soldiers halt and prepare their arms, we began instantly to disperse. A discharge of musketry followed us in a few moments, and a man fell at the entrance to the street, through which I was, with a strong throng, retreating from the fire. The fear of an indiscriminate massacre arose so naturally from this unprovoked assault, that everyone tried to look for safety in the narrow cross streets on both sides of the way. I hastened on towards my house, and having shut the front door, could think of no better expedient than to make ball pieces for a fowling-piece which I kept.

The Spanish novelist Galdós watched the ensuing bloodbath through the eyes of the victims. His account appears in the third novel of the multi-volumed *Episodios Nacionales* published in 1873.

The struggle, or, one should say, the bloodbath, was appalling in the Puerta del Sol. When the firing ceased, and the cavalry began to take action, the Polish guard and the famous Mamelukes (a small unit of cavalry under Murat's orders) fell with sabres on the people, those of us who were in the Calle Mayor getting the worst of the onslaught because the ferocious horses fell upon us from two sides . . . We had on our left hand the passage de la Duda as a strategic position which served us as a headquarters and the road to flight, and thence the noble gentleman and I directed our fire at the first Mamelukes who appeared in the street.

I must point out that we riflemen formed a kind of rearguard or reserve, because the truest and most resourceful warriors were those who fought with knives against the horses. From the balconies also there came many pistol shots and a great number of projectiles were

flying down, bricks, flowerpots, stewpots, clock weights
and so on.

'Come here, Judas Iscariot' – screamed La Primorosa,
directing her fists towards a Mameluke who was wreak-
ing havoc on the door of the house of Onate. 'And isn't
there anyone who can put a pound of gunpowder in his
body? What a sight you are! You worthless lump, put
fire in your gun or I'll scratch out your eyes.'

The impreciations of our general obliged us to fire shot
after shot. But that badly directed fire was not worth
much because the Mamelukes had managed to clear a
great part of the street with their sabre slashes and were
getting further along every minute. 'At them boys!' cried
the maja, rushing forward to meet a pair of horsemen
whose mounts were carrying them towards us.

Then, as White witnessed, the executions began, the
pavements emptied, and the silence of fear took over the
streets of Madrid.

The dead silence of the streets since the first approach
of night, only broken by the trampling of horses which
now and then were heard passing along in large parties,
had something exceedingly dismal in a populous town,
where we were accustomed to an incessant and enliven-
ing bustle. The Madrid cries, the loudest and most varied
in Spain, were missed early next morning, and it was ten
o'clock before a single street door had been opened.
Nothing but absolute necessity could induce the people
to venture out.

The silence did not persist however. The Spaniards rose up
against the French elsewhere in the country, their patriotism
refuelled in 1808 by a series of military victories, particularly
that of the Battle of Bailen. And yet what the Spaniards called
their War of Independence was in fact shared with others,
namely the British who were to leave abundant record of their
participation as allies in the Peninsular War. The plan of
Major General Sir John Moore was to advance from Lisbon
to Burgos, and to meet up with a second force, commanded
by Sir David Baird, advancing from Corunna. Then, uniting

with the Spanish armies, the combined Anglo-Spanish force would rout the French. Robert Southey, in his *History of the Peninsular War*, wrote:

Before the troops began their march, Sir John Moore warned them in his general orders that the Spaniards were a grave, orderly people, extremely sober but generous, and easily offended by an insult or disrespect; he exhorted them to accommodate themselves to these manners, to meet with equal kindness the cordiality wherewith they would be received, and not shock by their intemperence a people worthy of their attachment, whose efforts they were come to support in the most glorious cause. His resolution to maintain order and proper discipline was farther evinced by punishing a marauder upon the march with death: the offender was one whose character gave no hope of amendment, and the General took that opportunity of declaring his determination to show no mercy to plunderers or marauders, in other words to thieves and villains. Further to gratify the Spaniards, the army, upon entering Spain, were ordered to wear the red cockade in addition to their own.

The march, however, was to become a retreat and by December 1808 British troops were retreating to Corunna, outnumbered, starving, and suffering a bitter winter. In the *Recollections* of Rifleman Harris, the author describes how exhausted, barefoot soldiers abandoned their weapons and packs and 'linked arm in arm to support each other, like a pack of drunkards.' In Galicia, the perceived treachery of the Spanish character was such that Harris could not sleep. 'I refused to relinquish possession of my rifle, and my right hand was ready in an instant to unsheath my bayonet.' Sir John himself was to report: 'If our army was in enemy country, it could not be more completely left to itself . . . The people run away, the villages are deserted.'

In Corunna lies Sir John Moore's tomb, overlooking ancient battlements and tower blocks hugging the skyline across the harbour. He was buried, in his trenchcoat, on 16 January 1809. The site marks no brilliant military victory, yet the courage and nobility in defeat of the English general has engaged romantic imagination. The Irish curate Charles Wolfe never set foot on Spanish soil but was nonetheless moved to write an elegy to Moore, the opening of which is resonant with schoolboy memories.

> Not a drum was heard, not a funeral note,
> As his corpse to the rampart we hurried;
> Not a soldier discharged his farewell shot
> O'er the grave where our hero was buried.

H.V. Morton visited the tomb in the early 1950s, remarking on the English garden of daisies, fuchsias and geraniums that still lies in the shade of some very Atlantic-looking palms.

> Children from the surrounding streets play round the grave of Sir John Moore, and nursemaids wheel perambulators into the little garden because it is shadier there than anywhere else in the old town. Sometimes an English tourist arrives, takes a photograph and audibly recites a few lines of the one poem of which every Englishman knows at least the opening lines. When Moore was being helped to his feet after the French cannon-ball had carried away his left shoulder, his sword became entangled in his legs and an A.D.C. began to unbuckle it. Moore stopped him. 'It is as well as it is,' he said. 'I had rather it should go out of the field with me.'

In 1871 the Galician poetess Rosalia de Castro wrote this in dedication to Moore:

> Please God, noble foreigner, that this be not an alien place for you! There is no poet or spirit of imagination that cannot but contemplate in autumn the sea of yellowing leaves which covers your tomb with love, or the fresh buddings of May . . . and say 'How I wish that when I die, I could sleep in peace in this garden of flowers . . . far from the cemetery . . .'

Sir John Moore was succeeded by Sir Arthur Wellesley, the Duke of Wellington. Fresh from gaining his military colours in India, the Iron Duke treated the Peninsular Campaign as a convenient military exercise to extend British power

and influence abroad at the same time as firmly checking
Napoleon's ambitions. Under him the British displayed a deep
cultural and racial antagonism towards the natives. In a
letter home, one of Wellington's soldiers, Private William
Wheeler, gives a more lighthearted account of the day Madrid
was liberated from the French by British troops. It was
12 August 1812.

I never before witnessed such a scene. At the distance
of five miles from the gates we were met by the
inhabitants, each had brought out something, viz. laurel,
flowers, bread, wine, grapes, lemonade, aguardiente,
tobacco, sweetmeats etc. etc. etc. The road represented
a moving forest, from the great multitude of people
carrying boughs. The intervals of our subdivisions
soon became filled up with men, women, and children.
In one place would be a brawny Spaniard with a pig-
skin of wine, filling vessels for us to drink, then
another with a basket full of bread distributing it around,
then a pretty palefaced black-eyed maid would modestly
offer a nosegay or sprig of laurel, then without ceremony seize our arm and sing some martial air to the
memory of some immortal patriot who had fallen in
the good cause. The immortal names of Crawford
and others would also sound in Spanish song.
   When we entered the city the shouting increased
tenfold, every bell that had got a clapper was set ringing, the windows were ornamented with rich drapery
embroidered with gold and silver, such as is only used
on great festivals when the Host is carried. The whole
of the windows and tops of the houses were crowded
with Spanish beauty, waving white handkerchiefs. The
people endeavoured to drag us into their houses. Suffice
it to say, that we were several hours going to the convent where we were to be quartered, that under ordinary circumstances might have been walked in fifteen
minutes. But amidst all the pleasure and happiness we
were obliged to submit to a custom so un-english that
I cannot but feel disgust now I am writing. It was to be
kissed by the men. What made it still worse, their

breath was so highly seasoned with garlic, then their huge moustaches well stiffened with sweat, dust and snuff, it was like having a hair broom pushed into one's face that had been daubed in a dirty gutter.

Richard Ford noted in *Wanderings* that the reality of Spain's warlike tradition has not always lived up to the noble images which pervade literature. He based these thoughts on his own experience of the Peninsular War during which the quintessential virtues of the Spanish male such as bravery, honour, and national pride were often less in evidence than military indiscipline, lawlessness and brutality. In a despatch from Madrid to the war minister Earl Bathurst on 18 August 1812, Ford's friend the Duke of Wellington wrote:

I don't expect much from the exertions of Spaniards, notwithstanding all that we have done for them. They cry *Viva*, and are very fond of us; and hate the French; but they are, in general, the most incapable of useful exertion of all the nations that I have known; the most vain, and at the same time the most ignorant, particularly of military affairs, and above all of military affairs in their own country . . . I am afraid that the utmost we can hope for is to teach them how to avoid being beat.

Wellington was particularly dismissive of the Spanish regular army which he considered to be run by a corrupt and inefficient officer class, prone to cowardice. He had more time for the guerilla bands, whose persistent campaign of sabotage broke down the morale of the French. One of Wellington's sergeants, Edward Costello, records in his *Recollections* the barbarity of the guerillas under their commander General Minas following an attack on French troops near the Basque city of Vitoria.

The prisoners, about twenty in number, were immediately marched into the mountains, but not before they had time to draw a dark augury of their own fate by seeing all their wounded comrades brutally stabbed to death on the ground where the skirmish had taken place. The prisoners, after having been stripped of nearly every article of wearing apparel, even to their boots, were confined in the space of ground encircled by pens or hurdles, and used for keeping cattle, round which were planted many sentries. In the evening the ferocious mountaineers, elated with the day's success, being joined by a number of females, their sweethearts and wives, made merry with drinking wine and dancing to the music of several guitars. During this merriment both men and women frequently taunted their wretched prisoners, recapitulated the wrongs the Spaniards had suffered at the hands of the French, until they gradually had excited their passions to a partial state of frenzy. In this state, the signal having been given by one of their number, they rushed in among the hapless prisoners, and commenced a general massacre, drowning the cries and supplications for mercy of their victims, as they gave each blow, by enumerating the different losses each had sustained in his family during the war. 'Take that for my father', 'that for my son', 'this for my brother' etc. until the work of death was complete. The most inhuman and perhaps most revolting trait in this general murder was some of the women having actively assisted in the slaughter.

This is an image of a country not just at war, but at war with itself, cruel, brutal, intolerant. The Peninsular War was to produce other cruelties, as further accounts by British soldiers demonstrated. Lieutenant George Gleig was only seventeen when he disembarked with the 85th Infantry Regiment near the town of San Sebastián on 18 August 1813. The young Scot was taken by the 'swarthy visages' of the Basque men and the expressive countenance of the Basque women, 'their fine dark laughing eye, their white teeth, and brunette complexion.' He has the fresh recruit's zest for life: Spain – its land and people – seem untouched by the war. And yet the romance is soon overtaken by the reality of Wellington's military campaign. This is his description of Wellington's liberation of San Sebastián:

As soon as the fighting began to wax faint, the horrors of plunder and rapine succeeded. Fortunately, there were few females in the place; but of the fate of the few which were there, I cannot even now think without a shudder. The houses were eventually ransacked, the furniture wantonly broken, the churches profaned, the images dashed to pieces; wine and spirit cellars were broken open, and the troops, heated already with angry passions, became absolutely mad by intoxication. All order and discipline were abandoned. The officers had no longer the slightest control over their men, who, on the contrary, controlled the officers; nor is it by any means certain, that several of the latter did not fall by the hands of the former, when they vainly attempted to bring them back to a sense of subordination.

The pillage lasted all day and into the night, during which the darkness was dispelled, so bright was the light from the burning buildings. San Sebastián has a long history of fires, but none compares to the one started by Wellington's troops. The population felt abused and humiliated at the destruction of the city by their 'allies'. It was, they suspected, a deliberate act to stifle northern Spain's commerce with France.

British troops made some amends in 1833 when they helped defend the town during the Carlist War. Some of the bodies of these volunteers lie in a small cemetery above the city on the slopes of Monte Urgall. The collective memory however remains focused on that terrible night in 1813. The San Sebastián-born novelist Pio Baroja in his book on the Basque country and its people, *El Pais Vasco*, published in 1953, wrote with characteristic understatement:

The small town of San Sebastián, built over a peninsula against the background of the Castle of Mota was burnt by the English in August 1813, after they had had it in their hands, no one knows for what reason. Stupidities of war. The inhabitants quickly rebuilt it with a central square and various straight streets.

Badajoz is another city to have experienced the horror of rioting by British troops after they had successfully broken through the French defences. The scene of the British assault is still visible today: the ramparts surrounding a semi-derelict Moorish castle on a hill overlooking the town and the

Guadiana river. 'Badajoz! What queer, far-off, schoolboy memories that word calls up!' wrote Gerald Brenan in *The Face of Spain*, first published in 1950. 'The boring classroom and the smug tone of the history master's voice as he spoke of its sack by Wellington's troops – the pun in Thomas Hood's poem, printed in a little red school edition that cost 6d – the look of the name itself, so absurd in its English pronunciation!'

George Hennell, who joined Wellington's army as a volunteer two days before the storming of Badajoz, described with remarkable self-restraint what happened once the British had broken out of the French-occupied citadel liked caged animals.

> Soon after daylight, the bugle sounded for two hours plunder. The men were pretty quiet all night, but when the bugle sounded they could not get out of the citadel. They, however, soon broke down the gate and sallied forth. The first door that presented itself was dashed in with the butt end of a musket. I hear our soldiers in some instances behaved very ill – I only saw two (behaving ill) and stopped them both; one was beating an old man, the other ill-using an old woman. One of our officers saw a man go among a number of women and force off all their ear-rings. Those that would not give way [he] broke off a bit of their ear.

During the nineteenth century, Spain suffered more years of war than any other European nation. Almost permanent civilian and military strife coincided with a period of growing European interest in a country that had hitherto remained outside the Grand Tour. Some 200 books appeared in England on the five-year Peninsular War campaign and its aftermath. Ford spent much of his time in Spain sending intelligence reports on military movements to Addington, the British minister in Madrid. Borrow by contrast often found himself an innocent bystander, caught up in the conflict, the complexities of which he made no attempt to unravel, but which he followed with a keen journalistic eye. It was while staying in Lisbon that Borrow got his first insight into what was in store for him once he crossed the border. The rector of the

English College warned him: 'Surely you have chosen a strange time to visit Spain; there is much blood-shedding in Spain at present, and violent wars and tumults.'

Spain survived one war only to be plunged into another. The Carlist War pitted the supporters of Don Carlos, the brother of the late Ferdinand VII against the regime of the Regent María Cristina, supported by an ill-equipped British auxiliary legion. Spanish Quixotism returned to the fray, as depicted by an English officer's account of the Carlist conduct in battle:

> Many would caper and dance *Fandango* on the tops of the breastworks, with balls and shells flying on all sides . . . They would clap their buttocks in derision as the guns fired, waving their caps and black flags and shouting 'Down with Queen! Carlos for Ever.'

On 14 August 1836, 100 years before Franco's troops advanced on the Republican-held Madrid, the Queen Regent Cristina faced a no less dramatic assault on her summer residence of La Granja. To this palatial idyll, set among the pine forests of the Guadarrama hills, the Queen had retired from the turmoil and chaos of the Carlist War, hoping to enjoy, as Borrow put it 'rural air and amusements in this celebrated retreat, a monument to the taste and magnificence of the first Bourbon who ascended the throne of Spain.' Yet it was not to be. Early one morning members of the Queen's personal guard led by a Sergeant Garcia forced their way into her apartment and ordered the absolute monarch to sign the Constitution of the *Liberales*. Cristina refused to sign and ordered the guards to withdraw. Borrow takes up the story:

> . . . the soldiers at length took her down to one of the courts of the palace, where stood her well-known paramour, Munoz, bound and blindfolded, 'Swear to the constitution, you she-rogue,' vociferated the swarthy sergeant. 'Never!' said the spirited daughter of the Neopolitan Bourbons. 'Then your *cortejo* shall die!' replied the sergeant. 'Ho! Ho! my lads; get ready your arms, and send four bullets through the fellow's brain.' Munoz was forthwith led to the wall, and compelled to

kneel down, the soldiers levelled their muskets, and another moment would have consigned the unfortunate wight to eternity, when Cristina, forgetting everything but the feelings of her woman's heart, suddenly started forward with a shriek, exclaiming, 'Hold, hold! I sign! I sign!'

The day after this event Borrow, accompanied by a correspondent for the *Morning Chronicle*, witnessed the final rearguard action by the Queen Regent's military protector General Quesada as a demonstration spontaneously broke out near the Puerta del Sol.

He was closely followed by two mounted officers, and at a short distance by as many dragoons. In almost less time than is sufficient to relate it, several individuals in the crowd were knocked down and lay sprawling upon the ground, beneath the horses of Quesada and his two friends, for as to the dragoons, they halted as soon as they had entered the Puerta del Sol. It was a fine sight to see three men, by dint of valour and good horsemanship, strike terror into at least as many thousands; I saw Quesada spur his horse repeatedly into the dense masses of the crowd, and then extricate himself in the most masterly manner. The rabble were completely awed, and gave way retiring by the Calle del Comercio and the Calle de Alcala. All at once, Quesada singled out two nationals, who were attempting to escape, and setting spurs to his horse, turned them in a moment, and drove them in another direction, striking them in a contemptuous manner with the flat of his sabre. He was crying out, 'Long live the absolute queen!' When, just beneath me, amidst a portion of the crowd which had still maintained its ground, perhaps from not having the means of escaping, I saw a small gun glitter for a moment; then there was a sharp report, and a bullet had nearly sent Quesada to his long account, passing so near to the countenance of the general as to graze his hat. I had an indistinct view for a moment of a well-known foraging cap just about the spot from whence the gun had been discharged, then there was a rush of the crowd, and the shooter, whoever he was, escaped discovery amidst the confusion which arose.

This is the Quixotic stereotype in full flight, El Cid taking on the barbaric masses, courage and impetuosity alone capable of arresting, if only briefly, the avalanche of revolution. No action of any conqueror or hero on record, Borrow commented, could approach Quesada's final act of glory. The Spanish writer José Martinez Ruiz 'Azorín' has referred to the 'perpetual tumult of opposing passions' which runs through Spanish history. On the one side, a disorganized rabble shouting for liberty, on the other a uniformed strongarm leader or *caudillo* quite literally cutting the people down to size.

Spaniards have rarely been entirely responsible for their own destiny. In reflecting on the years leading up to the Spanish Civil War, Walter Starkie drew on the nightmarish imagery of some of Goya's drawings and cartoons to describe the successive scenes of conflict with which Spain appeared to be moving inexorably towards a collective catharsis. In an essay of introduction to Ramon Menendez Pidal's *The Spaniards in Their History*, Starkie wrote:

> The whole country was in the throes of a monstrous witches' Sabbath conjured up by a host of foreign agents eager to lead the dance. The tunes and rhythms these minions of the moon played up hill and down dale throughout the country were Spanish, but so deformed and twisted by the malignant ingenuity of these minstrels of chaos that it seemed as though the spirit of Spain had been obliterated. But through the mocking cacophony I could hear the solemn booming of the Dies Irae announcing the approaching doom.

11

THAT ARID SQUARE

The Civil War

Spain lost the last of her colonies – Cuba, Puerto Rico, and the Philippines – in 1898. This 'disaster' spawned one of Spain's greatest literary movements – the so-called 'Generation of '98' – made up of a small group of intellectuals which attempted to analyse the symptoms of Spain's decline and prescribe remedies. 'A new, intenser stage began of that long interior dialogue and self-examination that had occupied the best Spanish brains since the eighteenth century,' wrote Gerald Brenan in the *The Literature of the Spanish People*. 'Spain became more than ever the patient on the pyscho-analyst's couch.'

An important influence on this group were the writings of Angel Ganivet, an Andalusian diplomat and essayist whose *Idearium Espanol*, published in 1897, anticipated much of the soul searching that was to follow the final collapse of the Spanish Empire. In it Ganivet tried to identify those permanent features of Spanish life which had emerged from a turbulent history of Arab expulsion, South American conquest, and war, by drawing an analogy between the nation and Segismundo, the prince in Calderón de la Barca's seventeenth-century play, who awakes from the sleep of reason and discovers life is a dream.

> Spain, like Segismundo, was taken violently from that deep cavern of dark existence of fighting against the Arabs, thrown into the centre of European life and

converted into the lady and mistress of a people she hardly
understood; and when after many and extraordinary
events, which seemed more fantastic than real, we
recovered the reason of our deep cavern, to which we find
ourselves now, chained to misery and poverty, we ask
ourselves whether all our previous history has been reality
or just a dream . . .

A nation cannot, and shouldn't live without glory, but
it has many ways of conquering it, and glory manifests
itself in various forms: there is the ideal glory, which is
the most noble one, which is conquered through intelligence; there is the glory of the triumph of ideals of one
people over another; there is the glory of ferocious combat
where all that is at stake is mere material dominance; and
then there is the saddest glory of all in which a people
destroys itself in domestic strife. Spain has known all the
possible forms of glory, and for much of its history has
experienced to an excessive degree the saddest glory of
them all: we live in a state of perpetual civil war. Our
national temperament, fuelled but ultimately weakened
by endless periods of conflict, never manages to transform
itself, to find a more peaceful, ideal means of expression
and to speak in more human ways than with arms.

In *The Tragic Sense of Life*, published in 1912, Miguel de
Unamuno puts his faith not in any 'actual flesh-and-bone
philosopher' but in a creation of Spanish fiction, Don Quixote,
whom he believes comes closest to epitomizing the positive
spirit expressed by Spaniards in crucial points in their history.

There is one figure, a comically tragic figure, a figure in
which is revealed all that is profoundly tragic in the
human comedy, the figure of Our Lord Don Quixote,
the Spanish Christ, who summarises and includes in
himself the immortal soul of my people. Perhaps the
passion and death of the Knight of the Sorrowful Countenance is the passion and death of the Spanish people, its
death and resurrection. And there is a Quixotesque ethic
and a Quixotesque religious sense – the religious sense of
Spanish Catholicism . . .

There is undoubtedly a philosophical Quixotism, but

there is also a Quixotic philosophy. May it not perhaps be that the philosophy of the Conquistadores, of the Counter-Reformers, of Loyola, and above all, in the order of abstract but deeply felt thought, that of our mystics, was in essence, none other than this? What was the mysticism of St John of the Cross but a knighterrantry of the heart in the divine warfare?

On the other hand the journalist/philosopher Ortega y Gasset advocated modern Europe as the social model on which backward Spain should build its future. 'Our generation has never negotiated with the topics of patriotism' Ortega proclaimed in a speech delivered on the stage of Madrid's La Comedia theatre in March 1914. 'When it hears the word Spain . . . it does not remember the victories of the Cross, it does not call forth the vision of a blue sky, and under it a splendour – it merely feels, and what it feels is grief . . . The old Spain, with its governing and governed classes is now dying.'

In an essay published in 1930 entitled *The Revolt of the Masses*, Ortega spelt out his solution to his country's decline. Spain the nation-state should give way to the greater Europe.

Only the determination to construct a great nation from the group of peoples of the Continent would give a new life to the pulses of Europe . . . In my opinion the building up of Europe into a great national State is the one enterprise that could counter-balance a victory of the 'Five Years Plan'. Communism is an extravagant moral code, but it is nothing less than a moral code. Does it seem more worthy and more fruitful to oppose to that Slavonic Code a new European Code, the inspiration towards a new programme of life?

Unamuno and Ortega came to represent two ways of looking at Spain and its history. The first was intensely Spanish in its search for the spiritual soul of Spain; the second was commitedly European, rooted in the present, hostile to many aspects of Spanish culture. For a while their debate caught the imagination of many Spaniards, but in the end it was unable to alter the course of Spanish politics. Jan Morris describes how Spain limped into the third decade of the twentieth century

'with one half of her being, for the other half was still linger-
ing wistfully with the Cid and the conquistadores.'

She was a mess of a country: addled by bitter politics at
home – between 1814 and 1923 there were forty-three
coups d'état; embroiled in constant wars in the pathetic
remnants of her empire, now confined to a few sandy or
foetid enclaves in Africa; diplomatically a cipher, strategically so inessential that the First World War contemp-
tuously passed her by. Conflicting ideologies tortured
her – dogmas of monarchy, theocracy, despotism, demo-
cracy, socialism, anarchism, Communism. Her rural
poverty and urban squalor periodically erupted into
violence. Her colonial policies were so inept that in 1921
her Moroccan army was annihilated in the Rif. A dictator, Primo de Rivera, came and went; in 1931 the last
of the Bourbons, bowing himself out of the chaos, gave
way to a left-wing Republic; and in 1936 all these centuries of failure, schism, and frustration gave birth to that
ultimate despair, the Spanish Civil War.

The Spanish Civil War broke out in July 1936. Although it
came to involve foreign powers in a prelude to the Second
World War, its origins were endemic to Spain. The novelist
Ramon Sender described in *Seven Red Sundays*, published in
1936, the heady pre-revolutionary atmosphere that existed in
early 1930s Madrid.

We must force the whole city to go into mourning for
the murder of our three comrades. I come to the Puerta
del Sol. In the corner to the left, those out of work
belonging to the building trade are airing themselves in
the sun as usual. Very few of the *bourgeoisie* are to be seen
in the streets. Workmen are much more numerous, and
they proclaim themselves strikers by the mixture of
amusement and suspicion with which they walk the
streets. The streets belong to no one yet. We shall see
who are going to conquer. The Civil Guard, the Public
Safety Agents, the Shock Police lurk in the entrance halls
of public buildings and in the usual stations, the doors of
which are half closed. In the Home Office there are black

visors, chin-straps fastened, and eagle eyes looking in every direction . . .

Voices, disturbances. This Puerta del Sol is like a bay of the sea, always in agitation. I have sometimes seen all the street openings occupied by troops which had cleared the open space completely, and suddenly men, coming as it were from the asphalt itself, began to gesticulate and shout. Suddenly, firing. The rebels appear on the great electric light standards and in the entrances of the metro. What happens in the Puerta del Sol happens all over Spain. The strength of our tactics is that the Government never knows where the enemy is. And these tactics are not our own, but come from the Spanish temperament. They say that the monarchy fell in that way. A moment comes when passion has infected the air, and no one can breathe, and the most extraordinary events happen independently of any of the preparations which have been made.

The South African born Roy Campbell was in the vanguard of those who believed a great crusade was needed to resist the utopian Marxists. Campbell – who considered that industrialization was inimical to man – saw the Spanish Republic and its 'materialist' allies as a threat to the religious and social fabric of Catholic Spain. In June 1935, Campbell, his wife, and two daughters settled in Toledo, a town he felt was the 'whole embodiment of the crusade for Christianity against Communism.' The final pages of Campbell's autobiography, *Light on a Dark Horse*, are taken up with a farcical account of his last public act of 'anti-Red defiance', a month before the outbreak of civil war. It took place in the local bullring, for Campbell's orthodox Catholicism was surpassed in its fanaticism only by his love of wine and the bullfight.

As a last act of anti-Red defiance we had plaited red and yellow ribbons into the manes and tails of the horses. Tess and Anna [Campbell's daughters] rode beautifully, both while escorting the beauties, and opening the *corrida*. The Governor asked us all up into the box for the rest of the fight.

On the outbreak of the Spanish Civil War, the historian

Salvador de Madariaga in his book on Spain, says that it was 'the combined effect of two typically Spanish *pronunciamentos*: that of Don Francisco Largo Caballero, Commander-in-Chief of the revolutionary wing of the General Union of Workers (UGT) which was not communist and that of Don Francisco Franco, Commander-in-Chief of the rebellious General Union of Officers (UME) which was not Fascist.'

The cast of other characters involved, and the way their actions combined to ensure that what began as a military rising developed into a much wider conflict was summarized by Gerald Brenan in *The Spanish Labyrinth*.

> The Military Junta and group of Right-wing politicians which rose against the Government in July expected to occupy the whole of Spain, except Barcelona and perhaps Madrid, within a few days. They had at their disposal the greater part of the armed forces of the country – the Civil Guard, the Foreign Legion, a division of Moorish troops from Spanish Morocco, four-fifths of the infantry and artillery officers and a certain number of regiments recruited in the north and therefore reliable. They had also the Carlist levies of *requetes* which had for some time been drilling secretly and the promise of Italian and German tanks and aeroplanes if necessary. Against these the Government had only the Republican Assault Guards and a small and badly armed air force. But the plans of the rebels were defeated by the tremendous courage and enthusiasm with which the people rose to defend themselves and by the loyalty of the naval ratings who at a critical moment deprived them of the command of the sea. Each side being then left in control of one half of Spain, a civil war became inevitable.

The opening act of General Franco's participation in the military rising – his flight from the Canaries to Spanish Morocco from where he rallied his troops – has been described in terms that transform him into the Great Crusader of Spanish mythology. Luis Bolin, a right-wing journalist who accompanied Franco on his 'flight to history' on board a light aircraft operated by an English pilot Captain Begg, wrote in *Spain the Vital Years*:

Dawn was breaking when we reached the airport, where Mouchenino [an Algerian who ran it] was already bustling around. The gates of the hangar slid heavily on their metal wheels. We saw the Dragon Rapide, itching like a falcon for the air. We pushed it outside. It took Begg only a moment to get the propellers spinning. As we waited for the engines to warm up, Mouchenino spied a distant group, walking towards us in the morning haze. '*Filez vite!*' he said to me, 'they are policemen and Customs officials who will surely make a nuisance of themselves. Get into your plane and fly!' It was five o'clock. His advice seemed sound, and I estimated its value at something like five hundred francs. Our plane rose quickly from the ground and departed without leaving any trace of Casablanca. Fate and Mouchenino had treated us kindly.

We sped high over lowlands the lushness of which contrasted with the barren, mountainous country allotted to Spain the Protectorate under its care. Franco was silent now, and hardly a word passed between the rest of us. We had been on our way for about an hour when the General, reckoning that we were over the Spanish Protectorate, opened his suit case, discarded the dark grey suit in which he had travelled from the Canaries and changed into his khaki uniform. A lump rose in my throat when I saw him wind around his waist the scarlet, gold-tasselled sash which in the Spanish Army constitutes the most distinctive symbol of a General's rank. This was it. In his usual quiet and unassuming manner he had attired himself to take command of the forces that awaited his arrival. Years were to elapse ere he donned civilian clothes again.

For the Republican side, the first hours of the Civil War delivered no such certainties. The atmosphere of confusion is vividly captured in the novel *Days of Hope* by André Malraux when the mixed signals reaching the central telephone exchange in Madrid during Franco's overnight rising put to the test loyalties of centuries. Malraux himself served as a volunteer pilot and organized the supply of guns to the anti-Francoiste forces.

All Madrid was astir in the warm summer night, loud
with the rumble of lorries stacked with rifles. For some
days the Workers' Organizations had been announcing
that a Fascist rising might take place at any moment, that
the soldiers in the barracks had been 'got at', and that the
munitions were pouring in. At 1 a.m. the Government
had decided to arm the people, and from 3 a.m. the production of a union-card entitled every member to be
issued with a rifle. It was high time, for the reports
telephoned in from the provinces, which had sounded
hopeful between midnight and 2 a.m., were beginning
to strike a different note.

The Central Exchange at the Northern Railway Ter-
minus rang up the various stations along the line. Ramos,
the Secretary of the Railway Workers' Union, and
Manuel were in charge. With the exception of Navarre
– the line which had been cut – the replies had been
uniform. Either the Government had the situation well in
hand, or a Workers' Committee had taken charge of the
city, pending instructions from the central authority. But
now a change was coming over the dialogues.

'Is that Huesca?'

'Who's speaking?'

'The Workers' Committee, Madrid.'

'Not for long, you swine! *Arriba Espana!*'

Fixed to the wall by drawing-pins, the special late edition of the *Claridad* flaunted a caption six columns wide:
Comrades to Arms!

'Hullo, Avila? How's things at your end?
Madrid North speaking.'

'The hell it is, you bastards! *Viva El Cristo Rey!*'

'See you soon. *Salud!*'

An urgent message was out through to Ramos.

The Northern lines linked up with Zaragoza, Burgos,
and Valladolid.

'Is that Zaragoza? Put me through to the Workers'
Committee at the station.'

'We've shot them. Your turn next. *Arriba España!*'

'Hullo, Tablada! Madrid North here, Union Delegate.'

'Call the jail, you son of a gun. That's where your

friends are. And we'll be coming for you in a day or two; we want to have a word with you.'

'Bueno! Let's meet on the Alcala, second door on the left. Got it?'

It was in Andalusia that the first of the military risings occurred in response to General Franco's call to arms. Among those residing in Andalusia at the time were Gerald Brenan and his wife Gamel Woolsey. They had only recently moved to Churriana, near Malaga. The surprise and excitement of the first hours of the Civil War were described by Gamel in her autobiographical novel, *Death's Other Kingdom*.

Someone was singing 'London Bridge is burning down, burning down' – 'They're getting it all wrong,' I thought. 'It's falling down, isn't it? Or is it burning down?'

Then I started awake. Maria was standing at the foot of the bed. 'Why are you sleeping,' she said, 'when Malaga is burning down?'

We leapt out of bed asking 'What has happened? What is it?' still half asleep.

'There's been a rising,' she said, 'and they've set fire to the city.'

We rushed to the window. Malaga lying spread out across the bay was under a pall of smoke. The city was hidden and the smoke drifted far out over the sea. Malaga is burning down.

'But what has happened?' we kept asking and no one could tell us. Lorries full of armed workmen began to appear, rushing down the road. As they passed they threw up their left arms in the Popular Front salute, the clenched left fist and bent arm. With the pistols in their right hands, loaded and cocked and ready to go off, they waved to us gaily.

'Someone will get killed soon,' said Enrique sardonically, 'and it won't be a Fascist, but one of us if we don't stay indoors.'

No Spanish town was to be saved the trauma of civil war. Granada became the setting for an early and bloody battle between opposing factions. The Civil Governor was urged by the Republican government in Madrid to resist the military rising. Among those in the town at the time was Helen Nicholson, Baroness Zglinitski. Her daughter Asta, with whom she was staying, was married to a Spaniard and lived in a house situated on the Alhambra hill. In the garden were magnolia trees and in July 'the air was heavy with the perfume of the great white waxen blossoms'.

This idyll was wrecked when the working-class quarter of the Albaicin, directly beneath the Alhambra, became the scene of bloody street fighting with innumerable casualties as troops loyal to Franco moved in to crush the popular resistance. Nicholson watched from a distance, her worry being that 'all of us who are not communist might be massacred at any moment'. In her memoirs, *Death in the Morning*, she records:

> . . . I was conscious of the unnatural stillness that hung over the Alhambra. It was about six o'clock, and ordinarily at that hour there were abundant sounds of life from the road and from an open-air café near-by – guitar music, snatches of song, women's laughter, children's cries and men's deeper voices. But now that our dogs, Nita and Teddy, had ceased barking, there was utter silence. It was so abnormal that I felt uneasy. And at that moment I heard the sharp crack of rifle shots, from the Plaza Nueva . . .
>
> The shots lasted only a few moments, and Kathleen, my English maid, coming in with my tea on a tray, declared that she had heard nothing. Downstairs in the kitchen, she explained, with the Spanish servants all chattering together, and the fountain in the patio making so much noise, it was hard to hear anything else. While she arranged the tea-things on a table, I walked up and down my bedroom and the sitting-room adjoining it, and those were among the worst moments I have ever spent.

It was in Granada that the civil war claimed perhaps its most memorable literary victim, the great contemporary Spanish poet, Federico García Lorca. His execution by forces loyal to General Franco in August 1936 is described by Ian Gibson in his biography of the poet.

He and the three other condemned men were taken, before sunrise, further along the road to Alfacar. There was no moon – Federico, lunar poet that he was, did not have even that consolation. The lorry stopped not far from the famous spring known as the Fuente Grande, or 'Big Fountain' . . . It seems appropriate that the Fuente Grande, sung of by the Islamic poets of Granada, should continue to bubble up its clear waters close to the last resting place of the greatest poet ever born in this part of Spain. For it was here, just before reaching the pool, that the killers shot their victims, leaving their bodies beside an olive grove on the right side of the road coming from Viznar. A few moments later the gravedigger arrived, a young communist called Manuel Castilla Blanco whom Captain Nestares was protecting. The lad immediately recognized the bullfighters, noticed not without surprise that another of the victims had a wooden leg, and observed that the last one wore a loose tie, 'you know, the sort artists wear'. He buried them in a narrow trench, on top of each other, beside an olive tree. When he returned to the 'Colonia', they told him that the man with the wooden leg was a schoolteacher from a nearby village, and that the one with the loose tie was the poet Federico Garcia Lorca.

The Republican government failed to oppose the military rising with constitutional means. The bulk of the forces of law and order joined the Francoiste side, and an attempt to use loyal members of the navy to mount a counter-offensive proved short-lived. In towns were there were no garrisons loyal to Franco, trade unionists and left-wing activists took the law into their own hands and opted for revolution. Hugh Thomas in his masterly book *The Spanish Civil War* described the climate of political turmoil that gripped Spain.

So now there was to spread over Spain a cloud of violence, in which the quarrels of several generations would find outlet. With communications difficult or non-existent, each town would find itself on its own, acting out its own drama, apparently in a vacuum. There were soon to be not two Spains, but two thousand. The geographical differences within Spain were a prime factor in the social disintegration of the nation. Regional feeling had sown the wind, and now reaped the whirlwind. Sovereign power ceased to exist and, in its absence, individuals, as well as towns, acted without constraint, as if they were outside society and history. Within a month, thousands of people would have perished arbitrarily and without trial. Bishops would be murdered and churches profaned. Educated Christians would spend their evenings murdering illiterate peasants and professional men of sensitivity. These events inevitably caused such hatreds that, when order was eventually established, it was an order geared solely for the rationalization of hatred known as war.

Arthur Koestler, the Anglo-Hungarian journalist, in *The Spanish Testament* blamed the violence of the Civil War partly on the Spanish character.

The Spaniards show an undeniable tendency towards cruelty; the celebrating of bull fights as national festivals is hardly an engaging trait in the character of the people. I am convinced that enough acts of brutality have been committed on both sides to satisfy Europe's demand for horrors for the next hundred years . . . The 'black-is-black' and 'white-is-white' technique of many propagandists of the Left – Fascist devils on the one hand, democratic angels on the other hand – is just as absurd as the 'red-and-white' technique of the rebel propagandists. The stories of the burning of churches in Barcelona and the villages of Andalucia are no fable; I have seen such churches with my own eyes. A good many of them served as hiding-places for rebels and priests armed with rifles. Others, however, did not, and were burned nevertheless. Let me repeat: only demagogues and abstract doctrinaires with no first-hand experience of the Civil War can deny that a great number of abominable acts have been committed on both sides.

Among Spanish writers, José María Gironella stands out for having attempted to portray objectively the events preceding the Civil War and its impact on Spanish society. In his novel

The Cypresses believe in God, Gironella focused on what he considered a constant of the Spanish character, a tendency toward the instinctive, the individualistic, the anarchic. 'Spaniards follow men,' he wrote in the Introduction, 'better than they follow ideas . . . this accounts for the inclemency of personal relationships, the small respect for laws; this too is what causes our periodic civil wars.'

It is the Spanish character thus defined, rather than any idea or political dogma, that informs this description by Gironella of the first executions in July 1936 in the town of Gerona. As in the rest of Catalonia, power here was retained for much of the Civil War by the left.

Thirty-six bodies were dragged from their houses and driven to the cemetery. Some died in terror, others bravely – Roca and Haro shouting: *'Arriba España!'* Benito Civil calling his wife's name; the three doctors with utter amazement painted on their faces; the priest of San Felix wanting to forgive his enemies, but without achieving it; the lawyer of the *Espasa Encyclopedia* begging them on his knees to spare his life; Padilla taking leave of his wife with these words: 'See that the little one lets her braids grow out again'; Rodriguez saying to the militiamen: 'But Spain will win, don't make any mistake'; the assistant manager firmly convinced that his death had been decreed by the Lodge of the Calle del Pavo.

Half of the city learned during the night what was going on. The neighbours of those who were taken from their homes; those who peered fearfully out of windows when they heard the cars stop; those who heard the screams of the victims on the stairs; those who sensed something strange and menacing in the slamming of the doors; those who without stirring from bed recognized in the steps on the sidewalk something hard and belligerent from which there was no appeal. The other half knew nothing. They assumed that the searches were going on, that the militiamen were getting drunk on the pleasure of driving a Fiat or a Cadillac, and that women were mixed up in the business.

Most of the militiamen were amazed to see how easy

it was to kill a man or five men. One had only to think of the word 'fascist', take aim at the heart or the head, and fire – and that was all there was to it.

Just across the waters of the Mediterranean on the Balearic Islands, it was the Nationalists who imposed control from an early stage. Their particular brand of terror, repeated in many parts of the mainland, was recorded by the French Catholic writer Georges Bernanos in *Les Grands Cimetières sous la Lune*. At first Bernanos was sympathetic to the Nationalist cause. He was staying at the time in the home of a leading local Falangist and believed that the rebellious generals would assure the moral and religious unity of the country. But Bernanos became increasingly horrified with the summary executions carried out on left-wing sympathisers with the complicity on many occasions of priests and bishops.

> I have seen – I've seen with my own eyes, I tell you – a small Christian people, with peaceful traditions, extremely, almost absurdly friendly – I've seen them suddenly turned to stone, seen their faces hardening, even their children's faces . . . For months, in Mallorca, killer-gangs, swiftly transported from village to village in lorries requisitioned for the purpose, shot down in cold blood for everybody to see, thousands of persons who were held to be suspect, but against whom the military tribunal itself could not produce the faintest legal allegation . . .
>
> When the job was finished, the Crusaders piled their cattle in two heaps – those who'd been given absolution and those who hadn't – then sprinkled petrol over them, which they call gasolene over here. It is quite likely that this Purification by Fire may then have taken on, by reason of the presence of the priests officiating, a liturgical significance. Unfortunately I only saw these blackened, shiny creatures two days after that, contorted by the flames, some of them counterfeiting obscene poses in death, which must have been very distressing for the ladies of Palma and for their eminent confessors. A reeking tar oozed out of them, and smoked there in the August sunshine.

Few wars in modern times have stirred political conscience and fired literary imagination as much as the Spanish Civil War. Spain in the period 1936–9 became not so much a country at war with itself as a stage on which a wider ideological and religious struggle was played out by men of many nationalities. The poet, Miguel Hernández, was a shepherd who joined the Communist Fifth Regiment militia and defended Madrid from strongholds in the surrounding sierras against attacks by land and air from the Francoiste forces. He drew his images of freedom from the fighters of Spain, as in this, one of his most famous verses, 'The Winds of the People':

> The winds of the people sustain me,
> Spreading within my heart.
> The winds of the people impel me,
> And roar in my very throat . . .
> I come not from a people of oxen,
> My people praise
> The lion's leap,
> The eagle's straight swoop,
> And the strong charge of the bull
> Whose pride is in his horns.

The American socialist John Dos Passos was in Madrid as the city, under Republican control, withstood the most prolonged siege of the Civil War. In *Journeys Between Wars* he gives this account of how the capital, defended by troops which included foreign volunteers of the International Brigade, was transformed by 1937:

There are trenches made with sandbags in the big recently finished Plaza de España. The huge straggling bronze statue of Don Quixote and Sancho Panza look out oddly towards the enemy position in Carabanchel. At a barracks building on the corner a bunch from the International Brigade is waiting for chow. French faces, Belgium faces, North of Italy faces, German exiles, bearded men blackened by the sun, young boys; a feeling of energy and desperation comes from them. The dictators have stolen their world from them; they have lost their homes, their families, their hopes of a living or a career; they are fighting back.

Up another little hill is the burned shell of the Montana Barracks where the people of Madrid crushed the military revolt last July. Then we're looking down the broad rimmed street of the Paseo de los Resales. It used to be one of the pleasantest places in Madrid to live because the four- and five-storey apartment houses overlooked the valley of the Manzanares and the green trees of the old royal parks and domains. Now its no man's land. The lines cross the valley below, but if you step out on the paseo you're in the full view of the enemy on the hills opposite, and the Moors [Spanish Moroccans] are uncommonly good riflemen.

For many non-Spaniards it became difficult in the late 1930s not to see the involvement of foreign powers in the Spanish Civil War – Germany and Italy on the side of Franco, and the Soviet Union on the Republican side – as prelude to a worldwide conflict. W.H. Auden expressed the urgency in the call to active participation in the Spanish Civil War in his poem 'Spain'.

Many have heard it on remote peninsulas.
On sleepy plains, in the aberrant fishermen's islands
Or the corrupt heart of a city
Have heard and migrated like gulls or the seeds of a flower.

They clung like burrs to the long expresses that lurch
Through the unjust lands, through the night, through
    the alpine tunnel;
They floated over the oceans;
They walked the passes. All presented their lives.

On that arid square, that fragment nipped off from hot
Africa, soldered so crudely to inventive Europe;
On that tableland scored by rivers,
Our thoughts have bodies; the menacing shapes of our
    fever

Are precise and alive. For the fears which made us respond
To the medicine ad. and the brochure of winter cruises
Have become invading batallions;
And our faces, the institute-face, the chain-store, the ruin

Are projecting their greed as the firing squad and the
    bomb.

Madrid is the heart. Our moments of tenderness blossom
As the ambulance and the sandbag;
Our hours of friendship into a people's army.

There were many for whom the Spanish Civil War provoked
the resolution which Auden hoped for in serious literature: it
made 'action and its nature clear.' In the nineteenth century,
European writers who crossed the Pyrenees into Spain had done
so looking for the exotic and the picturesque. The young
travellers of the 1930s who crossed over the mountains into
Spain during the Civil War were romantics too. Yet their
journey was made in a spirit of sacrifice and solidarity. It sprang
from a deliberate if Utopian choice to help further the lot not
just of ordinary Spaniards but of mankind generally even if it
meant dying for it.

Laurie Lee left Spain in 1936 after being caught in the outbreak of war while travelling round the country as an amateur
minstral. In *As I Walked Out One Midsummer's Morning* he
signals with sadness his departure from the 'great gold plains,
the arid and mystical distances, where the sun rose up like a
butcher each morning and left curtains of blood each night'.
But by the end of 1937 he was back in Spain to join the
International Brigades. Lee's later disillusionment with the war
'of antique muskets and jamming machine guns' was to prove
more conclusive than his commitment.

The turning point for Laurie Lee, and for many others, came
at Teruel. The walled capital of Aragon's south-eastern province is set among steppe-like plains cut by jagged ravines
which in winter record the coldest temperatures in Spain. Lee,
fighting alongside the militias with the International Brigades,
was among those who survived the bloody battle of Teruel.
It lasted all winter. For Franco the capture of Teruel became
a matter of military honour. Lee was at the receiving end of
the Nationalist counter-offensive, an experience he describes in
A Moment of War.

> . . . in the morning they came. A long burst of shellfire
> straddled over us just before daylight, followed by the
> rattling metal of tanks and their sharp coughing guns, and
> the swooping buzz of Italian aircraft above. The main
> attack of the armour was up ahead of us, even so we were

briefly overrun; our machine-gun blew up, and we pulled
back down the gully, scrambling and falling over the ice.
First I remember a running close-up of the enemy – small,
panting little men, red-faced boys, frantically spitting
Moors. There was the sudden bungled confrontation, the
breathless hand-to-hand, the awkward pushing, jabbing,
grunting, swearing, death a moment's weakness or slip of
the foot away. Then we broke and raced off, each man
going alone, each the gasping centre of his own survival.
I headed for the old barn where I'd spent my first night.
I lay in a state of sick paralysis. I had killed a man, and
remembered his shocked, angry eyes. There was nothing
I could say to him now. Tanks rattled by and cries
receded. I began to have hallucinations and breaks in the
brain. I lay there knowing neither time nor place. Some
of our men found me, I don't know who they were, and
they drove me back speechless to Tarazona.

Was this then what I'd come for, and all my journey
had meant – to smudge out the life of an unknown young
man in a blur of panic which in no way could affect victory or defeat?

Lee ended the Civil War in a cell, rejected by the very people
he had come to fight alongside. His experience of the conflict
is one in which heroes did not exist and where more often than
not Spaniards and foreigners alike became corrupted and ideals
were gradually lost.

In every war, the first casualty is truth. Much of what was
written at the time was crude propaganda couched in literary
pretence. But the war was also a source of inspiration. The poet
Stephen Spender spent his first days in Spain as a propagandist,
broadcasting on behalf of the Republican cause in Valencia. But
the requirement to project a political message was disarmed by
a poetic sensibility repelled by history and its abstractions. In
an essay published just after his return from Spain in the summer of 1937, Spender criticized the 'propagandist lie which
makes the dead into heroes in order that others may imagine
that death is really quite pleasant.' The need of war writing was
to tell one essential truth, that 'for most of those who participate in it, a war is simply a short way to a beastly death.'

Spender's recollection of the Spanish Civil War as an event in which one million people lost their lives in a mess of money, arms, and ideology is aptly summed up in his poem 'Ultimo Ratio Regnum'.

> The guns spell money's ultimate reason
> In letters of lead on the spring hillside.
> But the boy lying dead under the olive trees
> Was too young and too silly
> To have been notable to their important eye.
> He was a better target for a kiss.

By the end of 1936 there was growing enthusiasm among the European left for the libertarian atmosphere of the anarchist occupation of Barcelona. Gustav Regler gave this account in his autobiography, *The Owl of Minerva*:

Only on this occasion have I known that sense of free-dom, a feeling of unconditional escape, of readiness for absolute change; it was the daydream of a whole people. Everything was in readiness for the unexpected, and the unexpected happened . . . There was a spirit of intoxica-tion in the people, an infectious eagerness for sacrifice, a hot-blooded unreason and fanatical belief in freedom, which could never lead to the constitution of an orderly State on an earlier pattern. To judge by their outward aspect, the militiamen might have been pushed out into the streets by the French Revolution, and no doubt many of the acts of violence of the first days of the war had been prompted by unconscious imitations . . . Anarchist doctrines were far more widespread than one would have ever supposed. They loved to see flags waving, and they built barricades which obstructed traffic more than they served the revolution. They drove in requisitioned Cadillacs up and down the Gran Via with sashes round their waists and Phrygian caps on their heads. No one knew whether the war was going well or ill.

George Orwell's sympathies for the international struggle of the working class had been strengthened by his experience down British coal mines. His decision to go to Catalonia in 1936 sprung from a desire to fight rather than write. After arriving in Barcelona, Orwell joined a POUM column on the Aragon front where he was wounded in battle and from where he eventually returned to England in June 1937. The Spanish Civil War was for him essentially a class conflict, part of a much wider international struggle. 'If it had been won,' he wrote, 'the cause of the common people everywhere would have been strengthened. It was lost, and the dividend-drawers all over the world rubbed their hands.' He never regretted having been a part of it. 'Curiously enough the whole experience has left me with not less but more belief in the decency of human beings.'

Orwell recognized early on that the crusade was also a cheat and a delusion; and because he reported the war without omissions, his work was turned down by left-wing publishers. There were times when Orwell, in the best tradition of Wellington and Ford, could be particularly blatant about the very people he came to fight alongside.

> The Spaniards are good at many things but not at making war. All foreigners alike are appalled by their inefficiency, above all their maddening unpunctuality. The one Spanish word that no foreigner can avoid learing is *mañana* – 'tomorrow' (literally, 'the morning'). Whenever it is conceivably possible, the business of today is put off until *mañana*. This is so notorious that even the Spaniards themselves make jokes about it. In Spain nothing, from a meal to a battle, ever happens at the appointed time.

Occasionally a sense of innocence filters through the harsh realities of Civil War writing. In *The Spanish Cockpit* Franz Borkenhau, the Austrian sociologist, travels by train from Valencia to Madrid. It is August 1937, and there is much killing yet to be done. He first meets a group of anarchists.

> They were on an errand of their organization. I travelled third class while they were going first class, on free tickets procured by the anarchist organization. We had a meal together in the dining-car, and then they invited me to their first-class compartment. I could not help remarking on the change in their station in life, but they only laughed about my criticism of their becoming 'bourgeois'.

After all, the change had not gone very far yet. Although they sit in a first-class compartment, they still wear their working men's suits, and one of them had brought his rifle with him and put it into a luggage rack. Opposite sat a couple very different from my companions, obviously not travelling on a free ticket; they were probably well-to-do Valencia shopkeepers, and the woman was scared to death by his handling of the rifle, though there was actually not the slightest danger. When he noticed her nervousness, he boyishly began to demonstrate the handling of the rifle; as he loaded and unloaded it, the couple on the opposite bench became more and more desperate. But there was no real enmity between the two camps, the old and the new upper class, which here met in such a queer and amusing way.

Robert Jordan, the hero of Ernest Hemingway's Civil War novel, *For Whom the Bell Tolls*, is on the side of the Republicans, yet the experience of war dents his uncompromising loyalty, as it did his creator's. He becomes critical of the corruption of Soviet officers and of executioners attached to the International Brigades. He also considers that the Spaniards, for all their bravery, betray themselves, through what he sees as insubordinate individualism, petty feuding, and treachery. 'There is no finer and no worse people in the world. No kinder people and no crueller,' reflects Jordan after witnessing acts of heroism and brutality committed by both sides.

Hemingway first sailed to Spain in February 1937 to report the war for the North American Newspaper Alliance chain. It was the first of several assignments, each of which coincided with crucial stages of the war. Soon after he arrived he witnessed the euphoria of Republican troops after an early victory over the Italians in Brihuega near Alicante. He described the Italian dead in a dispatch for NANA in March 1937.

The hot weather makes all dead look alike, but these Italian dead lay with waxy faces in the cold rain looking very small and pitiful. They did not look like men, but where a shell burst had caught three of them, the remains took on the shape of curiously broken toys.

Hemingway subsequently instructed members of the International Brigades stationed outside Madrid in weapon drill and made frequent visits to the line during the spring of 1937 at a time when the Republican military defences seemed to be holding.

The main characters that surround Jordan in *For Whom the Bell Tolls*, set in the summer of 1937, are a group of Republican guerrilla fighters. Their area of operation is behind the Franco lines in the Guadarrama hills north-west of Madrid. Many aspects of Hemingway's attitude to the Civil War are encapsulated in the action which takes place during the four days which the novel spans. The last stand of the guerrilla leader El Sordo depicts the quintessential pride and fearlessness in the face of death which Hemingway admired as much in soldiers as in bullfighters, and which is founded in his own romantic view of Spain.

> Dying was nothing and he had no picture of it nor fear of it in his mind. But living was a field of grain blowing in the wind on the side of a hill. Living was a hawk in the sky. Living was an unearthen jar of water in the dust of the threshing with the grain flailed out and the chaff blowing. Living was a horse between your legs and a carbine under one leg and a hill and a valley and a stream with trees along it and the far side of the valley and the hills beyond.
>
> Sordo passed the wine bottle back and nodded his head in thanks. He leaned forward and patted the dead horse on the shoulder where the muzzle of the automatic rifle had burned the hide. He could smell burnt hair. He thought how he had held the horse there, trembling, with the fire around them, whispering and cracking, over and around them like a curtain, and had carefully shot him just at the intersection of the crossline between the two eyes and the ears. Then as the horse pitched down he had dropped down behind his warm, wet back to get the gun going as they came up the hill.
>
> '*Eres mucho caballo*,' he said meaning, 'Thou wert plenty of horse.'

Sordo is finished off by aerial bombardment led by German

planes; he is then decapitated by a Nationalist lieutenant who wears the Sacred Heart on his left lapel. The landscape has not changed much since Hemingway's time. More than fifty years after the end of the Civil War, it is still possible to retrace Robert Jordan's footsteps in the pine forests of the Guadarrama hills, beyond the pass of Navacerrada some forty miles north of Madrid, on the main road to Segovia. It is not far from the Basilica of the Valley of the Fallen built by Republican prisoners for the victorious General Franco.

The historian Hugh Thomas has noted that Spain may have put the experience behind her, but she didn't forget it completely. 'The Spanish Civil War was the Spanish share in the tragic European breakdown of the twentieth century, and the sense of optimism, which had lasted since the Renaissance, was shattered.'

While the Civil War lasted, thousands of men from all over the world voluntarily sacrificed themselves in a conflict that did not directly concern them. In the aftermath of war, the survivors looked back. Some of them wondered whether it had all been worth it. Cyril Connolly had reported on the 'extraordinary mixture of patriotic war-fever and revolutionary faith' that engulfed Spaniards at war. In a retrospective published as part of the collection, *The English Colonnade*, he recalled:

> It was in Spain, as a matter of fact, that I first came across really frightened people: bourgeois trembling for their lives, men whose hands shook, a group of mercenary pilots in a Barcelona hotel drinking before taking up their obsolete planes in doomed missions . . . The war correspondents wandered with charm lives through the blacked-out city while the anarchist cars tore through the Ramblas to pick up suspects and bear them off to the lonely execution grounds. Civil war . . . brother against brother, the most deeply satisfactory of all explosions of aggression.

12

BLOODY PASTIMES

Bullfighting

In 1650, a 'spectacle very wonderful' was described by Edward Hyde, the Earl of Clarendon. This former British ambassador – he served under Charles I – attended a bull-fight staged in Madrid's Plaza Mayor, temporarily converted into a bullring. Clarendon described how aristocrats on horseback practised their military skills by lancing the bull, and how their plebeian footmen, 'nimble fellows', performed feats after their masters. The English royalist was less shocked than impressed by the deep-seated popularity of the spectacle.

> Then one of the four gates which lead into the streets is opened, at which the toreadores enter, all persons of quality richly clad, and upon the best horses in Spain, every one attended by eight or ten more lackeys, all clinkant with gold and silver, who carry the spears which their masters are to use against the bulls; and with this entry pay very dear. The persons on horseback have all cloaks folded up upon their left shoulder, the least disorder of which, much more the letting it fall, is a very great disgrace; and in that grave order they march to the place where the King sits, and after they have made their reverences, they place themselves at a good distance from one another, and expect the bull . . . When the bull enters, the common people, who sit over the door or near it, strike him, or throw darts with sharp points of steel

to provoke him to rage. He commonly runs with all his fury against the first man he sees on horseback, who watches him so carefully, and avoids him so dexterously, that when the spectators believe him to be even between the horns of the bull, he avoids by the quick turn of his horse, and with his lance strikes the bull upon a vein that runs through his poll, which in a moment falls down dead . . . Sometimes the bull runs with so much fierceness (for if he scapes the first man, he runs upon the rest as they are in his way) that he gores the horse with his horns that his guts come out, and he falls before the rider can get from his back. Sometimes by the strength of his neck he raises horse and man from the ground, and throws both down, and then the greatest danger is another gore upon the ground. In any of these disgraces, or any other by which the rider comes to be dismounted, he is obliged in honour to take his revenge upon the bull by his sword, and upon his head, towards which the standers-by assist him by running after the bull and hocking him, by which he falls upon his hinder legs; but before that execution can be done, a good bull hath his revenge upon many poor fellows. Sometimes he is so unruly that nobody dares to attack him, and then the King calls for the mastives, whereof two are let out at a time, and if they cannot master him, but are themselves killed, as frequently they are, the King then, as the last refuge, calls for the English mastives; of which they seldom turn out above one at a time; and he rarely misses taking the bull and holding him by the nose till the men run it; and after they have hocked him, they quickly kill him.

Clarendon's journal has sometimes been described as the first description of a *corrida* in English. In fact, an earlier account still was produced by a Welshman, James Howell, who in 1622 was in Madrid negotiating the release of a captured vessel. Howell was not impressed by the Count of Olivares, the king's adviser, still less so by the bullfight he observed in honour of Prince Charles and the Duke of Buckingham. The blood and guts, however, gave him a tale on which to hang a papal pun.

Commonly there are men killed at it, therefore there are
priests appointed to be there ready to confess them. It
hath happened that a Bull hath taken up two men upon
his horns with their guts dangling about them. The
horsemen run with lances and swords, the foot with
goads. As I am told, the Pope hath sent divers Bulls
against the sport of Bulling, yet it will not be left, the
Nation hath taken such an habitual delight in it.

Another royal bullfight was witnessed in the Plaza Mayor by
the Reverend Edward Clark in July 1760. The Anglican cleric
watched a horse run across the square with its entrails hanging
out. At one point a goat skin was inflated to look like a human
body and placed teasingly in front of the bull. But there were
also men on foot who swirled their capes or pricked the bull
with *banderillas* in what Clark judged acts of skill and bravery.
He considered the bullfight one of the finest spectacles in the
world.

I do not deny that the *corrida* will not bear the speculations
of the closest or the compassionate feelings of a tender
heart. But after all one must not speculate too nicely lest
we should lose the hardness of manhood in the softer
sentiments of philosophy.

On 11 October 1833, the Marquess of Londonderry, while
on a tour of Spain, attended his first and last bullfight in Seville.
By then bullfighting was no longer the preserve of aristocrats,
but had been taken over by the lower classes as a fight on foot.
The aristocracy was still represented but only, as befitted a
class in decline, by the mocking antics of the picador, a
resurgent Don Quixote seated on a nag. The Marquess noted
that while there was a large representation of the lower classes
assembled, there was very little if any quarrelling or drunk-
enness. 'It is the character of the people,' he noted, 'to amuse
themselves with innocent pastimes rather than vice and
rioting.'
Before the bullfight proper was the *encierro*, the running of
the bulls through the city streets and into the bullring where
for a few minutes every amateur could try his luck amidst a
general air of mockery and chaos. There was much cheering

and screaming, and oranges and handkerchiefs showered down on the arena from all sides. Several novices were tossed high in the air as a 'punishment for their awkwardness and temerity.' Then the 'medley of mischief and confusion' gave way to the regular event, as only one bull was left in the ring to fight to the death.

> . . . Though the spectacle as at present is sufficiently revolting, it has, according to competent authority, lost, in the course of time, and in the confusion and distresses of the whole country, very much of the splendours that formerly rendered the bull-fight of Spain so celebrated in other lands as well as in its own. When the flower of chivalry of the proudest nation in the world descended into the arena, and the highest names of Spain sought distinction and renown by their exploits in the circus, the barbarity of the amusement was in great degree veiled from the eye, or compensated by the extreme magnificence of the appointments, and often by the real dangers attendant on the scene. But now that the whole has sunk into a mere exhibition of hired combatants, men of a very low caste in society, instead of the chiefs and heroes of former days, and that the noble war-steed of olden time have given way to the wretched and miserable hacks that alone are now brought forward, the harness and trappings of the horses, and the decorations of the picadors, matadors, and banderilleros – in short, the whole display being deteriorated to a mere paltry show, the spectacle is anything but ennobling, and affords no better idea of the former glories that illustrated it, than the processions and tinsel glitter of a booth at the fair gives of a royal pageant in its reality.

The Marquess concluded that bullfighting, far from being considered an 'exhibition of festivity and gratification', should be 'banished for ever from the eyes of a civilised nation.'

During a six-month tour of Spain in 1818, George Ticknor was so shocked by the sight of his first *corrida* that he fainted and had to be carried out of the bullring by an attendant guard. But curiosity got the better of him and he returned to watch the spectacle a second time, this time with the intention of analysing what the bullfight had to say about the Spaniards themselves. He concluded that the *corrida* was a useful safety valve for a people prone to individualistic acts of defiance and violence. 'The masses', he noted, 'feel their own strength. They enter into the rights of their own importance and power. Their exclamations often seem revolutionary.' When one bull refused to show his bravery by charging at the picador, the crowd shouted that the animal was as cowardly as the King of Spain.

In the *corrida*, it is the bullfighter as much as the bull that is there to be abused and praised in turn. To the *aficionado*, man and beast form part of an inseparable whole; for some they perform a ceremony of pagan values; for others a tragedy in three acts. And while the case against bullfighting has always seemed essentially straightforward – a natural reaction of the usually non-Spanish mind to bloodshed and cruelty – the case for it has always seemed more complex, having to do with culture, psychology, and even religion.

In his novel *Fiesta*, Ernest Hemingway describes the ease with which the bullfighting crowd can switch from adulation to fanatical condemnation. Here the bullfighter in the firing line is Juan Belmonte, among the most famous of Spain's twentieth-century bullfighters whose legendary reputation raised expectations as easily as it crushed them.

Belmonte, in his best days, worked always in the terrain of the bull. This way he gave the sensation of coming tragedy. People went to the *corrida* to see Belmonte, to be given tragic sensations, and perhaps to see the death of Belmonte. Fifteen years ago they said if you wanted to see Belmonte you should go quickly, while he was still alive. Since then he has killed more than a thousand bulls. When he retired they knew how his bullfighting had been, and when he came out of retirement the public were disappointed because no real man could work as close to the bulls as Belmonte was supposed to have done, not, of course, even Belmonte.

Also, Belmonte imposed conditions and insisted that his bulls should not be too large, nor too dangerously armed with horns, and so the element that was necessary to give the sensation of tragedy was not there, and the public, who wanted three times as much from Belmonte, who was sick with a fistula, as Belmonte had ever been able to give, felt defrauded and cheated, and Belmonte's jaw came further out in contempt, and his face turned yellower, and he moved with great difficulty as his pain increased, and finally the crowd were actively against him, and he was utterly contemptuous and indifferent. He had meant to have a great afternoon, and instead it was an afternoon of sneers, shouted insults, and finally a volley of cushions and pieces of bread and vegetables, thrown down at him in the plaza where he had the greatest triumphs.

On the subject of bullfighting, Hemingway was more successful than most writers in setting aside his own cultural prejudices and getting inside the feelings of the crowd. He appreciated bullfighting as an art form, but most of all he touched on that elemental tension which gives the *corrida* its fatal attraction: the delicate balance between life and death, and the power of the crowd to make or break a bullfighter. In his autobiography, Belmonte describes the fate that befell his great rival Joselito the day after both bullfighters narrowly escaped a lynching from the Madrid crowd. They had been accused of eliminating the risk and getting rich with impunity. Shaken by the experience, Belmonte decided to stay at home and play cards rather than make another appearance. Joselito broke his contract and performed in a smaller bullring in Talavera de la Reina. He was gored to death while going in for the kill.

According to Belmonte, Joselito's death had an inevitability which can only really be understood in terms of the Spanish attitude to fate. Spaniards defy death, but fear it too.

Upon Joselito's death the bullfighting public experienced a curious sense of collective remorse. Then I was able to observe that suddenly an exaggerated fear and a most zealous concern for the bullfighter's life had been awakened in the audience. For some time there was a strange nervous strain in the bullrings. The public was more afraid than the bullfighter. Every time, during the performance, that the latter faced a dangerous or unexpected onslaught of the beast, an anxious 'ah' from the crowd put the bullfighter on his guard. It seemed as if those men who had the day before the tragedy at Talavera attacked us madly, asking us to let us be killed, or almost killed, now considered themselves guilty of that mishap and their remorse compelled them to avoid a repetition.

The popularity of bullfighting is to be found in the risk as much as the spectacle. Spaniards go to the bullring not just to watch a bull being killed but also to accompany a bullfighter to the brink. It is when the goring takes place that the bloodlust turns to collective panic as the following passage from Vicente Blasco Ibañez's novel *Blood and Sand* shows. In it, the bullfighter Gallardo tries to win back the favour of a hostile crowd by killing the bull in a manner that exposes him to maximum danger.

He placed himself opposite the animal, who seemed to be waiting for him, steady on his legs. He thought it useless to make any more passes with the *muleta*. So he placed himself 'in profile' with the red cloth hanging on the ground, and the rapier horizontal at the height of his eye. Now to thrust in his arm! With a sudden impulse the audience rose to their feet, for a few seconds the man and the bull formed one single mass, and so moved on some steps. The connoisseurs were already waving their hands anxious to applaud. He had thrown himself in to kill as on the best day. That was a 'true' *estocada*. But suddenly the man was thrown out from between the horns by a crushing blow, and rolled on the sand. The bull lowered his head, picking up the inert body, lifting it for an instant on his horns to let it fall again, then rushing on his mad career with the rapier plunged up to the hilt in his neck. Gallardo rose slowly, the whole Plaza burst out into uproarious, deafening applause, anxious to repair their injustice. *Olé* for the man! Well done the lad from Seville! He had been splendid!

But the *torero* did not acknowledge these outbursts of enthusiasm. He raised his hand to his stomach, crouching in a painful curve, and with the head bent began to walk forward with uncertain steps. Twice he raised his head as if he were looking for the exit and fearing not to be able to find it, finally staggering like a drunken man, and falling flat on the sand.

Four of the Plaza servants raised him slowly on their shoulders, El Nacional joining the group, to support the *espada's* pale livid head, with its glassy eyes just showing through the long lashes. The audience started with surprise, and their plaudits ceased suddenly. They looked around at each other unable to make up their minds as to the gravity of the accident . . . Soon optimistic news circulated, but no one knew from where it came . . . It was nothing, only a tremendous blow to the stomach which had deprived him of consciousness, but no one had seen any blood. The populace, suddenly tranquilized, sat down, turning their attention from the wounded *torero* to the bull, who, though in the agonies of death, still remained firm on his feet.

El Nacional helped to place his master on a bed in the infirmary. He fell on it like a sack, inanimate, his arms hanging over either side of the bed. Sebastian, who had so often seen the *espada* bleeding and wounded, without ever losing his calm, now felt the agony of fear, seeing him lifeless, with his face of a greenish whiteness as if he were already dead. 'By the life of the blue dove!' he groaned. 'Are there no doctors? Is there no help anywhere?'

At times like these it would seem that the Spaniards have succumbed to bloodlust and descended into a kind of collective insanity. Why, one wonders, do they allow such pointless sacrifice for the sake of a sport? André Gide could see no possible justification as this brief judgement on bullfighting in his 1893 journal makes clear.

> To kill someone because he is angry is alright; but to anger someone in order to kill him is absolutely criminal. The bull is killed in a state of mortal sin. He has been forced into that state. He himself only wanted to graze.

One of the more prolific Spanish writers on the bullfight, Eugenio Noel, wrote in a newspaper article published in 1914 that the national 'sport' was both a symptom and a cause of all that was wrong with Spain.

From the bullring we get the following characteristics of
our race: the majority of crimes committed with a knife;
the *chulo* [lower class inhabitant of Madrid]; the man who
puts the personal impression he creates above any other
moral consideration . . . the cruelty of our feelings, the
desire to make war; our ridiculous Don Juanism . . .

The truth is that bullfighting has never been considered a
sport by those who participate in it, nor does it suit illumina-
tion by rational analysis. Rather it is, in the words of Timothy
Mitchell, author of a study on bullfighting, 'built on the
volatile terrain of passion and subject to the blind workings of
chance.' Those who have got to grips with bullfighting are
those who have managed to set aside their own pre-judge-
ments and instead immersed themselves in the feelings of the
crowds. Ford, like other Hispanists, believed bullfighting to
be deeply engrained and capable of being properly understood
only on Spanish terms. He wrote in *Gatherings from Spain*:

It is poor and illogical philosophy to judge of foreign
customs by our own habits, prejudices, and conventional
opinions; a cold, unprepared, calculating stranger comes
with the freemasonry of earlier associations, and criticises
minutiae . . . They have heard the bullfight not praised
from their childhood, but condemned; they see it for the
first time when grown up; curiosity is perhaps a feature
in sharing an amusement of which they have an indistinct
idea that pleasure will be mixed with pain. The first sight
delights them; a flushed, excited cheek betrays a feeling
that they are almost ashamed to avow; but as the bloody
tragedy proceeds, they get frightened, disgusted, and
disappointed. Few are able to sit out more than one
course, and fewer ever re-enter the amphitheatre.

In *Death in the Afternoon*, Hemingway describes how the
Spanish attitude to bullfighting is inextricably linked to
geography and culture, and thus to a deep sense of regional
identity.

In Castilla the peasant has nothing of the simple-
mindedness, combined as always with cunning, of the
Catalan or Gallego. He lives in a country with as severe

a climate as any that is farmed, but it is a very healthy country; he has food, wine, his wife and children, or he has had them, but he has no comfort, nor much capital and these possessions are not ends in themselves; they are only a part of life and life is something that comes before death . . . The people of Castilla have great common sense . . . they know death is the inescapable reality, the one thing of which any man may be sure; the only security; that it transcends all modern comforts and that with it you do not need a bathtub in every American home, nor, when you have it, do you need a radio. They think a great deal about death and when they have a religion they have one which believes that life is much shorter than death. Having this feeling they take an intelligent interest in death and when they can see it being given, avoided, refused and accepted in the afternoon for a nominal price of admission they pay their money and go to the bullring, continuing to go even when, for certain reasons that I have tried to show in this book, they are most often artistically disappointed and emotionally defrauded.

In the early 1950s Honor Tracy watched a bullfight during the fiesta of Algeciras, an experience she subsequently recorded in her book *Silk Hats and No Breakfast*. There were, in her view, bullfights so graceful and artful that the spectator could go away 'treading on air', in awe at the 'so magnificent, so needless display of human courage'. But this was a rarity. The majority of bullfights were 'affairs of humbug and attitude, a cautious butchery marked by bravura.' She went on:

At such times one is inclined to wonder if the whole institution is not merely another aspect of the Spaniards' endless preoccupation with their virility, as empty and tedious as the eternal prating of sexual competence and triumph. It soon became all too clear into which category this afternoon would fall. There was not a single clean kill: the picadors were inept and savage by even their own debased standards, arousing storm after storm of protesting whistles from the crowd: the matadors went slowly to pieces, as even the finest do when the

mysterious fates of the ring are against them, posturing
and strutting the more as their hearts failed. The people,
as ever, were merciless. A roar of derision went up as
Giron, after theatrically kissing the blade of his sword,
made a thrust that went wide of the mark. Scathing
advice was bawled at the unfortunate man from all parts
of the amphitheatre. A bull who gave one of them a nasty
bang with his horn, splitting the breeches from thigh to
knee, was cheered to the echo. In no other circumstances
are Spaniards quite so Spanish.

When Kate O'Brien travelled to Spain in 1936 the only
account she had read on the subject of bullfighting was a
description in D.H. Lawrence's *The Plumed Serpent*, a Mexican
affair steeped in Aztec mythology. *Death in the Afternoon* still
lay in her suitcase, unread. The first bullfight she watched,
accompanied by an English couple, was a *novillada* – where the
bulls are under five years old – in Santander. One of the
bullighters was a woman, Juanita de la Cruz.

It was a bad fight actually, though Juanita acquitted
herself very well and three of our party became very
feministic and worked up about her. But there was a lot
of silly nonsense and one young matador disgraced
himself. Difficult to believe from that afternoon's
experience that one would want to see another corrida.
Harry didn't. That was definite. He took a sportsman's
view of it, and by National Hunt Rules or what have you
he dismissed it as silly and brutal. I was interested and
perplexed from the word 'Go!' Ruth was quiet and, I
suspect, made uneasy, but her imagination surrendered, I
guess, while she held debate. Harry's wife was taken out
of herself, was excited and thrilled and amused too,
exactly as if she were a Spaniard. Wanted the explanation
of everything and cheered Juanita like mad.

O'Brien herself found the spectacle embarrassing, dis-
tressing, distasteful, but was ultimately seduced by it.

Bravery, grace and self-control; the cunning of cape and
sword against incalculable force; sunlight and the hover-
ing of death; comedies and tragedies of character; tinny

music timing an old and tricky ritual; crazy courage
and sickening failure and the serenity of great matadors
curving in peril among the monstrous horns. There is no
defence. Either it gets you, or you're sick.

Kenneth Tynan counted himself among those who bullfighting got. He was unable to reconcile the logical reasons
for loathing the bullfight with what he described as his
own obstinate awareness that it represented the summit of
human aspiration. The *aficionado* believes that the bull and the
bullfighter must be in harmony with each other if the tragedy
in three acts is not to descend into farce. Tynan, a dramatist,
was keenly aware of this as he followed another legendary
Spanish bullfighter, Antonio Ordoñez, to a *corrida* in Ronda.
The bullring there was among the first to be built in Spain. It
was erected in 1775 by the Real Maestranza de Caballeria
(Riding Club of Noblemen) as a place where the aristocrats
could keep themselves entertained and fit in times of peace.

Ordoñez was seen as the synthesis of two heroes of bullfighting's Golden Age, Belmonte and Joselito: the first could
do everything well, and the second could do a few things
unforgettably. On that hot August afternoon in 1971, Tynan
witnessed in Ordoñez the 'high definition performance' which
he looked for in authentic stars. He defined this as the ability
to communicate the essence of one's talent with economy,
grace, no apparent effort, and hard-edged clarity.

Pointless to list the passes. The fight unfolds in an atmosphere of intoxication, with Antonio the cool centre of
the tumult. As with all great displays in the ring, it's as
if bull and man were both drawing on the same profound source of energy – animal impulse compressed and
canalizèd into deliberate beauty. The cape slowly billow-
ing, the bull surging with it, never less and seldom more
than a foot from its folds; the whole making an image like
a great ship under sail. At this level bullfighting temporarily heals the rift, dissolves the tension, between
reason and instinct, intellect and passion. The animal, by
the end, is part of us. We no longer regard it as an alien
force, outrageous in its violence, at all costs to be vanquished. Beneath an apparent contradiction – the bull's

power versus the man's intelligence – we perceive a deeper harmony.

An equally important aspect of bullfighting culture is the running of and with the bulls in which an entire village or town takes part. Here bullfighting returns to its ancestral roots, predating the aristocratic horsemen by centuries. The bull is transformed into a community's totem. Hemingway in *The Dangerous Summer* described the most famous running of the bulls.

Pamplona is no place to bring your wife. The odds are all in favour of her getting ill, hurt or wounded or at least jostled and wine squirted over her, or of losing her; maybe all three. If anybody could do Pamplona successfully it would be Carmen and Antonio but Antonio would not bring her. It's a man's *fiesta* and women at it make trouble, never intentionally of course, but they nearly always make or have trouble. I wrote a book about this once. Of course if she can talk Spanish so she knows she is being joked with and not insulted, if she can drink wine all day and all night and dance with any groups of strangers who invite her, if she does not mind things being spilled on her, if she adores continual noise and music and loves fireworks, especially those that fall close to her or burn her clothes, if she thinks it is sound and logical to see how close you can come to being killed by bulls for fun and for free, if she doesn't catch cold when she is rained on and appreciates dust, likes disorder and irregular meals and never needs to sleep and still keeps clean and neat without running water; then bring her. You'll probably lose her to a better man than you.

13

PARALYTIC OF THE MOON

Flamenco

In June 1922 the dusty esplanade that fronts the Alhambra, the Plaza de los Aljibes, played host to the two-day festival of *cante jondo* – genuine flamenco – organized by, among others, Federico García Lorca and the composer Manuel de Falla. The aim of the festival, which was enthusiastically attended, was to draw the attention of Spaniards and foreigners alike to the musical heritage of southern Spain. Competitors included Diego Bermudez 'El Tenazas' ('Pliers'), who had walked some 140 kilometres across country from his village of Puente Genil, and a child prodigy nicknamed 'El Caracol' ('The Snail') who would in time become one of the greatest flamenco singers Spain had ever produced. John B. Trend, the Cambridge don and a personal friend of Falla, was among those present at the festival. He described *cante jondo* as the song of the tragic sense of life, 'tragic because, by the beginning of the nineteenth century, it had come down to being the music made in prisons and *prostibulos* [brothels].' He wrote up his experience in an article for *The Nation & Athenaeum* in July 1922.

The stage itself had been erected under the trees which line the rusty red walls of the Alzaba and the Tower of Homage. Behind the little, tiled well-house was a low wall on the edge of a precipice, with the stream of the Darro clattering over the stones at the bottom; while, on the hill opposite, the dark gardens and greenish white walls of the dimly lighted Albaicin seemed as if they were part of a gigantic tapestry curtain which might have have been hung from two tall trees which stood at the corners. At the back of the audience was the noble but unfinished palace of Charles V, while the Alhambra lay hid in the darkness behind. But the most enchanting part of the spectacle was that presented by the ladies of the audience, who had put on their traditional clothes in the traditional way. Wherever one looked there were exquisite figures in gay, flowered shawls and high combs, while many had put on the silks and satins of bygone days, and appeared in the fashion of the thirties and forties – the Spain of Prosper Merimée and Théophile Gautier, of Borrow and Ford . . .

The singing suggested once again that primitive Andalucian song is a secular counterpart to plain-song; at any rate the melodies of *cante jondo* are made of much the same material as some of the Gregorian melodies of the Church; while the wailing Ay! or Leli, leli! with which many of them began, had a definitely Oriental suggestion. A cold analysis can give little idea of the musical effect, the passionate exaltation of the singing, the profound tragedy of the words, and the sheer beauty of style of the whole performance. The songs were not curious and interesting survivals from an Oriental past, but living pieces of music charged with every emotion which tradition, memory, surroundings and pure musical beauty could give them.

Romantic Spain, in other words, was alive and well at a time when the rest of Europe seemed bent on territorial expansion and industrialization. In Granada an intense debate was under way on the musical soul of a rural community. Falla proposed that the Andalusian song had its roots in Byzantine chant, Moorish music, and the gypsy tribes who settled in Spain in the fifteenth century after arriving from India. For Lorca, flamenco was 'one of the most gigantic creations of the Spanish people', with the verse form of the *cante jondo* or *copla* characterized by its striking imagery, conciseness, and emotional extremism.

One of the most notable characteristics of the texts of the *cante jondo* is the almost complete absence of half tones.

In the songs of Asturias, of Castille, of Catalonia, of the Basque country, and Galicia there is a certain equilibrium of sentiments . . . We *andaluces* are rarely aware of half tones. The *andaluz* either screams at the stars or else kisses the red dust of his paths . . . The *cante jondo* sings nearly always at night. It has neither morning nor afternoons, neither mountains nor plains. It only has the night, a night that is wide and profoundly starlit. It doesn't need anything else.

Its a song without landscape, and therefore, concentrated on itself, and terrible in the midst of the shadow it resembles a formidable blue archer who never runs out of arrows.

To sing, play, dance, or write flamenco in its most genuine form, one needs to have neither great intellect nor discipline. What is important is the magic that comes from within, called *duende*. In everyday usage *duende* can mean a fairy, a poltergeist spirit, a goblin. But in the context of flamenco, the word defies such strict definition. To have *duende* describes a state of being, deep in the soul, and the power to communicate the full mystery and anguish of life and death.

An old guitarist once told Lorca, Ian Gibson recalls in his biography of the poet, that the *duende* was 'not a question of power or ability, but of a truly living style; that is to say of blood, of living culture, of instant creation.' Lorca himself commented in 1933:

The *duende* acts on the body of a dancer like air on sand. It transforms with magical power a young girl into a paralytic of the moon, or fills with adolescent flushes a broken old man who goes begging in the wine shops, it gives the hair the smell of a nocturnal port, and at every instant moves the arms in an expression which is the mother of the dance of all times.

To the purists, flamenco begins and ends with *cante jondo*. But flamenco in its widest expression is a composite of song, spirit, rhythm, each of which have developed over the centuries into a musical idiom which defies strict definition. The mystery surrounding the etymology of flamenco has been summarized by James Woodall in the first detailed book in English on the subject, *Firedance*, published in 1992.

> It might be of Arab derivation; *felagmengu* means 'fugitive peasant', *fela men eikum* an Andalusian worker of the Muslim occupation. If there is an association here, then from the beginning 'flamenco' had clear roots in the notion of flight, opposition, of being subordinate in some undesirable way, of being on the outside. The words '*fanfarron*' and '*farruco*' also have overtones of the strange, the wild, the excessive, the over-passionate, all of which might have been first reactions to the spectacle of gypsy dance and behaviour that could be considered 'Moorish' or outlandish. In a later period, Charles V brought his court retinue from Flanders to Madrid, and it may be that their foreignness was transferred by association to the gypsies, other foreigners who sang strange songs; or that the colours of the Flemish (flamenco in Spanish) costumes reminded the indigenous population of the brightly dressed itinerants of the South. His Chapel singers were also always Flemish, these flamenco-cantores becoming famous in their time, so there is at least a tenable musical connection . . . Flamenco is the sum of its interpretations. Just as its etymology is unstable, so is its existence through the words of those who live it . . . For the vast majority who know nothing about it, nor care to, it is a vague, colourful blur in the corner of the eye. For those who know something about it or profess to, it is a unique music with social ramifications. For those who perform it, it is something to die for.

While in Spain in the early nineteenth century, Richard Ford drew a historical link between Andalusian dancers and the *puellae Gaditanae*, the dancing girls of Phoenician Cadiz who were so celebrated by ancient Rome. The most pertinent references to these performers are to be found in the epigrams of Martial. At one of his own dinners, Martial bemoaned not having enough money to pay for 'girls from wanton Gades [who] with endless prurience swing lascivious loins in practised writings'. Martial saw the sensuous spirit of Gades in his mistress Telethusa:

> She who was cunning to show wanton gestures to the sound of Baetic castanets and to frolic to the tunes of Gades, she who could have roused passion in palsied Pelias, and have stirred Hecuba's spouse even by Hector's pyre – Telethusa burns and racks with love her former master . . .

It was the French romantics who laid emphasis on the undercurrent of orientalism in flamenco. Thanks to them, the music of Spain came to be rediscovered – some would say reinvented. Blanca, the heroine of Chateaubriand's *Les Dernier des Abencérages*, chooses to show off her charms to her Muslim prince in the fairyland setting of the Alhambra by dancing a Zambra, the most popular fusion of Andalusian and Islamic dance elements from which flamenco draws some of its characteristics. The Zambra was not only much loved by the caliphs of Cordoba, but it earned great respect among the Christian kings who insisted on keeping Moorish dancers among their performers. Blanca, wrote Chateaubriand, 'chose an expressive dance which the Spaniards borrowed from the Moors'. He continued:

> The harmony of her steps, her singing and the sounds of her guitar were perfect. Her voice lightly veiled had the very tone to move the passions to the depth of the soul. Spanish music, made up of sighs, quick movements, sad refrains, suddenly halted songs, offers a peculiar mixture of gaiety and melancholy.

Gautier developed the theme in his *Wanderings in Spain*, drawing a striking contrast, while watching a performance in Madrid, between the free flowing expression of the Spanish dance and the stilted artifice of the French school. In the dancers of Spain Gautier found an essential poetic gift which filled him with wonder.

> In Spain, the feet hardly leave the ground; there are none of those wide circular or spreading movements of the legs, which make a woman look like a pair of compasses

stretched to its limits, and are considered down there revoltingly indecent. It is the body which dances, with curving motions of the hips, bending sides and a waist which twists and turns with the suppleness of a serpent or an Egyptian dancing-girl. When the body is thrown back, the dancer's shoulders almost touch the ground; the arms are faint and lifeless, with the flexibility and slackness of a trailing scarf; one would hardly believe that the hands could raise the clacking ivory castanets with their chords interwoven with gold; and yet at the given moment, this voluptuous languor is succeeded by bounds like those of a young jaguar, proving that these bodies, so silken-soft, enclose muscles of steel. The Moorish dance-girls of today still follow the same system: their dancing consists in harmoniously seductive undulations of the body, hips and loins, with the arms thrown back over the head . . . Spanish male dancers, though not very good, have a dashing, bold and gallant bearing which I far prefer to the insipid, equivocal graces of our own. They do not appear to be thinking either of themselves or the public; their glances and smiles are all for their partners, with whom they always appear to be passionately in love, and whom they seem prepared to defend against all comers. They have a certain savage grace, and an insolent curve of the body which is very characteristic. If they wiped off their paint, they might make excellent banderilleros and leap from the boards of the theatre on to the sands of the arena.

In the labyrynthine cultural background to the music of southern Spain, the gypsies are the race most closely connected with song and dance. The precise origins of these people remains a subject of some debate, although it is generally assumed that they migrated from India, reached the Bosporus and then around the beginning of the fifteenth century divided into two main groups, one entering Eastern Europe, the other travelling along the southern shores of the Meditteranean.

An early reference to the gypsy presence in Spain is to be found in a short story by Cervantes published in 1613 called *The Little Gypsy Girl*.

Preciosa turned out to be the most accomplished dancer in all the gypsy world . . . she acquired a rich heritage of carols, songs, seguidillas and sarabands, and of other verses, especially ballads, which she sang with great charm. For her cunning grandmother realized that these tricks and graces, along with the youth and the great beauty of her granddaughter, would contribute to the increase of her fortune. So she sought out and got hold of these poems in any way she could, and there were plenty of poets to produce them: for there are poets who condescend to deal with gypsies and sell them their works, just as there are poets who write poems for the blind, and invent miracles for them to get a share of the profits. It takes all sorts to make a world, and hunger can drive clever people to do unheard of things.

Listening to a Castilian seguidilla while staying in Consuegra in 1775, Henry Swinburne noted that the singer's 'ability and expression' were somewhat marred by her mode of dressing. This gave her 'a most prominent belly, a defect few Spanish women are free from.' On the Valencian coast he found the guitar playing very coarse and monotonous. He could find no other comparison for its rhythm than that of the 'beating of a frying pan, to call down a swarm of bees.' In Andalusia, however, he was stirred from his stiffness. His first experience of a fandango proved a sexual awakening.

It exceeds in wantonness all the dances I ever beheld. Such motions, such writhings of the body and positions of the limbs as no modest eye can look upon without a blush! A good fandango lady will stand five minutes in one spot, wiggling like a worm that has just been cut in two.

And it was not just English men who were stirred so. Matilda Betham-Edwards, while in Granada in 1868, changed for an evening with her fellow travellers into her best gown. Once in the gypsy quarter of the Albaicín, however, all the dignity of her proconsular progress dissipated in the course of a flamenco evening. The prudishness of the company of ladies and gentlemen 'whose utmost vagabondage had not exceeded boiling a picnic kettle in Epping Forest, or more likely taking tea on our own lawns' was exposed to an abandoned display of elemental passion.

> This was music one had never dreamed of. His fingers but touch the chords and your breath is taken away . . . You are indeed for the nonce a gypsy, your pulses are quickened to gypsy pitch, you are ready to make love or war. We felt thankful to Senor Antonio for having given us so full an experience of wild life in the space of a few minutes.

In his 1910 journal, André Gide noted that 'nothing since, not even the songs of Egypt, has touched a more secret part of my heart.' The Frenchman judged no entertainment more depressing than visiting a Spanish cinema during a downpour when the traveller longed for sun and dancing and singing. He recalled with nostalgia a visit to Granada some twenty years previously.

> It was at night, in the vast hall of an inn, a gypsy boy singing; a chorus of men and women, in an undertone, then sudden pauses, punctuated that panting, excessive, painful song, in which one felt his soul expiring everytime he caught his breath. It seemed a first draft of Chopin's last ballade; but it remained almost outside of music; not Spanish but gypsy, and irreducably so. To hear that song again, as, I would have travelled over three Spains! But I shall flee Granada for fear of not hearing it again there.

Vita Sackville-West one May evening in Seville felt the ghost of her maternal grandmother Pepita lay a soft hand on her shoulder during a gypsy party organized by an artist friend.

> Someone struck a few chords on the guitar. An immensely fat woman, the fattest woman I had ever seen, strode out from under the balcony and, planting herself down on a perilously small chair beside the fountain, her knees wide apart and a hand splayed on each knee, began to sing. She sang what appeared to be an interminable lament, in a voice like a trombone, and as she sang she began to sway backwards and forwards, as though she indeed bewailed some personal grief too intolerable for her mountainous

flesh to bear. The combination of her grotesque appearance and the magnificently profound notes of her com-
plaint, suggested some primeval sorrow untranslatable
save into the terms of that bellowing song.

She ceased as abruptly as she had begun, and sat there
complacently mopping the sweat from her brow. The
guitar took up again, in another strain this time, a twanging strain, and one by one the indistinct figures came out
from the shadows. I saw then that they were all gypsies,
for by their lineaments and their garments they could have
been nothing else. They were without exception the
most beautiful human beings I ever wish to see. Some of
them, of course, were old and wrinkled, but even those
still bore the traces of their youthful looks in the bony
architecture of their features and in the tragic dignity of
their sunken eyes. Others were in their prime, adult and
arrogant; but others were divinely young, elusively
adolescent, like wild things that never ought to have
submitted to the coaxing of even the kindliest hand . . .

The guitars by then were twanging in unison; the
little patio was filled by those strange minor cadences;
feet were beginning to tap; the enormous singer, still
planted on her tiny chair by the fountain, was beginning
to sway again and to clap her hands together in the
monotonous, exciting rhythm. Little by little, and as if
it were impelled by no organized intention, they began
to dance. At first it was little more than an instinctive
balancing of their bodies, then feet feel into measure,
fingers began to snap, and the patio was alive with these
strangely undulating and sinuous figures, dancing with a
curious intensity in which there was no thought of
anything but rhythm and dancing. They seemed, indeed,
to be part of the rough music and the scented night. There
was no thought of sex in it; or perhaps it might be said
that the whole thing was an expression of sex, love,
passion, so impersonal as to transcend anything trivial or
ephemeral in the emotion, and to translate it into eternal
terms with which the music, the night, and the colour
were inherently mixed. The extraordinary purity and
beauty of the performance was only enhanced by the vast

black figure seated by the fountain, a powerfully obscene goddess immortalised by some sculptor of genius.

Some foreigners have attempted to participate in flamenco, in Laurie Lee's case by playing a 'woozy *fandango*' on his fiddle to a poverty stricken family with whom he was staying in 1935.

The old man danced as if his life was at stake, while the woman was suddenly transformed, her great lumpen body becoming a thing of controlled and savage power. Moving with majestic assurance, her head thrown back, her feet pawing the ground like an animal, she stamped and postured round her small hopping husband as if she would trade him into oblivion.

Twenty years later Lee returned to Spain, determined to learn the more subtle forms of Spanish music. He judged that to be in Seville without a guitar was like being 'on ice without skates.' In *A Rose for Winter* the primordial spirit of Spanish music is captured by Lee in an account of a *cante flamenco* he stumbles across near Algeciras.

First comes the guitarist, a neutral, dark-suited figure, carrying his instrument in one hand and a kitchen chair in another. He places the chair in the shadows, sits himself comfortably, leans his cheek close to the guitar and spreads his white fingers over the strings. He strikes a few chords in the darkness, speculatively, warming his hands and his imagination together. Presently the music becomes more confident and free, the crisp strokes of the rhythms more challenging. At that moment the singer walks into the light, stands with closed eyes, and begins to moan in the back of his throat as though testing the muscles of his voice. The audience goes deathly quiet, for what is coming has never been heard before, and will never be heard again. Suddenly the singer takes a gasp of breath, throws back his head and hits a high barbaric note, a naked wail of sand and desert, serpentine, prehensile. Shuddering then, with contorted and screwed-up face, he moves into the first verse of his song. It is a lament of passion, an animal cry, thrown out, as it were over burning rocks, a call half-lost in air but imperative and terrible.

14

THE SPANISH KITCHEN

Food and Wine

Hard as it might be for them to admit it, those masters of European cuisine, the French, are indebted to their southerly neighbours for at least some of their dishes. 'Spain is a country with such a flair for creating stews,' wrote Maurice Cousin, Comte de Courchamps, in 1866 in his *Dictionnaire general de la cuisine française ancienne et moderne*, 'that the three best entrées of old French cooking, that is, *acollades d'anguiles à la royale*, *perdix à la Medina coeli* and *ollas podridas*, found their way into France with the retinue of Queen Ana' (the Spanish princess who became the wife of Louis XIII).

According to Auguste Escoffier, chef to Napoleon III, the Napoleonic general Junot during the Peninsular War spent some time studying a manuscript of recipes he salvaged from the monastery of Alcantara before sending them to his wife, Laure the Duchess of Abrantès. Among the Spanish culinary delights later noted by the Duchess in her Memoirs were consommé soup, and pheasant and partridge, both *à la mode de Alcantara*. The Spanish omelette or tortilla was another trophy of war that the French took with them. Soldiers found that eggs cooked easily in the hot Spanish sun.

Among the more amusing encounters with the tortilla on Spanish soil was that experienced by a young anonymous American traveller as he rode between Aranjuez and Toledo, a few years after the end of the Peninsular War, in 1868. The traveller had drawn into an inn for the night. His mulateers wasted little time in skinning a hare they had recently shot, but he himself chose to go for the dish of the house. The innkeeper, 'a coarse-haired, dark-eyed old woman,' said all she had was some eggs. The American ordered a tortilla.

The eggs were soon emptied into an earthen dish, where they floated at large in a sea of oil; the dish was placed on a low table, which, for want of a bench – the only one in the house being occupied by the party of the mulateer – drew close to the door, so as to take our seats upon the sill. Now that we had our meal before us, however, it was not so easy to eat it. The bread and the wine, indeed gave us no trouble, but the eggs were as much beyond our reach, as fishes that you have seen in the water, but have no means of catching. In vain did we ask for a spoon or a fork. Our hostess only regretted that she could do nothing for us. Until a week before, she had two wooden spoons and one horn one, for the accommodation of cavaliers, who did not carry their utensils, but some *quintas*, or conscripts, had passed by on their way to the frontier of Portugal, and halted during the heat of the day at her house. Since then, she had seen nothing either of her horn spoon, or the two wooden ones, and she never meant to buy another. As our invention was sharpened by hunger, José and I bethought ourselves to cut the bread into slices, and to use two pieces as chopsticks, after the manner of the Chinese. In this way, and by lending each other occasional assistance in catching a refractory egg, we were enabled to drive them, one by one, into a corner and draw them out until nothing remained but the oil.

Richard Twiss, a wealthy English traveller of the 1770s, found that the experience of tasting gazpacho for the first time more than made up for the inconvenience of having to sleep the night on a shopkeeper's wooden chest in the small Andalusian town of Los Barrios near Algeciras.

This is an excellent soupe-maigre. Nothing can be more refreshing during the violent heats: it is made by putting a sufficient quantity of oil, vinegar, salt and pepper into a quart of cold water and adding crusts of bread, garlick and onions shred small.

Théophile Gautier took a somewhat different view. He judged gazpacho the sign of a lesser race.

> In our country, no dog with the slightest breeding would deign to put his muzzle in such a mixture. It's the favourite food of the Andalusians, and even the prettiest of the women here have no hesitations in swallowing every evening large spoonfuls of this infernal brew.

The perception of Spanish food as unpalatable to civilized taste was an important element in the mythological baggage of the romantic travellers of the nineteenth century. Food, like bullfighting and flamenco, was what separated Spain from the rest of Europe, made it primitive and different. The cuisine was for tough constitutions, and the tasting of it carried a necessary element of risk. The food of Spain was one of the reasons it was never part of the Grand Tour, but rather part of the Grand Adventure. Dumas crossed the frontier and left behind him a France where 'hotels welcomed travellers at any hour, providing sumptuous profusion for two or three francs a head.' Once in Spain sustenance proved harder to come by. On the first day, the best a local innkeeper could provide for Dumas and his companions was 'five thimble-sized cups full of a thick black liquid, five glasses of clear water and a little basket containing small sticks of bread, pink and white.' Dumas considered the quality of Spanish chocolate superb, but thought there was not enough of it. He had to wait till he reached Vitoria before he could try out his first full Spanish meal. It was an experience he was never to repeat, so disastrous an effect did the food – a *puchero* – have on his digestion.

> It consists of a large joint of cow-meat, (in Spain the bull seems completely unknown as a source of food) a little mutton, a chicken, slices of a sausage called chorizo, all cooked with dripping, ham, tomatoes, saffron and cabbage. These would be acceptable enough if served separately, but I could never get used to eating them all together and in my opinion they form a most unfortunate mixture. Try to do better than I did, Madame, for if you cannot enjoy *puchero* you will be obliged to make do with *garbanzos*. These are hard, bullet-sized peas, quite beyond

my powers of digestion, but if you were to begin by eating one on the first day, two on the second, and on the third day three, it is just possible that you might survive . . .

Unlike Dumas, Gerald Brenan in 1957 was less concerned about his digestion than about what the national dish of Castile said about Spanish culture.

The chick pea, from which Cicero took his name, is a yellow bullet which explodes in the inside into several cubic feet of gas, while if the cook knows her job properly she will see that the meat is boiled till it has no taste left and that the fat, a yellowish white in colour, is rancid. A Spaniard feels when he eats this dish that he has vindicated his toughness of fibre. He has not degenerated from the breed of men who conquered a continent with a handful of adventures, wore hair-shirts day and night till they stuck to their flesh, and braved mosquitoes of the Picomayo and the Amazon.

In 1760, on eating *his* first *puchero*, Joseph Baretti declared that had he been in London he would 'scarcely have suffered my dog to eat of such a dinner.' However, he was pleasantly surprised by the new experience of drinking wine from a pig-skin *bota*.

It was full of a most excellent Cariñena wine and I sucked out of the cock so often and so kindly, that my spirits were entirely recruited, and my weariness forgot in half an hour.

The delights of drinking wine from a *bota*, as of drinking cold water from an earthenware *botijo*, were identified also by the poet Roy Campbell whose own drinking escapades became legendary in the Toledo of the 1930s. On the *botijo* he had this to say:

This way of drinking brings out of the flavour and perfume, both of wine and water, and once one has mastered the art without choking, drinking wine or water out of a glass seems flat and insipid compared to it. The longer, thinner, and more forcible the jet, the more it aerates the bouquet of the wine or the water. From two and a half feet away you can say: 'This water tastes of marble, of violets, of granite, of thyme, of iron, or of quartz; or of the shade of mulberry, white poplar trees, or olives.

During the nineteenth century wine generally continued to be made in a careless, unscientific manner, proving a disappointment to many a traveller. Sir Arthur de Capell Brook in *Sketches in Spain and Morocco*, published in 1831, left this account of his experience in the Castilian town of Valdepeñas, the heart of one of Spain's main wine-growing areas:

My fellow-travellers had looked forward to our halt at Valdepeñas with considerable pleasure, in order to regale themselves with its celebrated wine which had produced too strong an impression on me, from the acquaintance I had made with it at Cordova, not to wish to taste once more the contents of the wine-skins of La Mancha, and to quaff, on the very spot of its growth, the blood of the mighty giant, the spilling of which forms so pleasant a narration among the recorded adventures of the redoubtable knight [Don Quixote]. It turned out, however, that our palates were not doomed to be tickled in so agreeable a manner; for, having despatched the usual ragout of the Spanish cuisine, and called for some of mine host's best, upon conveying it to our lips we found it to be of so vile a quality that, although we were by no means squeamish, it was impossible to drink it. It was to equal purpose that we instituted a search in the different stores of the place. We did not succeed in obtaining a single drinkable bottle of wine, and were at last compelled to content ourselves with aguardiente [firewater].

While Richard Ford was more generally benevolent towards Spanish wines on his first encounter, he was dismissive when judging them from the distance of his English home. It was possible to come across good wine in Spain, but the product simply didn't travel, as he explained in *Gatherings*.

The thirsty traveller, after a long day's ride under a burning sun, when seated quietly down to a smoking peppery dish, is enchanted with the cool draught of these *vins de pays*, which are brought to him from the skins or amphora jars; he longs to transport the apparatus and its divine nectar to his own home, and wonders that 'the trade' should have overlooked such delicious wine. Those who have tried the experiment will find a sad change for the worse come over the spirit of their dream, when the long-expected importation greets their papillatory organs in London. There the illusion is dispelled; there is a cloyed fastidiousness of taste, to a judgement bewildered and frittered away by variety of the best vintages, how flat, stale and unprofitable does this much-fancied beverage appear! The truth is, that its merit consists in the thirst and drinking vein of the traveller, rather than in the wine itself.

In a league of its own among Spanish wines is of course sherry, whose English name is a corruption of Jerez, the Andalusian town from which the product has been exported for centuries. Towards the end of the nineteenth century, the sherry trade with Britain became embroiled in a very public controversy, the so-called 'plastering scandal', in which it was alleged that a harmful proportion of sulphuric acid had found its way into the wine. A visit to Jerez, by Mr Vasey, a health inspector, allayed public fears in a report published in *The Lancet* in 1898 which makes it clear that sherry had become a sophisticated wine subject to industrial process.

There are two facts in connexion with the production of sherry which are open to be construed an adulteration. The first is the addition of sulphate of lime to the crushed grapes before fermentation and the second the addition of a small proportion of spirit to wine intended for export. Against the former we do not think that a rational objection can be raised so long as the treatment is kept within limits, and this is invariably so. It may be called an artificial recourse, but so also is the adding of sugar-candy to champagne to make it sparkling or of gelatine, clay, and so on for the purpose of refining wines, beers, etc. We have described how the same thing may be to some extent naturally effected by the simple occurrence of an unusual proportion of vineyard dust adhering to the grapes prior to pressing. We venture to suggest that this has been the origin of the so-called 'plastering process'. The sulphate of the lime employed is a natural constituent of the soil contiguous to the vineyards. The question is, can this be regarded in the light of adulteration or fraud, since it does not add in any way to the bulk of the wine nor does it make it poisonous? On the contrary, it refines the wine and increases its power to develop those fragrant ethers which give to the wine its peculiarly pleasant characters in regard to bouquet, flavour, and agreeable stimulating qualities.

The town of Jerez itself has not always enchanted visitors. Swinburne, in 1776, described it as a 'large town, with winding streets, and horrible kennels of black stagnated water . . .' But by the time the British ambassador, Sir Samuel Hoare, came to it in 1942 on a visit to the vice-consul, the town had taken on a more seductive self-assurance. Hoare recalled in his autobiography, *Ambassador on a Special Mission*:

Jerez with its bright sun and white houses was to us one of the most attractive towns in Spain. The juice of the grape seemed to have entered into its life. Its baroque churches and palaces bore evidence to its former riches, whilst the vast *bodegas* as high and bony as Gothic cathedrals showed that the potential source of wealth was unabated. The father of the wine trade was the nonogenarian head of the Gonzalez family, the Marques de Torre Soto. Like most of the Spanish families in the Jerez wine trade his had frequently made English and Scottish marriages. Some of the firms still bore other British names. This was as it should be in a trade that had been developed by a sergeant-major in one of Wellington's regiments and had since found its main outlet in the British market.

The Marques de Torre Soto seemed to have found in the native grape an *elixir vitae perpetuae*. At the age of ninety, when we visited him, we sat down to dinner at 11 pm and left hale and hearty at 2.30 am.

From the perspective of some visitors to Spain, wine was as

essential to the local culture as bullfighting, but William Jacob,
on a visit to southern Spain in 1809, found that restraint in
drinking, and to a lesser extent eating, was the norm, a
remnant perhaps of the Islamic traditions that had once
prevailed. Jacob wrote in *Travels in the South of Spain*:

> Temperance seems the prevailing habit of the Spaniards in
> eating, but more especially in drinking. I have known
> many gentlemen who never drink any wine; and those
> who do, generally mix it with a large quantity of water.
> I am informed, however, that in the winter the lower
> orders indulge, but not to excess, in the use of brandy
> mixed with aniseed, and sweet wine. In England, every
> family has a store of beer, wine, and such other necessaries
> as they require for their daily use, ready at all times; but
> the best families in Seville keep nothing of the kind in
> their houses. If company accidentally drop in to a meal,
> a thing not common, they send to the shops for such food
> as they want, and to the wine-house for a pint or a quart
> of wine, so they are never provided with the commonest
> of those articles, and at the conclusion of the day no pro-
> vison is left in the house. Though I have visited a good
> deal at some of the best houses, and at all hours, I have
> seldom known where the comidero, or eating room, was
> placed. Where I have seen it, I have generally found it the
> smallest and darkest apartment, and in the most obscure
> part of the dwelling, whereas the rooms for the reception
> of company are usually spacious and lofty, but in them no
> refreshment is offered, except cool water for visitors to
> drink.

It is once again to Richard Ford that we must turn for
a wider perspective on the delights and shortcomings of the
Spanish kitchen. Ford instructed the visitor to Spain not to
'lumber himself with much *batterie de cuisine*; it is not much
needed in the imperfect gastronomy of the Peninsula, where
men eat like the beasts which perish.' And yet he wrote more
about food than about any other single aspect of Spanish
culture, with the exception of architecture, devoting numerous
pages both in his *Handbook* and *Gatherings* to such details of
local cuisine as the sauce used in stews – 'it carries that rich

burnt umber, sienna tint, which Murillo imitated so well' –
and Catalan soup – 'this mess is called *sopa de gato*, probably
from making cats, not Castilians, sick.'

Ford considered garlic the 'foundation of the national
cuisine', although the very name 'was enough to give offence
to most Englishmen' at the time. The Reverend Richard
Roberts was one of them. During an autumn tour of Spain
taken in 1859, not even the delights of a hotel near the
Alhambra were enough to distract him from the overwhelming
fumes emanating from the breath of Pepe the waiter.

> He could eat garlic to such a degree, that his presence at
> meals was quite intolerable, being only one remove from
> having to eat that abominable esculent ourselves.

Roberts suffered Pepe for two days before persuading him,
'being a very good natured creature', to go out into the garden
before each meal and eat parsley.

Next to garlic it was the mistrust of olive oil that set another
barrier between the visitor to Spain and the indigenous community. Swinburne noted the Spanish fondness for an oil that
had a 'rank smell and taste' and which was used indifferently
for cooking or lighting lamps. Such prejudices were noted
but not shared by George Cayley, an eccentric 25-year-old
Englishman who in 1851 was forced by ill-health to winter
in Seville. From his first day in Spain he made a habit of
munching garlic and taking spoonfuls of olive oil regularly for
medicinal purposes. Cayley wrote a chapter entitled 'Butter vs.
oil' in his entertaining travelogue, *Bridle Roads of Spain*.

> The English have a strange unfounded prejudice against
> oil, and in favour of butter, which is as near as possible
> the same thing, only that oil is clean, pure, vegetable fat,
> which keeps better, and is infinitely easier to have good
> than butter; while butter is the result of a greasy animal
> secretion, milked out of unpleasant udders by a dirty-
> fisted wench. Butter is not good after three days' keeping;
> and accordingly, is much oftener eaten bad than good.
> Nevertheless good butter is a good thing; and we eat it,
> because we know it to be so, in spite of all the disagreeable
> ideas which are connected with its origin. But of oil,

from unfamiliarity, we have an abhorrence. Our first
acquaintance with it in childhood is through the unen-
couraging sample called after the elder of the constel-
lated twins; our next is the smell of the lamp. When
subsequently we see oil in a salad, it shocks our prejudices.
On tasting it with a candid determination, we find it
good; but still there are few Englishmen who, in tasting
a sample of oil, would swallow a spoonful, which a
Spaniard could do as unconcernedly as we should a spoonful of cream. I have the national horror of oil, but I cannot
say that, on honest experiment, I find that in good
cookery it is a bit worse than the best butter; and in some
cases it is better.

Such prejudices, however, were the privilege of those who
could afford to pick and choose what to eat. Spaniards on the
whole have spent most of their history, at least well into the
twentieth century, making do with what is available, when not
close to starvation. From the middle ages onwards, the theme
of hunger runs persistently through Spanish writing, making
the mere act of eating a very special experience. In *La Vida de
Lazarillo de Tormes*, a picaresque novel published anonymously
in 1554, much of the action revolves around the efforts of a
young starving urchin to obtain food from his masters. Because
they are usually as hungry as he is, and miserly, Lazarillo has
to devise tricks like the following to get his share.

When we were staying at an inn in Escalona, a town
belonging to the duke of that name, my master gave me
a piece of sausage to roast. Once the sausage was dripping
and he had eaten some bread dipped in its fat, he took a
penny from his purse and sent me to the inn for wine.
Now the devil presented me with the opportunity, and
opportunity, as they say, makes the thief. There happened
to be a little turnip beside the fire, a poor thing that must
have been thrown out as unfit for the pot. Now as he and
I were alone in the room and my appetite had been
aroused by the smell of the sausage – which I knew was
all I was to enjoy of it – without a thought for the
consequences I threw aside all my fear in order to get my
desire. So when the blind man was extracting the money

from the purse I seized the sausage and rapidly put the aforementioned turnip on the spit in its place. After giving me the money for the wine my master took it and began to turn it in front of the fire, setting out to roast this object that was so miserable as to have escaped being boiled. I went for the wine and quickly gobbled the sausage on my way, and when I returned I found that old sinner holding the turnip between the two slices of bread. Not having touched it he had not discovered what it was. But when he took the slices and put his teeth into them, expecting to bite into the sausage, he felt the sudden chill of the cold turnip.

If the art of good cooking lies in improvization, the capacity to make, as Ford put it in *Gatherings*, 'something out of nothing', there have always been good cooks in Spain. Gautier may have been disgusted by the taste of gazpacho, but he was impressed by the quantity of food made available to him when he crossed the frontier from France into the Basque country staying the night in the village of Astirraga. Instead of the expected 'omelettes adorned with hairs dating from Merovingian days, mixed with feathers and claws, gammons of rancid bacon with all the bristles on them, equally suitable for making soup or for cleaning shoes . . .' he was treated to a veritable banquet.

As for the wine, we are bound to admit that it was of the finest possible bishop's violet, so thick that it could be cut with a knife, and the decanters which held it lent it no transparency . . . After the soup, they brought the puchero, an eminently Spanish dish, or rather the only Spanish dish for it is eaten every day from Irun to Cadiz, and vice versa . . . Next come chickens fried in oil, for butter is unknown in Spain, fried fish – trout or haddock – roast lamb, asparagus, and salad; and for dessert, little macaroons, almost roasted in the pan and exquisitely flavoured goat's cheese – queso de Burgos – which has a great, and sometimes deserved reputation. At the end, they bring on a tray with wine of Malaga, sherry, and a brandy, or aguardiente, which is like coal, to light the cigarettes.

Similar culinary surprises greeted Laurie Lee when in the 1930s he set off for the first time to Spain, turning his back on the cheap lodgings in London's Lower Richmond Road where his diet had consisted of kippers, meat pudding and bubble-and-squeak. On his first visit Lee was drawn to the 'sweet tang' of Spanish cooking. When he returned to Spain during the Civil War, Laurie Lee encountered a country on the point of starvation, but he found that hunger sharpened the senses and stimulated the Spanish talent for improvization. On one occasion, as described in *A Moment of War*, the act of testing soup becomes a rite of passage.

> A fat old crone, crouching by the fire in the corner, was stirring soup in a large black cauldron, and as she seemed to be in charge I went up to her and made a sign for food. Without a word she lifted a ladleful of the soup and held it up to my mouth. I tasted and choked; it was hot, strong, and acrid with smoke and herbs. The old lady peered at me sharply through the fumes of the fire. She was bent, leather-skinned, bearded and fanged and looked like a watchful moose. I wiped my burnt mouth, nodded my head, and said 'Good' in clear loud English.

Spanish improvisation – indeed imagination – in the kitchen was contrasted with the dull restraint of English cooking by Nancy Mitford in *The Pursuit of Love*. The stuffy Edwardian atmosphere of Alconleigh, traumatized by war-time rationing, is transformed by the arrival of Juan, a Communist refugee from the Spanish Civil War, and former cook to a cardinal. Let loose on the Radlett household's kitchen, Juan brings off a culinary revolution.

> He was more than a first class cook, he had an extra-ordinary talent for organisation, and soon, I suspect, became king of the local black market. There was no nonsense about foreign dishes made out of little bits of nothing at all; succulent birds, beasts, and crustaceans appeared at every meal, the vegetables ran with extra-vagant sauces, the puddings were obviously based on real icecream . . . Juan also pickled and bottled and preserved from morning till night, until the store cupboard, which

he had found bare except for a few tins of soup, began to look like a pre-war grocer's shop. Davey called it Aladdin's Cave, or Aladdin for short, and spent a lot of his time there, gloating. Months of tasty vitamins stood there in rows, a barrier between him and that starvation which had seemed, under Mrs Beecher's regime, only just round the corner.

When Gijs van Hensbergen arrived in Spain in 1986 he came across an old recipe for tortilla from the 'Hungry Years' of the 1950s. It was totally devoid of potatoes, eggs, olive oil and onions; the 'culinary miracle' relied on the 'cook's ability to transform orange zest, flour, and water into something resembling the same.' In the Spain of the 1980s, he encountered no such need for radical abstinence. On the contrary, Spaniards seemed to be making up for lost time, inventing canny ways of getting round the only remaining restriction on their appetite, the Catholic fast of Lent.

On Friday morning you wake up exhausted. All night long, because you know that you're not allowed to have one, you dream of a giant tender *solomillo* steak surrounded by a few of the spicy green peppers from the village of Padron. You're sweating with greed and not a little guilt. What do you do? Easy. You go to confession and talk to the priest. You bow your head in shame for the sin you are about to commit, and say:

'Father. I beg God's forgiveness. It is Lent and on top of that it is Friday. In about approximately four hours twenty minutes, after I've had a first course of asparagus with a generous helping of mayonnaise – good Lenten fare, don't you agree, Father . . .?'

'Yes, my son, speak up. What is your sin?'

'Well . . . I will consume a *solomillo* with spicy green peppers and covered in a thick layer of *jamon serrano*.'

The sinner buys his *bula* from the priest, a fine that bears some relation to the ten per cent service charge added to a bill in London restaurants, and is automatically forgiven his forthcoming sin.

In the novels of Montalban the hedonistic private detective Pepe Carvalho regards Catalan food as an excuse for indulgence and sheer erotic delight. In *Murder in the Central Committee*, Carvalho tours Barcelona's restaurants.

> The Ramblas were about to start channelling people in search of restaurants and snack bars. Casual strollers and groups of pensioners were making way for the newspaper kiosks. A slow-moving, garrulous and more cheerful mass of people were shaping up for the gastronomic mysteries concealed in the dark side-streets where new restaurants appeared every day – one more proof of the democratic pluralism made available by the liberation from domestic gastronomic paternalism. At the height of the crisis of patriarchal society, heads of families were out in search of new restaurants, their hearts thumping at the forbidden adventure of a cream sauce with Olot truffles, dishes with tight and black, transparent underwear, four-course oral-genital meals in which the tongue is ready for the prevalency of aromatic herbs and quick-fried dishes enlivened by bites of pine-kernel.

Gautier's account of the café life of nineteenth-century Madrid is equally sensuous. He would patronize the Café de Bolsa, full of life even in the heat of summer.

> Here is the list of bebidas heladas, sorbetes, and quesitos: the bebida helada (iced drink) is contained in glasses distinguished into grande and chico, and offers a very great variety; there is the bebida de naranja (orange), limon (lemon), fresa (strawberry) and guindras (cherry), which are as superior to those horrible decanters of genuine gooseberry and citric acid with which they are not ashamed to serve you in the most brilliant cafés in Paris as real sherry is to the original wine of Brie: it is a sort of liquid ice, or snowy pulp of the most exquisite flavour: the bebida de almendra blanca (white almonds) is a delicious drink, unknown in France, where, under the pretext of barley water, one swallows goodness knows what medicinal compounds; one is also given iced milk, half filled with strawberry or cherry, which enables your throat to enjoy all the snows and hoar-forests of Greenland while your body is drinking in the torrid zone.

During the day, when the ices are not yet ready, you have agraz, a kind of drink made from green grapes, and contained in bottles with disproportionately long necks; the slightly acid flavour of agraz is highly agreeable; you may also drink a bottle of cerveza (beer) de Santa Barbara con limon, but this requires certain preparations: you are first brought a bowl and a great ladle, like those with which they stir punch, then a waiter advances, bearing the bottle, sealed with wire, which he uncorks with infinite care; the cork flies out, and he pours the beer into the basin, into which a decanter of lemonade has first been emptied. Then it is stirred up with the ladle, one fills one's glass and drinks. If this mixture is not to your taste, you have only to go into the orchaterias de chufas, which are generally kept by Valencians. The chufa is a little berry, a sort of almond, which grows near Valencia; they roast them, pound them and compose an exquisite drink, especially when it is blended with snow; this preparation is extremely refreshing.

In a country periodically subjected to invasion by foreigners and divided by regional loyalties, bread has proved the great equalizer. In 1830, Henry Inglis wrote in his book *Spain* that he had nowhere tasted bread that could compare with that of Spain. It was the 'most excellent . . . in Europe . . . and this applies not only to the cities and towns, but even villages; in the village of San Lorenzo, in the midst of the Sierra Guadarrama, I found bread equal to any that can be purchased in Madrid or Seville.'

In times of hunger, bread has proved a lifeline while in times of plenty it has been the medium, together with wine, through which the delights of Spanish cooking can be fully appreciated. Commentators through the centuries have discoursed at length about its qualities. 'Bread is the staff of the Spanish traveller's life, who have added raw garlic, not salt, to it, then journeys on with security,' wrote Ford. Spanish poets for their part have infused bread with a lyrical quality. As he viewed the red earth of the hills of Andalusia in winter, Lorca said he felt like spreading it on bread as if it were top-quality pork dripping.

Bread is the soul of the small white-washed village of Moguer. It is from here that Columbus recruited some of the crew for his Atlantic crossing to an America that would send back corn, tomatoes, potatoes, and spices. In his portrait of a Spanish rural and fishing community, *Platero y Yo*, Spain's Nobel prize winner Juan Ramón Jiménez wrote:

Moguer is just like wheat bread, white on the inside, and golden on the outside like the crust . . . At midday, when the sun is at its strongest, the whole village starts to steam and smell of pine and warm bread. The whole village opens its mouth. Its like a big mouth that eats a big piece of bread. The bread goes into everything: into the oil, into the *gazpacho*, into the cheese and the grape, to give the taste of a kiss, in the wine, in the soup, in the ham, and in itself, bread with bread.

15

TIMES PAST AND TIMES PASSING

Expatriates and Eccentrics

In 1927, the English poet Robert Graves said goodbye to all that was England, resolving never again to make it his home. Graves left behind him a repressive public school education, painful memories of the First World War, and a broken marriage. He went to Majorca

Because its climate had the reputation of being better than any other in Europe. And because I was assured, correctly it proved, that I should be able to live there on a quarter of the income needed in England. And because it was large enough – some 1,300 square miles – not to make me feel claustrophobic. Then from all Majorca I chose Deyá, a small fishing and olive-producing village on the mountainous north-west of the island – the rest is mostly plain and rolling country – where I found everything I wanted as a background to my work as a writer: sun, sea, mountains, spring-water, shady trees, no politics, and a few civilized luxuries such as electric light and a bus service to Palma . . .

I wanted to go where town was still town; and country, country; and where the horse plough was not yet an anachronism. There were other *desiderata*, naturally, such as good wine, good neighbours, and not too great a distance from the Greenwich meridian . . . On consulting the atlas, I saw that Majorca lay almost dead on the Greenwich meridian, in the centre of the most consistent fair-weather area in Europe, and that it had one mountain at least as high as any in England . . .

Escape from a censorious society, dreams of an Arcadian idyll, the need for literary inspiration, were in part what had brought George Sand to Majorca a century earlier. She was also driven by the tension of a secret love affair that longed to flourish in a different setting.

I set out in order to satisfy a need to repose which I was feeling more keenly than usual. Since in this world that we have made for ourselves time is always short, I fancied once again that I should find some faraway retreat where there should be no notes to write, no newspapers to peruse, no callers to entertain; where I could always wear my dressing gown, where every day would last twelve hours . . .

George Sand arrived in November 1838 with her two young children, Maurice and Solange, and her lover, the Polish composer Frédéric Chopin. What she found fell well short of her romantic expectations. Her dream was marred by the inclemency of the weather, her sense of alienation in the midst of a conservative community (her alleged affair with a local priest and her habit of riding a horse like a man shocked the Mallorquinos), and Chopin's low libido due to bad health. There were no noble savages on the island, only sad and squalid refugees from the Carlist War. Customs officials confiscated Chopin's piano. The heavy rain and snow instilled an atmosphere of damp melancholy. Sand suffered the weather together with the tuberculous Chopin and the equally sickly Maurice in an old Carthusian monastery in the hills of Valdemosa.

It was for this landscape that Sand reserved her few words of praise, it was 'simple, calm . . . a green Switzerland beneath a Calabrian sky, and with the silent solemnity of the Orient.' By contrast, in her book *A Winter in Mallorca* she poured scorn on Majorcan society: the ignorant nobility, 'more African than European', the 'imbecile' hermits, and the thieving nave inhabitants.

The Mallorcan peasant is a gentle, kind creature, with peaceful habits and a tranquil, patient nature. He has no love of evil, and no knowledge of good. He goes to confession, prays, and thinks incessantly of how to enter Paradise, yet is ignorant of the true obligations of human kind. You can no more hate him than you could an ox or a sheep, for he is close to a savage, whose soul is lulled in animal innocence. He recites his prayers like the superstitious savage; but he would eat his fellow-man without a qualm, were that the custom of his country, and were he unable to satisfy himself fully with pork. He cheats, exhorts, lies, abuses and plunders without the least scruple, where foreigners are concerned, not regarding these as fellow-men. Though he would never rob his neighbour of so much as an olive, he believes that in God's scheme of things the only use for human beings from overseas is to bring the Majorcans nice little profits.

And yet it was in Majorca that Chopin completed his Preludes, a romantic masterpiece, whose sentiment only his lover could adequately interpret. Sand called them the work of a masterhand. To her, many of the Preludes suggested a 'vision of deceased monks and the sound of funereal chants accompanying them to the cemetery.' Others were melancholy and tender. They came to Chopin 'in the hours of sunshine and good health, while the children were laughing under the window, and guitars twanging far off, and birds singing in the wet trees, and little pale roses bloomed against snow.'

It was in Chopin that Graves found his own feelings reflected. He belonged to a second wave of English romantics who sought escape and deliverance in Spain in the first half of the twentieth century. Amongst the early pioneers was Gerald Brenan, at the age of twenty-six another escapee from the horrors of the First World War and the conventions of Edwardian England. Unlike Graves, however, he initially chose Spain by default. His conversion to the country was gradual. In *South from Granada* he wrote of his arrival in Spain in September 1919.

. . . My choice of Spain rather than of Greece or Italy was not due to any special feeling I had for it. Almost all I knew about the country was that it had been neutral in the war and would therefore, I imagined, be cheap to live in. This was essential, for the longer I could make my journey last, the longer I should have in which to enjoy my leisure. My first impressions after landing at Corunna were discouraging. I spent a few days walking in Galicia, then travelled across the tableland by a mixed goods and passenger train that stopped for ten minutes at every station. As we crawled over the endless yellow expanse I was painfully struck by the emptiness and monotony of the country. Not a bush, not a tree, and the houses built of sun-dried bricks that were the colour of the earth. If the whole of Spain were like this I did not see how I could settle down in it.

And yet settle down he did in the village of Yegen in the Alpujarra hills south of Granada, land of the Moorish kingdom to which so many earlier travellers had made their pilgrimages of discovery. In Yegen, Brenan lived a simple rustic life surrounded by the many books he had brought with him from England, including those of Borrow and Ford. The harsher realities of Spanish life that occasionally intruded were partially offset by resorting to the non-Spanish 'civilised' culture he had left behind. Brenan recalled this period of his life in his second book of memoirs, *Personal Record*.

Yegen was a place of light and air and it was also a place of water. Streams ran down its slopes from the mountain above and were diverted into irrigation channels which in early summer, when the snow on the high summits was melting, filled the air with a continual burbling. The soil too, whenever it got through the water, was fertile. Nowhere have I seen wheat grow thicker or taller than on its *bancales* or terraces, nowhere were the figs and apricots and persimmons and melons and trellis-grown grapes better to the taste. A little higher up the slope, above the chestnut level, there grow cherry trees whose dark red succulent fruit no one bothered to pick, while from the next village came walnuts and pears and apples. This meant that in summer, if one liked fruit and vegetables, one lived well. The whole village blossomed out, the air was full of the songs of the men riding their mules to work and at night guitars twanged in the streets as the young men serenaded their *novias*.

Brenan's biographer, Jonathan Gathorne-Hardy, thought that it was the 'stagnation, the conventionality of the deep sleep of English upper-class country life' which gave Brenan a special appreciation of the 'great boredom of Spain', what Gathorne-Hardy identified as the 'infinite boredom of a *pueblo* at midday beneath the hammer of the summer sun, its timeless quality, whom not even the flies can move.'

It was the image of Spain as different from the rest of Europe, a land that was very much 'abroad', challenging and exciting because of its backwardness, that persisted in the imagination of Englishmen who crossed the Pyrenees in the aftermath of the First World War. The Sitwell brothers, Osbert and Sacheverell, went to Spain in 1919. Demobbed, they found in neutral Spain the symbol of their newly-won independence. Osbert recalled in his memoirs, *Left Hand, Right Hand*:

We had chosen Spain of all other countries, because we had never hitherto visited it, and because, through the First World War, it had seemed an unattainable island of peace, and, as always, to be compact of idiosyncracy and austere beauty – as well as of a kind of masculine and aristocratic common sense, because, so long as it is not a matter of religion, the Spaniard is always willing to mind his own business . . . Even the journey over the frontier, from Hendaye to Irun, was exciting, unlike any other: the great mountains, the towering clouds overshadowing them, and suddenly releasing bursts of dramatic sunlight, the women, who could be seen carrying pitchers to the wells, the men, with enormous straw hats as big as wheels, the hog-skins filled with wine, the sub-Alpine dwarfs – all possessed the indefinable tang of an ancient and historic country that was new to us.

At the same time, Lytton Strachey, together with Dora Carrington and her husband Ralph Partridge, were on their way back to England after staying with Gerald Brenan. In a letter to Mary Hutchinson in April 1920, Strachey enthused about Brenan's house.

> Look at a map of Spain and find Granada. Thence draw a line of 40 miles in a southwesterly direction, across the Sierra Nevada, and you will arrive – here. Yegen is a village among the mountains, high up with a view of the Mediterranean in the distance, and all round the most extraordinary Greco-esque formations of rocks and hills. Never have I seen a country on so vast a scale – wild, violent, spectacular – enormous mountains, desperate chasms – colours everywhere of deep orange and brilliant green – a wonderful place, but easier to get to with a finger in a map than in reality!

Strachey spent most of the time at Yegen recovering from the rigours of the journey out. The *ménage à trois* showed signs of disintegration under the Spanish sun. Carrington accused the energetic Ralph of using Spain as an 'open-air gymnasium' in which to test his endurance. Strachey took to refusing to talk to the 'natives' at all times.

The trio's final approach to Yegen consisted of a three-day journey involving a frantic bus ride and a day's trek across flooding rivers and along paths overhanging precipices. Such things had been conquered by earlier travellers, but to Strachey they were an immense ordeal. It is described in his biography, *A Life Apart*, by Michael Holroyd.

> The day was very hot, and thirty miles of difficult and precipitous country lay before them, filling them all with the darkest forebodings. No sooner had they dismounted from the carriage and descended into the river valley, than Lytton, who was suffering by this time from piles, discovered that he could not ride on mule-back. Every half-mile or so the band of them would arrive at a river, he would perilously mount his animal, be agonizingly conveyed across, and then climb off again – all the while balancing an open sunshade high above his head. This procedure repeated itself with a montonous frequency throughout the day, so tiring Lytton and so delaying their progress that at last they agreed unanimously to break

their journey and put up for the night at the small village of Cadiar. But one look at the best bed available at the posada, and they quickly changed their minds and dragged themselves off again along the bed of the same river which they continued, as in a nightmare, to cross and recross on their mules, and so on and so on by narrow tracks, up and up into the hills until the day began to fade and the stars appeared in the sky.

Once safely back in England, Strachey offered blunt advice to Virginia Woolf, herself about to set off on the Brenan trail with her husband Leonard in March 1923. 'Spain is absolute death,' he warned.

Woolf was nevertheless not only prepared to push ahead with her itinerary but with 'infinite labour' to describe it for the inaugural issue of the *Nation & Athenaeum* magazine. In an article entitled 'To Spain', Woolf describes herself leaving behind, not without initial apprehension, the conventions and certainties of London society – 'it is from them that we must escape; the hours, the works, the divisions, rigid and straight, of the old British week.' It was the first time the Woolfs had left England in eleven years. The train took them down to the border via Paris and Bordeaux and, as it crossed over, Virginia encountered for the first time primitive, elemental Spain. Words become 'flimsy things' when confronted with such beauty.

> . . . A chaotic, and alarming chasm filled – for the eyes pour it all in – with white towns, with mules in single file, with solitary farms, with enormous churches, with vast fields crumbling at evening into pallor, with fruit-trees blazing askew like blown matches, and trees burning with oranges, and clouds and storms. Beauty seems to have closed overhead, and one washes this way and that in her waters. It is always on the shoulders of a human being that one climbs out; a profile in the corridor; a lady in deep mourning who steps into a motor-car and drives across an arid plain – where and why? A child in Madrid throwing confetti effusively upon the figure of Christ; an Englishman discussing, while his hat obscures half the Sierra Nevada, Mr Churchill's last article in The Times.

'No,' one says to the beauty – as one rebukes an importunate dog – 'down, down; let me look at you through the eyes of human beings.' But the Englishman's hat is no measure of the Sierra Nevada. Setting out next day upon foot and mule – back this wrinkled red and white screen, this backround for hats, this queer comment (especially at sunset) upon Mr Churchill's article in The Times, is found to consist of stones, olive trees, goats, asphodels, irises, bushes, ridges, shelves, clumps, tufts, and hollows innumerable, indescribable, unthinkable. The mind's contents break into short sentences. It is hot; the old man; the frying pan; it is hot; the image of the Virgin; the bottle of wine; it is time for lunch; it is only half past twelve; it is hot. And then over and over again come all those objects – stones, olives, goats, asphodels, dragonflies, irises, until by some trick of the imagination they run into phrases of command, exhortation, and encouragement such as befit soldiers marching, sentinels on lonely nights, and leaders of great batallions. But must one give up the struggle? Must one relinquish the game? Yes, for the clouds are drifting across the pass; mules mind not what they carry; mules never stumble; they know the way. Why not leave everything to them?

V.S. Pritchett felt his life changed on encountering the Spanish landscape and its spiritual expression in the writings of Miguel de Unamuno. He went to live in Madrid in 1924 and spent the following five years travelling around the country, including a memorable walk from Badajoz through Extremadura to Vigo in Galicia. In his memoirs, entitled *Midnight Oil*, V.S. Pritchett recalls the fundamental change which contact with Spain provoked in him as a young man.

Until now I had picked up my education as I went along. In Spain the matter became more serious . . . I was to get one of those moral shocks that make one question everything that one has taken for granted . . . Italy is richer, but here . . . one can see the bare flesh and bone of the earth . . . the sight of wide stretches of country and sky liberate the mind and lift some of the load off it . . . The earth did not fade into the transcendental, rock was rock, trees were trees, mountains were mountains and wilderness was wilderness. There was nothing of the 'deeply interfused'; there was something that could be known and which it was necessary to know. There was a sense of the immediate and finite, so much more satisfying than the infinite, which had really starved me. I felt I was human.

V.S. Pritchett concluded that even if he hadn't read Unamuno's *A Tragic Sense of Life*, he would have still seen that Spain was the 'old and necessary enemy of the West'. Only in Spain could one be so 'frankly frightened' by history, and experience the 'passions of human nature' unleashed. With its history of wars Spain was destined to disintegrate into social turmoil. On the consequences of the Spanish Civil War, Professor Raymond Carr has written in his *History of Spain*:

Order was the indubitable achievement of General Franco's rule: yet it can be bought at a price that societies in the long run cannot afford. As previous exponents of the craft of the iron surgery have experienced, the marginal costs of authoritarianism are high and to recross the Rubicon is a delicate operation.

For some the crossing proved easier than for others. Robert Graves had first arrived in Majorca during the dictatorship of General Primo de Rivera. He returned to the island – after the interlude of the Second World War – with another authoritarian ruler, General Franco, in power. Graves found his house in Deyá untouched and unchanged but for the immensity of the tangerine bushes in the garden and the loquat trees already bearing fruit.

Everything I had left behind had been looked after – linen, silver, books and documents – though the moths had got into my socks; and if I felt so inclined, could have sat down at my table, taken a sheet of paper from the drawer and started work again straight away. Deyá certainly rolled out the red carpet for me; my return made everyone hope that prosperity was once again around the corner.

The next three years were, I admit, pretty hard. Spain had not profited from World War II as from World War I. On the contrary, rationing was now far severer than in England, a family loaf cost as much as a bottle of champagne, and effective steps could not yet be taken to suppress the flourishing black market. The flow of tourists remained negligible . . .

Brenan returned to his house in Churriana to find that it too had survived the Spanish Civil War and the Second World War. He seemed to have few regrets about leaving England behind again, as he recorded in *Personal Record*.

It was a great change to find myself occupying once more a large house whose rooms were airy and spacious instead of a diminutive cottage where I had to stoop every time I went through a door. It was also a change to leave the cold, grey English winter for the warmth and sunlight of southern Spain. I love large rooms and I love light. The garden too had come on surprisingly since we had laid it out twenty years before. The trees had grown taller and more spreading, roses and wysteria smothered walls and trellises and there was a look of semi-tropical exuberance breaking through the formality of the edged flower beds. This was the house that I had dreamed of so often during the war years, searching for it but never finding it, inquiring but always put off, and now that I at last had it I could say that it was even better than I had imagined it to be.

This was in 1951. Three years previously Brenan had travelled in central and southern Spain with the idea of taking notes on Spain from a non-political perspective, focusing instead on the 'more permanent and characteristic features of the country.' To his dismay he found that such an attitude – perhaps possible to maintain in the Spain of the 1920s – was no longer sustainable in the Spain of 1949. The memory of the Civil War was too recent, censorship too widespread, for Spaniards to use Brenan in any other way than as a convenient confessor for their deeply engrained sense of frustration, guilt, and fear. 'Spaniards of all classes and of all political ideologies,' Brenan wrote in his preface to *The Face of Spain*, 'are discouraged and exasperated.' In Cordoba

One sees men and women whose faces and bodies are coated with dirt because they are too weak or too sunk in despair to wash in water. One sees children of ten with wizened faces, women of thirty who are already hags, wearing that frown of anxiety which perpetual hunger and uncertainty about the future give. I have never seen such sheer misery before: even the lepers of Marrakesh and Taroudant look less wretched because, besides being better nourished, they are resigned to their fate. It presents one too at every step with a personal problem: what right has one to eat good meals, to drink coffee, to buy pastries when people are starving all round one? No right at all, and yet, being selfish by nature, I could not help doing so.

The destitution of post-war Spain had little impact on the young Alastair Boyd who escaped from the stuffy atmosphere of the City of London and arrived in Spain for the first time in 1948. Using his father's business contacts to get round the foreign exchange controls of the time and to borrow a car, Boyd and two friends drove through old and new Castile in the spirit of the Grand Tour.

What seized my imagination were the dramatically sited old cities that had hardly changed since the seventeenth century, the grand and solemn architecture, the sense of boundless space and light. As we drove with a feeling of light-headedness across the high-plain, rimmed by distant mountains, the towns with their barn-like churches, shimmering mirages from a distance, turned out on arrival to have a crumbling but real substance, fissured and frayed by long decay. Around them the rhythm of life and agricultural tasks seemed to descend directly from pre-Christian times.

Ancient history was also was what seized the imagination of another post-war visitor, Rose Macaulay, who noted in *The Fabled Shore* that Spain 'grows Roman walls and basilicas and tenth-century churches like wild figs, leaving them about in the most careless and arrogant profusion, uncluttered and unattended for travellers to stumble on at will.' In the year of her visit, 1949, the Costa Brava was still in the main a 'succession of little fishing ports and untenanted coves and rocks.' One of the few large hotels already built was La Gavina in S'Agaro – 'large and beautiful' – laid out with gardens, terraces, swimming pool, steps down to an isolated beach, and even a small chapel 'for the benefit of devout visitors.' Macaulay hazarded the prediction that if the Costa Brava was ever allowed to enter the twentieth century, it would be with a 'line of such fine hostelries, all down it, alternating with private villas, and beautifying every corner with white arcaded gardens.'

Moving south, Macaulay judged Torremolinos to be a pretty place. She stayed at the Hotel Santa Clara which was white and tiled and rambling and had a walled garden dropping down by stages to a virgin beach. The atmosphere seemed that of a South Sea isle, although a sense of profound change just around the corner comes through in this description of her stay there:

> A round full moon rose corn-coloured behind a fringe of palms. Swimming out to sea, I saw the whole of the bay, and the Malaga lights twinkling in the middle of it as if the wedge of cheese were being devoured by a thousand fireflies. Behind the bay the dark mountains reared, and here and there a light. It was an exquisite bathe. After it I dined on a terrace in the garden; near me three young Englishmen were enjoying themselves with two pretty Spanish girls they had picked up in Malaga; they knew no Spanish, the *señoritas* no English, but this made them all the merrier. They were the first English tourists I had seen since I entered Spain; they grew a little intoxicated, and they were also the first drunks I had seen in Spain.

Seven years later a London-based tour operator started its first charter flights to the Costa Brava and the Costa del Sol. Among those who came to Spain in the wake of the tourist invasion was Ian Gibson, an Irish academic, in 1978. He chose to experience the country not from without, but from within. Gibson not only settled in Spain, he also abandoned his nationality and took up Spanish citizenship. Gibson noted the perplexity and soul-searching he encountered in the Spain of the 1990s, and offered this comment on the nature of its people:

In Spain there is no option but to take the good with the bad, since both are inseperably related – the inhabitants' extremely attractive ebullience, for instance, being the cause of the fact that it may be difficult to get to sleep in the summer. If, as a result of EC membership, Spain were to change profoundly (to become, let's say, a Mediterranean Germany) I'd be tempted to pack my bags. But I don't envisage any such contingency. 'We in this country all have a depth of "Spanishness" that not even torture could wring from us,' wrote the Andalusian novelist Juan Valera in 1888. Those words, happily, are still true.

SOURCES AND ACKNOWLEDGEMENTS

Anonymous, *Lazarillo de Tormes*, Oxford University Press, 1924.

Alexander, Tamar and Romero, Elena (ed.), *Erase una vez . . . Maimondes*, Ediciones El Almendro, Cordoba, 1988.

Allison Peers, E., *Our Debt to Spain*, Burns & Oates, 1938; *Spain: The Church and the Orders*, Eyre and Spottiswoode, 1939. Reprinted by permission of Burns & Oates Ltd.

Amicis, Edmondo de, *Spain and the Spaniards*, 1881.

Aulnoy, Madame d', *Travels into Spain*, Routledge, 1930.

Avila, Teresa of, *The Life of Saint Teresa of Avila by Herself*, (translated by J. M. Cohen © J. M. Cohen 1950) Penguin Classics, 1957. Reprinted by permission of the publishers.

Baker, Carlos, *Ernest Hemingway*, Collins, 1969.

Barea, Arturo, *The Forging of a Rebel*, Reynal & Hitchcock, New York, 1946.

Baretti, Joseph, *A Journey from London to Genoa*, 1770.

Baroja, Pio, *El Pais Vasco*, Destino, Barcelona, 1953.

Beckford, William, *Italy, with Sketches of Spain and Portugal*, 1834.

Bell, Quentin, *Virginia Woolf*, Hogarth Press, 1972.

Belloc, Hilaire, *Many Cities*, Constable and Co. Ltd., 1920. Reprinted by permission of the Peters, Fraser & Dunlop Group Ltd.

Benson, Frederick, *Writers in Arms, The Literary Impact of the Spanish Civil War*, University of London Press, 1968.

Bentley, James, *The Way of Saint James*, Pavilion, 1992. Reprinted by permission of the author.

Bernanos, George, *Les Grands Cimetières sous la lune*, printed as *A Diary of My Times* (translated by Pamela Morris), 1938.

Besas, Peter, *The Written Road to Spain* (limited edition published by the author), 1988.

Betham-Edwards, Matilda, *Through Spain to the Sahara*, 1868.

Bexley, H. Willis, *Spain: Art-Remains and Art-Realities, Painters, Priests, and Princes*, London, 1875.

Blasco-Ibañez, Vicente, *Cañas y Barro*, Plaza & Janes, 1976; *La Barraca; Blood & Sand*, Cedric Chivers, 1973.

Bolin, Luis, *Spain, The Vital Years*, Cassell, 1967.

Bone, Gertrude, *Days in Old Spain*, Macmillan, 1938.

Borges, Jorge Luis, *Obras Completas*, Emece, Buenos Aires, 1979.

Borkenau, Franz, *The Spanish Cockpit*, Faber & Faber, 1937. Reprinted by permission of the publishers.

Borrow, George, *The Bible in Spain*, Dent, Everyman, 1907; *The Zincali*, Dent, Everyman, 1914.

Boulay, Shirley du, *Teresa of Avila*, Hodder & Stoughton, 1991. Reprinted by permission of David Higham Associates Ltd.

Boyd, Alastair, *The Sierras of the South*, Harper Collins, 1992. Reprinted by permission of the author.

Brenan, Gerald, *The Face of Spain*, Penguin, 1965; *The Literature of the Spanish People*, Cambridge University Press, 1951; *South from Granada*, Hamish Hamilton, 1957; *The Spanish Labyrinth*, Cambridge University Press, 1964; *Personal Record 1920–1972*, Jonathan Cape, 1974 © Lynda Jane Nicholson Price. Reprinted by permission of Margaret Hanbury.

Brodrick, James, *Saint Ignatius Loyola*, Burns & Oates, 1956. Reprinted by permission of the Society of Jesus.

Brooke, Sir Arthur de Capell, *Sketches in Spain and Morocco*, London, 1831.

Burgos, Antonio, *Guia Secreta de Sevilla*, Ediciones 29, Barcelona, 1991.

Burns, Tom, *The Use of Memory*, Sheed & Ward, 1993.

Burns, Tom G., *Spain: Everything Under the Sun*, Harrap Columbus, 1987.

Calvert, Albert F., *Toledo*, The Bodley Head, 1907.

Camba, Julio, *La Casa de Luculo o El Arte de Comer*, Espasa Calpe, Madrid, 1961.

Campbell, Anna, *Poetic Justice*, Typographeum, Francestown, 1986.

Campbell, Roy, *Collected Works*, ed. Donker, Craighall, 1985; *Light on a Dark Horse*, Penguin, 1971; *Poems of Saint John of the Cross*, Fount, 1979; *Flowering Rifle*, Longmans, 1939. Reprinted by permission of the estate of Roy Campbell.

Cano, Maria José, *Yishaq Ibn Jalfun: Poeta cortesano Cordobes*, Ediciones El Almendro, Cordoba, 1988.

Capek, Karel, *Letters from Spain*, Geoffrey Bles, 1931.

Caraman, P., *St Ignatius Loyola*, Collins, 1990.

Carr, Raymond, *Spain, 1809–1939*, Oxford University Press, 1966; *Modern Spain 1875–1980*, Oxford University Press, 1980.

Casanova, Giacomo, *Memoirs Vol. 6, 'Spanish Passions'*, Elek Books, 1960.

Castro, Americo, *La Realidad Historica de Espana*, Mexico, 1966.

Castro, Rosalia de, *Poesias*, Patronato, 1982.

Cayley, George John, *Bridle Roads of Spain*, 1853.

Cela, Camilo José, *The Hive*, Echo Press, New York, 1983; *Journey to the Alcarria* (translated by Frances M. Lopez-Morillas), Granta Books, 1990 © Camilo José Cela. Translation © the Regents of the University of Wisconsin, 1966. Reproduced by permission of Penguin Ltd. *Primer Viaje Andaluz*, Noguer, Barcelona, 1959; *Madrid*, Alfaguara, Madrid, 1966.

Cervantes, Miguel de, *Don Quixote* (translated by J. M. Cohen), Penguin Classics, 1950. Reprinted by permission of the publishers. *Novelas Ejemplares* (translated by C. A. Jones), Penguin Classics, 1972. Reprinted by permission of the estate of C. A. Jones.

Chateaubriand, Francois Auguste, *Le Dernier des Abencèrages*, 1826.

Chetwode, Penelope, *Two Middle-Aged Ladies in Andalusia*, John Murray, 1963. Reprinted by permission of the publishers.

Clark, William, *Gazpacho; or Summer Months in Spain*, 1850.

Clarke, Edward, *Letters Concerning the Spanish Nation*, 1763.

Columbus, Christopher, *Diario de Colón*, Cultura Hispanica, Madrid, 1968.

Connolly, Cyril, *The Evening Colonnade*, David, Bruce and Watson, 1973. Reprinted by permission of the estate of Cyril Connolly.

Costello, Edward, *Recollections of the Peninsular War*, Longmans, 1967.

Cunningham, Valentine (ed.), *Spanish Front: Writers on the Civil War*, Oxford University Press, 1986.

Dali, Salvador, *The Unspeakable Confessions*, W. H. Allen, 1975. Reprinted by permission of Virgin Publishing Ltd.

Dalrymple, Major William, *Travels through Spain & Portugal in 1774*, J. Almon, 1777.

Diaz, Bernal, *The Conquest of New Spain*, Penguin, 1963.

Disraeli, Benjamin, *Letters 1815–1834*, University of Toronto Press, 1982.

Dominguez, Francisco Garrido, *La Plaza de Toros de la Real Maestranza de Ronda*, Ronda, 1985.

Dos Passos, John, *Journeys between Wars*, Constable, 1938. Reprinted by permission of the publishers.

Dumas, Alexandre, *From Paris to Cadiz*, Peter Owen, 1958.

Dunn, Douglas, *A Choice of Byron's Verse*, Faber & Faber, 1974.

Elliot, J. H., *Imperial Spain, 1469–1716*, Edward Arnold, 1963.

Ellis, Havelock, *The Soul of Spain*, Constable, 1908.

Falla, Manuel de, *Escritos sobre Musica y Musicos*, Espasa Calpe, Madrid, 1972.

Fernandez-Armesto, Felipe, *Barcelona*, Sinclair-Stevenson, 1991.

Fielding, Xan, *Best of Friends: the Brenan-Partridge Letters*, Chatto & Windus, 1986.

Ford, Richard, *Handbook for Travellers in Spain*, John Murray, 1869; *Gatherings from Spain*, Dent, Everyman, 1906.

Foxa, Agustin de, *Madrid de Corte a Checa*, Madrid, 1976.

Fuentes, Carlos, *The Buried Mirror*, André Deutsch, 1992. Reproduced by permission of the publishers.

Gadow, Hans, *In Northern Spain*, 1897.

Galdós, Benito Perez de, *Fortunata & Jacinta* (translated by Agnes Moncy Gullon), Viking, 1987 © the University of Georgia Press, 1986. Reprinted by permission of Penguin Ltd. *El 19 Marzo y el dos de Mayo*, Madrid, 1873; *La de Bringas* (translated by Gamel Woolsey as *The Spendthrifts*), Weidenfeld & Nicolson, 1953. Reprinted by permission of the publishers.

Ganivet, Angel, *Obras Completas*, Aguilar, Madrid, 1961.

Garnett, David (ed.), *Carrington, Letters and Extracts from her Diaries*, Cape, 1970.

Gasset, José Ortega y, *Viajes y Paises*, Revista de Occidente, Madrid, 1957; *La Rebelion de las Masas*, Espasa Calpe, Madrid, 1976; *El Espectador*, Nueva, Madrid, 1943; *Espana Invertebrada*, Madrid, 1921. Reprinted by permission of the estate of Ortega y Gasset.

Gathorne-Hardy, Jonathan, *The Inner Castle: A Biography of Gerald Brenan*, London, 1992.

Gautier, Théophile, *A Romantic in Spain*, Alfred A. Knopf, New York, 1926.

Gellhorn, Martha, *The View from the Ground*, Granta, 1989.

Genet, Jean, *The Thief's Journal*, Blond, 1957.

Gentleman Volunteer, A, *The Letters of George Hennell 1812–13*, Heinemann, 1979.

Gibson, Ian, *The Assassination of Federico Garcia Lorca*, Harmondsworth, 1983; *Federico Garcia Lorca: A Life*, Faber & Faber, 1989; *Fire in the Blood*, Faber & Faber and BBC Books, 1992. Reprinted by permission of the author.

Gide, André, *The Journals*, Secker & Warburg, 1947.

Gilmour, David, *Cities of Spain*, John Murray, 1992.

Gironella, José Maria, *The Cypresses Believe in God*, Alfred A. Knopf, New York, 1956.

Gleig, George, *The Subaltern*, William Blackwood, 1826.

Gongora, Luis, *Obras Poeticas*, Hispanic Society of America, New York, 1921.

Gomez, Emilio Garcia, *Poemas Arabes en los Muros y Fuentes de la Alhambra*, Instituto Egipcio de Estudios Islamicos, Madrid, 1985.

Goytisolo, Juan, *Count Julian*, Serpent's Tail, 1989; *Landscapes after the Battle*, Serpent's Tail, 1987; *Marks of Identity*, Serpent's Tail, 1988; *Juan The Landless*; *Fiestas*, Alfred A. Knopf, New York, 1960; *Sands of Torremolinos*, Jonathan Cape, 1962; *Realms of Strife*, Quartet, 1990. Reprinted by permission of Quartet Ltd.

Graham, Robert, *Spain, Change of a Nation*, Michael Joseph, 1984. Reprinted by permission of the author.

Graves, Robert, *Goodbye to All That*, Penguin, 1965; *Majorca Observed*, Cassell, 1965, including Robert Graves' translation of George Sand, by permission of A. P. Watt Ltd on behalf of the Trustees of the Robert Graves Copyright.

Greene, Graham, *Monsignor Quixote*, The Bodley Head, 1982.

Gwynne, Paul, *The Guadalquivir*, Constable, 1912.

Hall, Trowbridge, *Spain in Silhouette*, New York, 1923.

Hanbury-Tenison, Robin, *Spanish Pilgrimage*, Hutchinson, 1990. Reprinted by permission of the Peters, Fraser and Dunlop Group Ltd.

Hare, Augustus, *Wanderings in Spain*, London, 1873.

Harris, Rifleman, *Recollections of Rifleman Harris*, Leo Cooper, 1970.

Hemingway, Ernest, *Death in the Afternoon*, Jonathan Cape, 1932; *Fiesta*; *For Whom the Bell Tolls*, Jonathan Cape, 1941; *The Dangerous Summer*, Hamish Hamilton, 1985 © the estate of Ernest Hemingway. Reprinted by permission of Random House, UK.

Hensbergen, Gijs van, *A Taste of Castille*, Sinclair-Stevenson, 1992. Reprinted by permission of the author.

Hernandez, Miguel, *Poemas Sociales de Guerra y de Muerte*, Alianza, 1977.

Hoare, Samuel, *Ambassador on Special Mission*, Collins, 1946. Reprinted by permission of the author.

Holland, Lady Elizabeth, *The Spanish Journal of Elizabeth Lady Holland*, 1910.

Holt, Edgar, *The Carlist Wars in Spain*, Putnam, 1967.

Holroyd, Michael, *Lytton Strachey: A Critical Biography*, Heinemann, 1986. Reprinted by permission of A. P. Watt Ltd. *Augustus John*, Heinemann, 1975.

Hopkins, Gerard Manley, *A Selection of his Poems and Prose*, Penguin, 1953.
Howell, James, *Familiar Letters*, David Nutt, 1892.
Hughes, Gerard, *God of Surprises*, Darton, Longman & Todd, 1985. Reprinted by permission of the publishers.
Hughes, Robert, *Barcelona*, Harvill, 1992.
Hughes, Terence Mason, *An Overland Journey to Lisbon at the Close of 1846*, 1847; *Revelations of Spain in 1845*, 1847.
Hynes, Samuel, *The Auden Generation*, Faber & Faber, 1976.

Inclán, Ramón de Valle, *Flor de Santidad*, 1904.
Inglis, Henry, *Spain*, Whittaker & Co, 1837.
Irving, Washington, *Tales of the Alhambra*, Carey & Lea, Philadelphia, 1832; *Diary in Spain 1828–1829*, Hispanic Society of America, New York, 1926; *Letters from Sunnyside and Spain*, Yale University Press, New Haven, 1928.

Jacob, W., *Travels in the South of Spain in 1809–10*, 1811.
Jacobs, Michael, *A Guide to Andalusia*, Viking, 1990.
Jiménez, Juan Ramón, *Platero y Yo*, Alianza, Madrid, 1981.
Josephs, Allen, *White Wall of Spain*, Iowa State University Press, 1983.

Knightley, Phillip, *The First Casualty*, Quartet, 1978.
Koestler, Arthur, *Spanish Testament*, Gollancz, 1937. Reprinted by permission of the Peters, Fraser & Dunlop Group Ltd.

Layton, T.A., *The Way of Saint James*, George Allen and Unwin, 1976.
Lee, Laurie, *As I Walked out One Midsummer's Morning*, André Deutsch, 1969; *A Rose for Winter*, Hogarth Press, 1955; *A Moment of War*, Viking, 1991. Reprinted by permission of the Peters, Fraser & Dunlop Group Ltd.
Levi-Provencal, E. & Gomez, Emilio Garcia, *El Tratado de Ibn Abdun*, Moneda y Credito, Madrid, 1948.
Liddel-Hart, B.R. (ed.), *The Letters of Private William Wheeler*, Michael Joseph, 1951.
Lithgow, William, *Rare Adventures and Painefull Peregrinations*, 1632.
Lomas, John, *Sketches in Spain*, Longmans, Green, & Co, 1888.
Longford, Elizabeth, *Byron*, Weidenfeld & Nicolson, 1976; *Wellington, the Years of the Sword*, Weidenfeld & Nicolson, 1969.
Lorca, Federico García, *Obras Completas*, Aguilar, Madrid, 1978.
Lyall, Archibald, *Well Met in Madrid*, Putnam, 1960.

Macaulay, Rose, *Fabled Shore*, Hamish Hamilton, 1949. Reprinted by permission of HarperCollins Ltd.
Machado, Antonio y Manuel, *Obras Completas*, Editorial Plenitud, Madrid, 1951; *Poesias Completas*, Espasa Calpe, 1981.
Madariaga, Salvador de, *Spain, a Modern History*, 1946.
Malraux, André (translated by Stuart Gilbert and Alastair Macdonald), *Man's Hope*, Random House, 1966.
Maragall, Joan, *Obras Completas*, Barcelona, 1981.
Marañón, Gregorio, *Obras Completas*, Espasa Calpe, Madrid, 1966. Reprinted by permission of Mabel Marañón Moya.

Marchand, Leslie A., *Byron, a Portrait*, John Murray, 1971.

Maugham, Somerset, *Don Fernando*, William Heinemann, 1971. Reprinted by permission of the publishers.

Maurois, André, *Chateaubriand*, Jonathan Cape, 1938.

Mendelson, E., *The English Auden: Poems, Essays and Dramatic Writings, 1927–39*, Faber & Faber Ltd. Reprinted by permission of the publishers.

Mendoza, Eduardo de, *City of Marvels*, Collins Harvill, 1986. Reprinted by permission of the publishers.

Mercadel, J. Garcia, *Viajes de estranjeros por Espana y Portugal desde los tiempos mas remotos hasta fines del siglo XV*, Madrid, 1952.

Mérimée, Prosper, *Carmen and Other Stories*, Blackie, 1966.

Mitchell, David, *Travellers in Spain*, Lookout, 1990.

Mitchell, Timothy, *Bloodsport*, University of Pennsylvania, 1991.

Mitford, Nancy, *The Pursuit of Love*, Penguin, 1949. Reprinted by permission of the Peters, Fraser & Dunlop Group Ltd.

Molina, Tirso de, *El Burlador de Seville*, Cambridge University Press, 1967.

Montalban, Manuel Vazquez, *Murder in the Central Committee*, Pluto, 1984. Reprinted by permission of Serpent's Tail Ltd.

Morris, Jan, *The Presence of Spain*, Faber & Faber, 1964. Reprinted by permission of the author.

Morton, H.V., *A Stranger in Spain*, Methuen, 1955. Reprinted by permission of Reed International Books.

Mottola, A., *The Spiritual Exercises of St Ignatius*, Doubleday, 1964.

Murphy, Martin, *Blanco White*, Yale University Press, 1989.

Murray, E. Dundas, *The Cities and Wilds of Andalusia*, 1849.

Neruda, Pablo, *Memoirs*, Farrar, Straus & Giroux, New York, 1977.

Newby, Eric, *On the Shores of the Mediterranean*, Picador, 1985. Reprinted by permission of HarperCollins Ltd.

Nicholson, Helen, *Death in the Morning*, Lovat Dickson, 1937.

Noel, Eugenio, *España nervio a nervio*, Espasa Calpe, 1924.

Nogales, Manuel Chaves, *Juan Belmonte, Matador de Toros*, Alianza, Madrid, 1969.

O'Brien, Kate, *Farewell Spain*, William Heinemann, 1937; *Mary Lavelle*, William Heinemann, 1936. Reprinted by permission of David Higham Associates Ltd.

O'Brien, Patrick, *Picasso*, Collins, 1976.

Oman, Carola, *Sir John Moore*, Hodder & Stoughton, 1953.

Orwell, George, *Homage to Catalonia*, Secker & Warburg, 1938 © the estate of Sonia Brownwell Orwell. Reprinted by permission of A.M. Heath & Co. Ltd.

Palacios, Miguel Asin, *Amor humano, amor divino, Ibn Arabi*, Ediciones El Almendro, Cordoba, 1990.

Pidal, Ramon Menendez, *The Spaniards in Their History*, Norton, New York, 1966.

Poitou, Eugene, *Spain and its People*, T. Nelson & Sons, Edinburgh and New York, 1873.

Pritchett, V.S., *The Spanish Temper*, Chatto & Windus, 1954; *Midnight Oil*, Penguin, 1974; *Marching Spain*, Ernest Benn, 1928. Reprinted by permission of the Peters, Fraser & Dunlop Group Ltd.

Prothero, Rowland, *The Works of Lord Byron, Letters & Journals*, John Murray, 1898; *The Letters of Richard Ford 1789–1858*, John Murray, 1905.

Regler, Gustav, *The Owl of Minerva*, Rupert Hart-Davis, 1959.
Roberts, Richard, *An Autumn Tour in Spain*, Saunders, Otley, 1860.
Robertson, Ian, *Los Curiosos Impertinentes*, Vallehermosò, Madrid, 1992.
Roland, The Song of, (translated by Glyn Burgess), Penguin Classics, 1990 © Glyn Burgess, 1990. Reprinted by permission of the publishers.
Ruiz, José Martinez, *España Clara*, Doncel, Madrid, 1966; *Lecturas Españolas*, Thomas Nelson, 1955; *España: Hombres y Paisajes*, Francisco Beltran, Madrid, 1909; *Madrid*, Avapies, Madrid, 1988; *Tiempos y Cosas*, Salvat, Madrid, 1970; *La Ruta de Don Quixote*, Losada, Buenos Aires, 1938.

Sackville-West, Vita, *The Eagle and the Dove*, Michael Joseph, 1943; *Pepita*, Hogarth Press, 1937. Reprinted by permission of Curtis Brown Ltd. on behalf of the estate of Vita Sackville-West.
Saenz-Badillas-Judit Targarona Borras, Angel (ed.), *Poemas: Desde el Campo de Batalla Granada 1038–56*, Ediciones El Almendro, Cordoba, 1988.
Sand, George, *A Winter in Majorca* (translated and edited by Robert Graves), Cassell, 1956.
Sender, Ramon, *Seven Red Sundays* (translated by Sir Peter Chalmers Mitchell), Faber & Faber, 1936.
Serna, Ramón Gomez de la, *Elucidario de Madrid*, Ayuso, Madrid, 1988; *Madrid*, Almarabu, 1987.
Serra, Victoria, *Tia Victoria's Spanish Kitchen*, Nicholas Kay, 1963.
Shakespeare, William, *The Complete Works*, Murrays Sales, 1978.
Sitwell, Osbert, *Noble Essences*, Macmillan, 1950 © Frank Magro. Reprinted by permission of David Higham Associates Ltd.
Sitwell, Sacheverell, *Spain*, B.T. Batsford, 1950. Reprinted by permission of David Higham Associates Ltd.
Southey, Robert, *History of the Peninsular War*, John Murray, 1823.
Spender, Stephen, *Collected Poems 1928–1983*, Faber & Faber. Reprinted by permission of the publishers.
Starkie, Walter, *Spanish Raggle-Taggle*, John Murray, 1934; *The Road to Santiago*, John Murray, 1957; *Don Gypsy: Adventures with a Fiddle in Barbary, Andalusia, and La Mancha*, John Murray, 1936.
Stoye, J.V., *English Travellers Abroad 1604–1667*, Jonathan Cape, 1952.
Swinburne, Henry, *Travels through Spain in 1775 and 1776*, 1787.

Thomas, Hugh, *The Spanish Civil War*, Hamish Hamilton, 1977; *Madrid, A Traveller's Companion*, Constable, 1988. Reprinted by permission of the author.
Ticknor, George, *Life, Letters, and Journals*, Boston, 1876; *History of Spanish Literature*, John Murray, 1855.
Townsend, Joseph, *A Journey through Spain in the years 1786 and 1787*, 1791.
Tracy, Honor, *Spanish Leaves*, Methuen, 1964; *Silk Hats and No Breakfast*, Methuen, 1957.
Trend, J.B., *Spain from the South*, Methuen, 1928; *A Picture of Modern Spain, Men and Music*, Constable, 1921.
Trotsky, Leon, *En España*, Akal, Madrid, 1975.

Twiss, Richard, *Travels Through Portugal and Spain in 1772 and 1773*, 1775.

Tynan, Kenneth, *Right & Left*, Jonathan Cape, 1967; *The Sound of Two Hands Clapping*, Jonathan Cape, 1975; *Bull Fever*, Quality Book Club, 1956. Reprinted by permission of Random House UK.

Unamuno, Miguel de, *Por Tierras de Portugal y España*, Espasa Calpe, Madrid, 1941; *The Tragic Sense of Life*, Macmillan, 1921. Reprinted by permission of the estate of Miguel de Unamuno.

Valera, Juan, *Pepita Jimenez*, Espasa Calpe, Madrid, 1986.

Vane, C.V., *Marquess of Londonderry, A Steam Voyage to Spain*, Henry Colburn, 1842.

Vines, Cristina, *Granada en los libros de viaje*, Miguel Sanchez, Granada, 1982.

Volunteer in the Queen's Service, A, *A Concise Account of the British Auxiliary Legion in the Civil War of Spain*, Scarborough, 1837.

Walker, Ted, *In Spain*, Secker & Warburg, 1987. Reprinted by permission of David Higham Associates.

Waugh, Evelyn, *Labels: A Mediterranean Journal*, Duckworth, 1974.

Wellington, Duke of, *Letters & Despatches*, Parker, Furnivall & Parker, 1844.

Williams, Michael E., *St Alban's College, Valladolid*, C. Hurst, 1986.

Wollaston, Nicholas, *Tilting at Don Quixote*, André Deutsch, 1990. Reprinted by permission of the author.

Woodall, James, *In Search of the Firedance*, Sinclair-Stevenson, 1992. Reprinted by permission of the author.

Woolsey, Gamel, *Death's Other Kingdom*, Longmans, 1939 © the estate of Gamel Woolsey. Reprinted by permission of Laurence Pollinger Ltd.

While every effort has been made to secure permission, we may have failed in a few cases to trace the copyright holder. We apologize for any apparent negligence.

The author and publishers would like to thank the following for their permission to reproduce pictures: 1, 11, 12, 13, 14: Courtauld Institute and Brinsley Ford Collection; 2: Hugh Newsam; 3, 5, 6 (left), 9, 15, 19, 20: Cervantes Institute; 6 (right), 7 (right), 22: Spanish Tourist Board; 8: Tom Burns; 16: National Army Museum; 17: Robert Hunt Library; 18: John Fitzgerald Kennedy Library; 21: J. Paul Getty Museum; 23: Frances Partridge; 24: Beryl Graves and Weidenfeld & Nicolson Archives.

INDEX